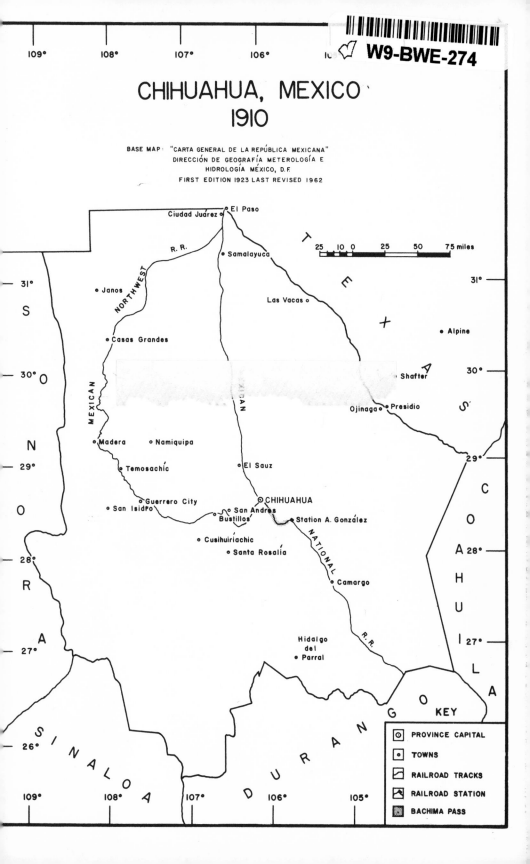

Insurgent Governor

Insurgent Governor

Abraham González
and the Mexican Revolution
in Chihuahua

William H. Beezley

UNIVERSITY OF NEBRASKA PRESS · LINCOLN

Some of the material in Chapter 4 was published in different form in "State Reform during the Provisional Presidency: Chihuahua, 1911," *Hispanic American Historical Review* 50 (August 1970): 524-37, and is used by permission. Copyright 1970 by Duke University Press.

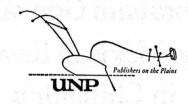

Publishers on the Plains
UNP

For Alda

Contents

A section of illustrations follows p. 112

Preface

Abraham González's political career spanned only four years, from 1909 to 1913, but that brief period witnessed sweeping changes in Mexican society, particularly in the northern state of Chihuahua, where González served as governor for two years after the 1910 revolution. Many events in Chihuahua epitomized the revolution: it was there that the revolutionaries routed the federal forces, toppling Porfirio Díaz's thirty-five-year federal dictatorship and bringing to power the moderate constitutional reformer Francisco Madero. It was there, too, that the dream of orderly, bloodless reform died in feuding among the revolutionaries which resulted in the assassination of González.

González's political life was simply a chapter in the history of the maderist movement—without the formation of Madero's Anti-reelectionist party he would have remained one of the educated, able men who lacked the necessary connections with the porfirian oligarchy to enter public life—and it paralleled the course of the revolution in Chihuahua in its origins, successes, and failures. Beyond exemplifying the maderist revolt in a crucial state, González's career illustrated the problems of establishing the legitimacy of the new government. Because he was governor, his policies represented the revolution to Chihuahua's people. Allegiance to González equaled support for the revolution; opposition to him was tantamount to rejection of the new national government.

As one of Madero's lieutenants, González accomplished many of the tasks necessary for the revolution. He recruited men, purchased supplies, created communications networks, and established provisional civil government in the wake of rebel victories in battle. His contribution did not include momentous political pronouncements or striking military command; rather he dealt with the daily problems that required immediate decisions. By handling details with some improvisation and a good deal of hard work, he contributed to the revolution's success.

When González became governor his program was little more than a restatement of the Anti-reelectionist party platform of 1910 (a moderate document in comparison with the rigidly nationalistic and quasisocialist Constitution of 1917), but he left a legacy of reform that revolutionaries in Chihuahua associated as much with their governor as they did with Madero. Rather than in originality, González's genius lay in adapting Díaz's methods to revolutionary goals and in recognizing the important role of state government in shaping both local economy and society. He displayed initiative and loyalty to Madero; he also demonstrated a genuine concern for the well-being of Chihuahua's working men. He tried to improve their lives and in his efforts revealed a reformer's paternalistic, but sincere, convictions.

González became an insurgent in spite of himself and he never altered his moderate beliefs. His middle position was difficult to maintain—caught as he was between the demands of extremists like Ricardo Flores Magón and Pascual Orozco on the one hand, and the almost conservative proposals of Madero on the other—but his strongest attribute was his loyalty to the Anti-reelectionist cause. He developed his reforms within the limits set by the president; indeed, rebellion against Madero by his former adherents seemed to strengthen González's resolve to remain moderate. González, like Madero, remained a reformer of the nineteenth-century type.

González was a tall, portly man with sharp features that made him appear stern; only his twinkling eyes betrayed his congeniality. Although direct in his manner, he smiled easily and made friends readily. He trusted people, but became vindictive when angered or betrayed. At the time Madero began the campaign against Díaz, González had just passed his fortieth birthday and was still a bachelor—he later explained that he had never married because "his sweetheart was the revolution."[1] To the extent that he succeeded, as

1. Daniel Moreno, *Los hombres de la revolución. 40 estudios biográficos* (México: Libro Mex, 1960), p. 63.

governor, in carrying out the designs of the revolution in his day-to-day decisions, he laid the legislative foundation for the aspirations of the rebels. His
death at the hands of a huertista assassin became a rallying point of opposition to the Huerta regime and started a crusade for the implementation of the
laws that the governor had created. At least in Chihuahua, González had
made legal realities of the slogans and promises of the Anti-reelectionist
party. His achievement provided a cause worth fighting for. In the struggle
that followed, Chihuahuans were transformed into Mexicans who made common cause with other Mexicans seeking national social revolution.

Examination of González's career adds a dimension to our knowledge of
the early Mexican Revolution. His early frustrations with the state oligarchy
affords one a view of the motives which drove men to rebel; his activities
during the struggle provide a glimpse of the workings of the revolution be-
neath the rhetoric of the movement's leaders. Of greatest significance, study
of González's governorship offers insight into a facet of the Madero revolution which has never been examined. After the rebel victory, Madero first
relinquished authority to a caretaker government, and even after assuming the
presidency did little to forge a national program to redeem the goals of his
party. The failure of national policies from 1911 to 1913 has obscured the
dynamic features of state government. Madero, perhaps by design, but more
likely by default, allowed the state governors to initiate reform programs
during his administration. It was at the state level, particularly in Chihuahua,
that a revolution was being effected during the Madero years by governors
like González.

In the turmoil of revolution that followed González's death, what little
evidence that did exist of his personal life, his thoughts, and his ambitions
was destroyed. Only the scattered records of his political activities and his
administrative duties remain. In this evaluation of González's public career, I
had the assistance of many people. Professor Michael C. Meyer of the University of Nebraska has offered encouragement from the early stages of this
study. Financial assistance for the project came from the National Defense
Education Act, Title IV, and a University of Nebraska travel grant.

In Mexico City, I received assistance from the directors and staffs of the
Archivo General de la Secretaría de Relaciones Exteriores de México, the
Hemeroteca Nacional, the Biblioteca Nacional, and the Biblioteca del Instituto Nacional de Antropología e Historia. Professor Richard E. Greenleaf,
then academic vice-president of the University of the Americas, extended

good counsel and friendship. In Chihuahua City three men assisted me: Juan Holguín Luján, president of the Sociedad Chihuahuense de Estudios Históricos, served as a guide to the city and its historical collections; Génaro Salazar Irigoyen offered help in the Archivo de Supremo Tribunal de Justicia; and Francisco R. Almada took time from his research and writing to discuss González's career. The United States consul in Chihuahua, John L. Martin, helped to arrange several interviews.

In the United States, the library staffs at the University of Nebraska and the State University of New York, Plattsburgh, obtained several volumes and microfilms on interlibrary loan. The staff at the Bancroft Library, University of California, Berkeley, extended every kindness; and the Southwest reference librarians of the El Paso Public Library, Mrs. Virginia P. Hoke, and Miss Lizabeth Lovelace, provided assistance. Miss Lovelace was especially helpful in selecting photographs from the Otis Aultman Collection. All the photographs in this book are from that collection and are used with the permission of the El Paso Public Library. Special thanks are also due Sr. Antonio Pompa y Pompa, of the Biblioteca Nacional de Antropología e Historia, for permission to reproduce the picture of González used on the dust jacket. Ignacio E. Lozano, Jr., editor of *La opinión*, permitted me to use the newspaper's files in the editorial offices in Los Angeles. Several colleagues assisted by reading drafts or discussing parts of this monograph. I received particular encouragement from Mark T. R. Gilderhus, Colorado State University; Ronald D. Tallman, State University of New York, Plattsburgh; Frederick C. Adams, Drake University; and Robert J. Haws, University of Mississippi. My typist, Mrs. Judy Dashnaw, proved patient and persevering. Paul M. Andrews prepared the map of Chihuahua. My thanks to all the persons mentioned here and others unnamed who have helped to improve this study. I alone am responsible for errors.

I owe a special debt of gratitude to my wife, Alda, and my sons, Paul, John, and Mark, for their patience and understanding.

William H. Beezley

Abbreviations

ABFC   Albert Bacon Fall Collection. Papers from the Senate Office Files of Senator Albert Bacon Fall Relating to Mexican Affairs. Huntington Library, San Marino, California. Microfilmed by the University of New Mexico, reels 30-40.

AGN   Archivo General de la Nación, Mexico City. Libros Copiadores de Francisco I. Madero.

AM   Instituto Nacional de Antropología e Historia, Mexico City. Archivo de don Francisco I. Madero. Microfilmed by El Centro de Documentación Histórica, 22 reels.

AREM   Archivo General de la Secretaría de Relaciones Exteriores de México, Mexico City. Various expedientes are cited in specific footnotes. Unless otherwise indicated, citations refer to Revolución Mexicana durante los Años de 1910 a 1920. Informaciones Diversas de la República y de las Oficinas de México en el Exterior. File Series H/513-1910-20/1.

ASTJ   Archivo del Supremo Tribunal de Justicia, Chihuahua. Records and Transactions, 1910-13.

BNAM   Biblioteca Nacional, Archivo Madero. Mexico City. Correspondencia del Presidente Francisco I. Madero. File number 9 (72) (003). Abril y Mayo, 1911. 2 boxes.

DHRM   Isidro Fabela, ed. *Documentos históricos de la revolución mexicana. Revolución y régimen maderista.* 5 vols. México: Fondo de Cultura Económica, 1964; Editorial Jus, 1965.

EPMT   *El Paso Morning Times.* 1908-14.

LO(LA) *La opinión* (Los Angeles, California). Various documentary collections and historical articles are cited from this Spanish-language newspaper.

NF   National Archives, Washington, D.C. Records of the Department of State, Numerical Files, 1906-1910, Record Group 59.

PO   *Periódico oficial del estado de Chihuahua.* 1911-13.

PR   National Archives, Washington, D.C. Post Records of Embassies and Consulates, Record Group 84, Correspondence of the Consulate General, Monterrey, Mexico.

RDS   National Archives, Washington, D.C. Records of the Department of State Relating to the Internal Affairs of Mexico, 1910-1929. National Archives Microfilm Publication (microcopy no. 274), 1910-1914.

STC   Silvestre Terrazas Collection. Correspondence and Papers. Bancroft Library, University of California, Berkeley. 119 boxes.

Insurgent Governor

1

Chihuahua
in the Díaz Era

For thirty-five years, from 1876 to 1911, Porfirio Díaz dominated the social, economic, and political life of Mexico. Ruthless in rooting out his opponents, he alternately bribed and prodded, alternately offering prominent Mexicans political and economic opportunities and threatening imprisonment, even death. Political challengers, rural bandits, churchmen, all received the choice of preferment or persecution. With *pan o palo*, the carrot or the stick, Díaz secured his dictatorial regime and simultaneously established peace and order as prerequisites for progress. Many Mexicans, grateful for an end to the half century of turmoil that had followed independence from Spain, eagerly traded political and civil rights for a stable society that could lure investment and technology from industrial nations. As Díaz's reign wore on, this general from Oaxaca ensured his authority by increased control of elections and appointments. All political power emanated from the Presidential Palace overlooking the Zócalo: his cronies gathered in the halls of Congress to provide conventional forms for legislation he had already approved; state governors held office at his will, and their success in maintaining order determined their reelection; even local officials felt his heavy hand in the appointment of prefects, the *jefes políticos*, to displace locally elected administrators. Business

1

and society both worked within the boundaries marked by Díaz. Franchises, tax exemptions, corporate organization, and bank credit, without which a business failed, required governmental sanction. Foreigners received favored treatment as Díaz promoted development with external capital and enterprise. Only in arranging a second marriage did he seem typically Mexican as he bore witness to the adage *A gato viejo, ratón tierno* (For the old tomcat, a tender mouse). Even then his nuptial contract with Carmen Romero Rubio, several decades his junior, served the practical purpose of allying him with an old, established family; and the new Señora Díaz assisted in arranging a reconciliation between Díaz and the Catholic Church and in gathering support for him from the Mexico City aristocracy.

Members of the Mexican gentry who stood in the dictator's shadow succeeded in business and politics. His favor brought concessions and property which regional leaders parlayed into land and commercial empires that only the foolish dared challenge. Men such as Ramón Corral in Sonora and Luis Terrazas in Chihuahua dominated local society and state politics while sharing economic benefits with North American and European developers. These regional aristocrats represented the Porfiriato as surely as the dictator. Thus, the porfirian government created a closed society, allowing only those who remained within Díaz's limits to compete for profits and positions. Nowhere were the privileges extended to favorites and the rivalry among the gentry for political and business preference more clearly evident than in the state of Chihuahua.

I

Located on the northern border, Chihuahua before the completion of the railroad in 1884 was free to some extent from national interference because of its isolation. Its desert wastes and rugged mountains discouraged settlement, as did sporadic raids by Apaches from the southwestern United States. The opportunities for mining and ranching attracted only a sparse population. The scattered residents, numbering 180,758 in 1877, adopted provincial, or *patria chica*, attitudes in the administrative and commercial centers of Chihuahua City, Guerrero City, and similar towns.[1] Political groups represented little more than cliques of self-seeking patricians—merchants, mine owners,

1. Chihuahua City, with eighteen thousand residents in 1879, was the only town in the state with a population over ten thousand (Moisés González Navarro, *Estadísticas sociales del porfiriato, 1877-1910* [Mexico: Talleres Gráficos de la Nación, 1956] p. 7, table 1.

and military officers—whose position as landowners provided both time and ambition to direct state affairs and to set social conventions. Family ties and local residence formed the basis for enduring loyalties; political parties were temporary factions lacking common ideals and long-range programs. In Chihuahua City, for example, Luis Terrazas, a wealthy, experienced politician, led one faction, while the Trías family, an old political power, formed the center of another. The extended Casavantes and González families forged a powerful group in Guerrero City, a service and shipping center for the rich mineral district in the Sierra Madre. Other state aristocrats headed similar loose alliances.[2]

Since most of the factions managed to hold at least one of the fifteen seats in the state legislature and to dominate their district governments, the political prize was the governorship. Although campaign rhetoric appealed to national issues, elections merely provided opportunities to advance local rivalries. In the gubernatorial election of 1873, for example, the candidates offered indistinguishable programs in support of national policies, the slate presented no choice except among the personalities of members of the state's oligarchy.[3]

The revolt and victory of Porfirio Díaz in 1876 brought political opportunity to the dissenting gentry in Chihuahua. Angel Trías, Jr., joined the Díaz rebellion in order to challenge Governor Luis Terrazas. With official support from Mexico City, he won the gubernatorial election of 1876, but he could neither destroy Terrazas's political influence nor impair his economic activities. Díaz's usurpation of national authority forced a new alignment of the state's upper class as the *terracistas* allied with their usual antagonists from Guerrero City to win about half of the seats in the legislature. Despite the national backing for Trías, the rival deputies attacked his program in the assembly chamber and in the newspapers. At the same time, they remained within the limits established by the dictator and seized every opportunity to obtain the concessions he offered. All the gentry benefited from the development programs of the porfirian government. Rivals in the legislature shared concessions for tax-exempt companies and divided vast tracts of land. The major land companies were the Ignacio Gómez del Campo Company of Luis

2. Information on Chihuahua during this period is contained in José Fuentes Mares, *. . . Y México se refugió en el desierto: Luis Terrazas, historia y destino* (Mexico: Editorial Jus, 1954), pp. 1-128, 181-98.

3. See two studies by Francisco R. Almada, *Gobernadores del estado de Chihuahua* (Mexico: Imprenta de la H. Cámara de Diputados, 1950), pp. 219-448, and *La revolución en el estado de Chihuahua*, 2 vols. (Mexico: Talleres Gráficos de la Nación, 1964), 1: 37-42 (hereafter cited as *Revolución en Chihuahua*).

Terrazas and his relatives and associates and the Jesús E. Valenzuela Company formed by prominent politicians from Guerrero City.[4]

Among the gentry, Terrazas was the most adroit at seizing both political and economic advantages. A middle-class native of Chihuahua, he had escaped from his small butchering business and minor civil service posts through the Wars of the Reform and the French Intervention. He had served Benito Juárez and been rewarded with military command. His part in minor but well-publicized military actions gave him widespread popularity that led to his election as governor in 1860. From that time his power in the state increased, but the vicissitudes of national politics—Maximilian's Empire, Juárez's Restoration, revolts against Juárez, and the seizure of power by Díaz—complicated Terrazas's efforts to establish political domination of Chihuahua.

During the porfirian years Terrazas was the prototype of the entrepreneur who prompted the extraordinary growth of the Mexican economy. His main wealth was in land, which in the arid North was used primarily for cattle raising. His latifundio stretched over some two and a half million hectares (one hectare = 2.47 acres), or about one-tenth of the surface area of Mexico's largest state. Terrazas stocked his haciendas with cattle and his herds grew to huge numbers. He shipped thousands of cattle to the United States through the El Paso port of entry, and according to popular stories he was willing to supply any number of cattle in matching colors to American importers. In Chihuahua City, he held a virtual monopoly over the supply, butchering, and distribution of beef.[5]

But in Chihuahua state, Terrazas could dominate neither politics nor the economy in the first decades after the porfirian takeover. Other families contested his every move. When the legislature increased the number of banking houses with the privilege of issuing currency, for example, the Terrazas clan obtained only two of the six new franchises, while the Guerrero faction re-

4. These statements are based on a collation of information in Almada's *Gobernadores*, pp. 336, 383, 405, with the concessions reported in Almada, *Revolución en Chihuahua*, 1: 57, 63-64. For a detailed examination of Díaz's efforts to centralize government and to strengthen his authority during his first presidential administration, see Daniel Cosío Villegas, *El Porfiriato: La vida política interior*, vol. 9 of *Historia moderna de México*, ed. by Daniel Cosío Villegas, 9 vols. (Mexico: Editorial Hermes, 1955-70).

5. There is no dispassionate account of Luis Terrazas and his influence in Chihuahua, but the following are serviceable: Francisco R. Almada, *Juárez y Terrazas (alaraciones históricas)* (Mexico: Libro Mex, 1958); Fuentes Mares, ... *Y México se refugió en el desierto*; for the development of Terrazas's landholdings, see Moisés González Navarro, *El Porfiriato: La vida social*, vol. 4 of *Historia moderna de México*, pp. 215-16; for his cattle herds, see Fernando Rosenzweig, et al., *El Porfiriato: La vida económica* vols. 7 and 8 of *Historia moderna de México*, 7: 152-53.

ceived one and other groups in the state got the remaining three. The faction-al rivalry became more intense in the mid-1880s as the old restraints on the state's economy—Chihuahua's isolation and susceptibility to Indian raids—were removed. The combined campaigns of the state militia and the United States Army broke the power of the Apaches and soon the telegraph linked Chihuahua with the rest of the nation. But the most significant event was the completion in 1884 of the Mexican Central Railroad running from El Paso, Texas, to Mexico City.[6]

The railroad connected Chihuahua with the southwestern United States and North Americans began to treat the Mexican borderland as an extension of their own territory. In the 1880s a small but growing number of foreigners drifted into the state to exploit its minerals, grazing land, and timber and to secure railroad concessions. El Paso merchants tried their luck in Chihuahua City. Typical was the Krakauer, Zork and Moye Hardware Company, which opened a general merchandise store in 1887 but soon expanded into banking, railroads, and mining. These entrepreneurs presaged a rush of foreign specula-tors at the end of the century.[7]

The telegraph, the railroad, and the elimination of the Indian threat made Chihuahua a frontier of unusual appeal which the federal government accen-tuated by promulgating new surveying and mining laws to facilitate the ex-ploitation of land and minerals. By the end of the 1880s land companies had obtained over four million hectares for the competing Terrazas and Guerrero factions. Both sides sponsored corporations ranging from telephone to trolley companies, dealing in goods from textiles to cigarettes, and obtained exemp-tions from state and local taxes as well as a monopoly of the market for periods of up to twenty years.[8]

The Guerrero party dominated state politics until 1892, but the Terrazas family, often in association with foreign investors, consolidated profitable ag-ricultural and commercial enterprises. With increasing financial strength, the

6. Fernando Jordán, *Crónica de un país bárbaro*, 3d ed. (Mexico: B. Costa-Amic, editor, 1967), pp. 229-41; Clarence C. Clendenen, *Blood on the Border: The United States Army and the Mexican Irregulars* (New York: Macmillan, 1969), pp. 85-86, 95-112.

7. Daniel Cosío Villegas, *El Porfiriato: La vida política exterior*, vols. 5 and 6 of *Historia Moderna de México*, 2: xxi, 37-38; U.S., Senate, Committee on Foreign Relations, *Revolutions in Mexico*, 62d Cong., 2d sess., 1913 (Washington: GPO, 1913), testimony of Charles M. Newman, pp. 113-17 (hereafter cited as *Hearings, 1913*). The entire volume is a catalog of North American investment in Mexico, particularly the northern states.

8. Almada, *Gobernadores*, p. 409; González Navarro, *Porfiriato: Vida social*, p. 191, note citing *Memoria que presentó el C. Gobernador del estado de Chihuahua, Lauro Carrillo en el año 1888*.

terracistas became restive under the Guerrero-dominated political administration. After unsuccessful local revolts in 1887 and 1889, they launched a determined effort to win the gubernatorial election of 1892. An incident in one of the mountain settlements provided them with an issue. Opposition to local officials had crystallized around an old couple in Tomochic who possessed a holy image reputed to have miraculous powers. The townspeople challenged the district prefect with intense religious fervor. For over a year, they resisted the authorities and ignored assurances of an investigation of their grievances by the *jefe político*. Just before the elections they defeated a detachment of troops sent to suppress their rebellion.

In its publication, *El Norte*, the Terrazas party attacked the state government. The ensuing newspaper war received a gruesome touch after an article in *El Norte* charged that the editor of the administration's newspaper, *El Diario de Chihuahua*, had offered to defect to the Terrazas side. Luis Díaz Couder, *El Diario*'s editor, printed a challenge to the author. Although the editor of *El Norte* attempted to protect his anonymous contributor, Díaz Couder shot to death his opponent, Pablo Ochoa.[9] Reports of the duel and the mismanagement of the Tomochic rebellion soon reached Mexico City. Because the incumbent regime had failed to maintain peace and order, Díaz intervened in Chihuahua. He removed the governor and refused to consider a local candidate, least of all Luis Terrazas, for office, deciding instead to appoint a regent who could control the state's intraclass struggle.

Under the watchful eye of the new governor, Miguel Ahumada of Jalisco, who ruled from 1892 to 1903, the legislature turned its attention almost exclusively to the distribution of economic favors. In eleven years the Ahumada government issued more than twice the number of concessions granted from 1876 to 1892. Since Díaz had made it evident that he would not accept Terrazas in a major political office, the old patriarch concentrated all his efforts on multiplying his financial and agricultural empire.[10] The Terrazas latifundium grew to be the largest in Mexico. Cattle exporting and local marketing through his own slaughter houses provided Terrazas with capital for investment in other commercial and manufacturing projects. He obtained concessions for such varied enterprises as a sugar beet refinery, a meat-packing plant, and a candle factory, while his relatives invested in beer production and streetcar lines, among other businesses. The clan also acquired a virtual monopoly of the state's finance and banking by merging rival banks,

9. Francisco R. Almada, *Resumén de historia del estado de Chihuahua* (Mexico: Libros Mexicanos, 1955), p. 350.

10. Terrazas did serve one term in the national Congress, but it appears to have been the exception to his elimination from politics; see Almada, *Gobernadores*, p. 266.

managing branches of national institutions, and controlling local pawn shops.[11]

During the Ahumada years developments resulting from the arrival of the railroad laid the basis for a Díaz-Terrazas rapprochement in 1903. As a railway division and shipping point, Chihuahua City experienced a boom in both population and business that accentuated its importance as the state capital. Guerrero City, which was not on the main line, declined until a spur joined it to the transportation network. Juárez, a railhead and port of entry, suddenly emerged as the state's second city.[12] The Terrazas family benefited from the growth of the state capital, long its headquarters, and from the developments in Juárez, where the family had provided most of the capital for commerce, utilities, and recreation facilities.[13]

An alteration of state politics occurred as the allocation of electoral and legislative districts mirrored the shifts of population. Chihuahua City received two additional seats in the legislature for a total of three, and the district that included Juárez was divided as a result of that city's growth.[14] Luis Terrazas could not personally take advantage of the situation because of Díaz's hostility toward him, but his sons and relatives obtained a number of district and legislative offices during the Ahumada administration. The family patriarch also gained an advantage as the Guerrero group dispersed. Some of its members went into graceful inactivity in the national Congress, but most were old men in the 1890s who either retired or died. Luis, of the same generation, proved longer-lived and moreover could rely on his son-in-law, Enrique C. Creel, under whose direction the family's economic and political fortunes prospered.

Creel began building carefully about 1892 to dominate the state. He perceived opportunities in a far different manner than his patron. Terrazas had built an agrarian empire without porfirian assistance, but Creel saw the pos-

11. Almada, *Revolución en Chihuahua*, 1: 64-70, 89; Fuentes Mares, . . . *Y México se refugió en el desierto*, pp. 155-77; Rosenzweig, *Porfiriato: Vida económica*, 1: 152-53; Reports by the U.S. consuls at Ciudad Juárez regularly recorded the exportation of Mexican cattle; see Charles W. Kindrick, U.S. consul, Juárez, to Secretary of State, January 12, 1898, NARG 59, Consular Dispatches, Ciudad Juárez, vol. 1, passim.

12. González Navarro, *Estadísticas*, pp. 67, 69. The capital city's population more than doubled, while the state's grew by only 81 percent in the years from 1877 to 1910. In 1900, Chihuahua City had slightly over 9 percent of the state's population. The growth of the city was as follows: 1877, 12,000; 1895, 18,279; 1900, 30,405.

13. Terrazas's investment in Juárez can be traced in the list of concessions granted by the legislature in Almada, *Revolución en Chihuahua*, 1: 64-80. The Terrazas activities reached a climax in 1909 when Luis's son Alberto established the Juárez Jockey Club, with a membership almost exclusively of New York financiers, to sponsor an annual race meeting and to promote business interests; see *El Paso Morning Times*, November 26 and 27, 1909 (hereafter cited as *EPMT*).

14. Almada, *Revolución en Chihuahua*, 1: 41; Almada, *Resumén*, p. 344.

sibilities of corporate enterprise. He arranged close association between foreign, especially North American, businesses and the Terrazas interests to obtain increased control of the state economy. Acquisition of complementary political authority required a rapprochement between his father-in-law and the dictator, and by 1903 Creel achieved an alliance of Díaz, Terrazas, and foreigners to monopolize politics as well as business in Chihuahua.[15]

With the encouragement of both state and national governments, foreigners surged into Chihuahua to obtain concessions for mining, ranching, and lumbering. A few came as individual speculators, but most were corporate representatives. Guggenheim's mining and smelting cartel dominated mining, and other international firms such as the Sierra Madre Land and Timber Company of William S. Greene, the Madera Lumbering Company of Lord Pearson, and the Palomas Land and Cattle Company joined in the exploitation of the state.[16] Industry was thrice favored with tariff protection, tax exemptions, and cheap labor. The Mexican Central played a major part in the economic growth as it shuttled agricultural goods, cattle, and ore from Chihuahua south to domestic markets or north to the United States.[17]

Only those thus favored by the legislature benefited from the boom economy, however. The rest of the nation suffered economically. Business expansion brought inflation that meager salary increases could not match, and the buying power of wage earners declined by as much as half during the Díaz years. In central Mexico some nine out of ten Mexicans lived on someone else's property, working for credit or coupons redeemable at a company store or utilizing spare lots as sharecroppers. In Chihuahua the situation was slightly better, but land concentration was taking place there and by the end of the Díaz regime, nineteen hacendados owned estates of more than one hundred thousand hectares each in the state.[18] One observer reported that the state's

15. Almada, *Gobernadores*, pp. 266, 426-34; Harold D. Sims, "Espejo de caciques: Los Terrazas de Chihuahua," *Historia mexicana* 18, no. 71 (1969): 379-99.

16. A detailed, although at times overstated, record of foreign investment is contained in the testimony in *Hearings, 1913*, passim; Luther T. Ellsworth, U.S. Consul, Porfirio Díaz, to Secretary of State, June 11, 1907, National Archives, Records of the Department of State, Numerical Files, 1906-1910, Record Group 59, case 69/15-20 (hereafter cited as NF). Charles M. Leonard, U.S. vice-consul, Chihuahua City, to Secretary of State, September 26, 1905, National Archives, Dispatches from U.S. Consuls in Chihuahua, 1830-1906 (microcopy 289, reel 2) includes a four-page list of American citizens and corporations engaged in business in the Chihuahua district; Enrique C. Creel prepared a list of Europeans who had contributed to the state's economic growth in *El estado de Chihuahua: Su historia, geografía, y riquezas naturales* (Mexico: Tip. el progreso, 1928), p. 27.

17. Leonard to Secretary of State, September 7, 1908, NF, case 13911/70-71.

18. Manuel González Ramírez, *Las ideas, la violencia*, vol. 1 of *La revolución social de México* (Mexico: Fondo de Cultura Económica, 1960), pp. 20-21; Almada, *Revolución en Chihuahua*, 1: 59-60.

workers lived under deplorable conditions, "with no alternative but to work for what they can get, and they get only what is necessary to support existence." A more callous writer added, ". . . the common laborer earning only one dollar per day, unless assisted by other members of the family has a hard struggle, but with his few and simple needs manages to make ends meet."[19]

Centralization of political power in the state coincided with the concentration of commercial and manufacturing enterprises. Using a national law of 1887, politicians attempted to synchronize local and state governments by making the *jefe político* the major administrator in local districts. Appointed by and responsible to the governor, the *jefes* had executive and judicial authority over minor criminal cases and in public health and economic affairs. In 1904 they were authorized to preside at meetings of local town councils.[20] Opponents of the system began to look to more extreme measures than the ballot to alter the status quo: the triad of Terrazas, Díaz, and the foreigners did not triumph without opposition in Chihuahua.

II

During the last years of the nineteenth century, intermittent insurrections stemming from local grievances marred the porfirian peace of Chihuahua: revolts followed unsatisfactory election returns, the imposition of *jefes políticos*, abuses by surveying companies, and the expansion of large estates. Guerrero earned a reputation as a particularly recalcitrant canton as violence erupted there in 1879, 1887, 1892, and 1899. From 1900 to 1911, Guerrero's citizens regularly petitioned state governors protesting the arbitrary administration by prefects.[21] Located on the margin of the established settlements of the plateau, Guerrero was a transition zone between the ranching country and the sierra district of Indian villages, mining settlements, and logging camps. The region had been the scene of incessant struggles between the indigenous population and Spanish, later Mexican, settlers. Its inhabitants often reacted forcefully to unpopular decisions by the state government; many would later enlist in the Revolution of 1910. Guerrero City was the

19. Thomas D. Edwards, U.S. Consul, Juárez, to Secretary of State, August 28, 1908, NF, case 13911/83-84; Leonard to Secretary of State, September 7, 1908, NF, case 13911/70-71.

20. Robert L. Sandels, "Silvestre Terrazas, the Press, and the Origins of the Mexican Revolution in Chihuahua" (Ph.D. dissertation, University of Oregon, 1967), citing Chihuahua's constitution of 1887; Alberto Calzadíaz Barrera, *Hechos reales de la revolución*, 3 vols., 2d ed. (Mexico: Editorial Patría, 1961), 1: 29.

21. Almada, *Revolución en Chihuahua*, 1: 93-94; Michael C. Meyer, *Mexican Rebel: Pascual Orozco and the Mexican Revolution, 1910-1915* (Lincoln: University of Nebraska Press, 1967), pp. 14-15.

most prominent settlement in the transition zone. Astride the 107th meridian that paralleled the axis of the Sierra Madre Occidental, the city was located on "the longitude of war."[22]

The alliance between Díaz and the Terrazas clan meant that local recourse to violence could not succeed, but as authority was tightened in Chihuahua, a newly organized political party rose to challenge the national government. The Mexican Liberal Party (PLM) called for a national revolt against the established order.[23] Exiled to the United States, its leaders in 1905 and 1906 launched a militant campaign against the dictatorship. They distributed a newspaper, *La regeneración,* and promoted the organization of Liberal clubs throughout Mexico in anticipation of a national insurrection. At the end of 1905, they drafted a program calling for the overthrow of the porfirian government and the securing of social justice for all Mexicans. Although they distributed propaganda and started clubs throughout Mexico, they encountered their greatest success in the states along the northern border. In Chihuahua *La regeneración* had a large circulation and several affiliated groups met regularly to plan cooperative action with the exiled leaders.[24]

In response to the PLM's activity, Creel, now governor of Chihuahua, coordinated efforts to extirpate the radical menace. He prepared border defenses to deter guerrilla attacks from the United States, placed informers among the Liberals, censored mail, and circulated pictures of prominent members of the PLM among district chiefs to prevent their infiltration into the state. Adding teeth to his program, he ordered troops to Cusihuiriáchic to maintain the peace in that potential danger zone, enlarged the police force in Juárez, and requested an additional army regiment from the national government.[25] The Mexican government enlisted the services of the United States, particularly the Post Office and Justice departments, to investigate violations of neutrality legislation. The Ministry of Foreign Relations retained American detectives,

22. Jordán, *Crónica,* chap. 27, passim; Moreno, *Hombres de la revolución,* p. 62; Florence and Robert H. Lister, *Chihuahua, Storehouse of Storms* (Albuquerque: University of New Mexico Press, 1966), 183-86.

23. Ward Sloan Albro III, "Ricardo Flores Magón and the Liberal Party: An Inquiry into the Origins of the Mexican Revolution of 1910" (Ph.D. dissertation, University of Arizona, 1967); James D. Cockcroft, *Intellectual Precursors of the Mexican Revolution, 1900-1913* (Austin: University of Texas Press, 1968), pp. 91-156.

24. Albro, "Flores Magón," p. 76, estimates that fifteen hundred copies of the newspaper were regularly sent into Mexico, largely to the northern tier of states. For the development of the PLM in Chihuahua, see Silvestre Terrazas Collection, Correspondence and Papers, Bancroft Library, University of California, Berkeley (hereafter cited as STC). Box 27, folder 11b, contains a list of subscribers to *Regeneración* compiled by the state government.

25. Creel to Ramón Corral, October 27 and November 6, 1906, STC, box 26, folder 7a.

including the famous Pinkertons, to complement the surveillance of informers located in border towns with the hope of having the PLM leaders arrested and extradited for trial in Mexico. Creel relied on the Thomas Furlong Agency of St. Louis, Missouri, for his calculated pursuit of the Liberals.[26]

The widespread circulation of its newspaper and the successful organization of Liberal affiliates emboldened the PLM, despite harassment in both Mexico and the United States, to attack the government directly. Twice they invaded border states attempting to incite a general revolution. In late 1906 they struck at Jiménez, Coahuila, and tried to launch a simultaneous expedition from El Paso into Juárez. Their efforts failed completely because of the well-prepared border defenses. Before another attempt could be made in 1907, Thomas Furlong apprehended the PLM leaders in Los Angeles, California, and turned them over to a federal court, which eventually sentenced them to prison. A small contingent captured Las Vacas, Chihuahua, for the PLM in late 1907, but federal troops forced them to retreat back across the border within a matter of hours.[27] Chihuahua's PLM members protested the arbitrary persecution of their leaders and even petitioned the president of the United States to intervene in behalf of the Liberals arrested there,[28] but their efforts came to nothing.

The PLM's failure to instigate a general uprising did not deter disillusioned railroad workers from striking in 1906 and 1908 in Chihuahua. The first action was in support of workers' demands in the central part of the nation, and the second concerned a state question. Trouble developed on the Chihuahua section of the Mexican Central in the fall of 1908 when the management began discharging illiterate Mexican trainmen and replacing them with North American workers. Most of the Mexicans who held posts as brakemen or firemen were forced into unskilled jobs at lower pay. The National Railroad

26. See letters from Creel to Corral, October and November, 1906, STC, box 26, folder 7a. Reports of the Furlong Agency to Creel are included in [José C. Valadés?], ed., "Siguiendo la pista a políticos mexicanos," *La opinión* (Los Angeles, Calif.) weekly from April 16 to June 11, 1939 (hereafter cited as *LO* (LA); reports from Furlong and other detective agencies are also scattered throughout the Archivo de Relaciones Exteriores de México, Mexico City, file series H/13-1910-1920/1 (hereafter cited as AREM).

27. [Ricardo Flores Magón] to José de la L. Soto, June 22, 1906, STC, box 26, folder 1; Albro, "Flores Magón," pp. 23-30; Charles C. Cumberland, "Precursors of the Mexican Revolution of 1910," *Hispanic American Historical Review* 22 (1942): 344-46, and "Mexican Revolutionary Movements from Texas, 1906-1912," *Southwestern Historical Quarterly* 52 (1948-49): 301-5; Lyle C. Brown, "The Mexican Liberals and Their Struggle against the Díaz Dictatorship, 1900-1906," *Antología MCC, 1956*, pp. 358-59. Furlong described his arrest of the PLM leaders in his *Fifty Years a Detective* (St. Louis: C. E. Barnett, 1912), pp. 137-48.

28. "Liberals of Chihuahua" to President [Theodore Roosevelt] of the United States, September 23, 1906, NF, case 100/100.

Brotherhood (La Gran Liga Mexicana de Empleados de Ferrocarril) supported the workers' protest and halted rail service for a short time in the North before the Díaz administration resolved the issue by promising some concessions.[29]

The failure of the Liberals and the railroad strikers resulted from the systematic suppression organized by Creel in Chihuahua. The PLM suffered from a lack of finances and its exile in the United States, where it was harassed by agents directed from Mexico, while the workers were easily coerced by the national government. The ease with which Creel eliminated threats to the established authority made the state government complacent and overconfident of its ability to crush opposition if it should reach serious proportions. That official attitude predominated in Chihuahua and throughout Mexico in the critical years preceding the Revolution of 1910, while for the future, the PLM left a legacy of resistance that could be utilized by a skillful organizer.

Meanwhile, the alliance between the federal dictator and the state oligarch, between Díaz and Terrazas, had made the government increasingly repressive and the economic monopoly even more grinding. Although some Chihuahuans had joined the Liberals and others had flirted with their conspiracy, most of the state's residents were not ready to overturn local and national governments until after the heated presidential campaign and election of 1910.

29. Cockcroft, *Precursors*, pp. 141-43; William F. Sands, U.S. Consul, Chihuahua City, to Secretary of State, October 20, 1908, NF, case 3289/15-16; González Navarro, *Porfiriato: Vida social*, p. 339.

2

*Early Career of an *Anti-reelectionist

Not surprisingly, it was a native son of Guerrero, Abraham González, who emerged as Chihuahua's leader of opposition to the Díaz dictatorship. His career represented the frustrated aspirations of the gentry who were not favored by the porfirian regime, and conditions in his home district were ideal for nurturing a revolutionary movement.

I

Guerrero City lies above Chihuahua's arid plateau in an upland valley of the Papigochi River, a rich agricultural zone with ample water and stands of pine, cedar, and evergreen oak. In the nineteenth century its residents engaged chiefly in farming and stock raising, but a few managed a profitable trade since the town served as a provisioning center for nearby mining communities in the Sierra Madre. As the district seat for the surrounding canton, Guerrero City had its courthouse politicians. Local patricians joined together to dominate the district and contended for control of the state government. Their strength came from their close association through commerce, intermarriage, and *compadrazgo*. Among the leading members of the Guerrero

13

gentry were the extended families of Casavantes, who had settled in the valley
in the mid-eighteenth century, and González, who had arrived in the 1840s.

The marriage of Dolores Casavantes and Abraham González, Sr., united
the two clans directing local politics. The eldest child of this union, José
Abraham Pablo Ladislao González, was born on the late spring evening of
June 7, 1864, in Guerrero City. Known simply as Abraham, the boy had
advantages because of the prominence of his relatives that were denied most
Mexicans. The Casavantes had a statewide reputation based on military service and political experience. Jesús José Casavantes had earned a general's
insignia while serving on the staff of the Liberal President Benito Juárez, and
before Abraham had reached his tenth year, this maternal grandfather had
served as interim governor of the state and as district prefect. The González
family was a newer, ascending member of the oligarchy. Abraham's uncle,
Celso, served in the district government and later as Guerrero's deputy in the
state legislature, where he secured a position that led on several occasions to
his appointment as interim governor. His political allies started a commercial
house with branches in Chihuahua City, Guerrero, and the nearby mining
camps. Other members of his family held positions in local and district administration that illustrated their domination of the province. Abraham also
had kinsmen throughout the state and in neighboring Sonora and Coahuila,
and the González family claimed relation to the influential Bacas across the
border in New Mexico.[1] Abraham, Sr., had not accumulated great wealth, but
his son grew up in a ranching family distinguished by financial independence,
land ownership, and association with the state's gentry.

In keeping with his family's position, Abraham received a formal education. During his early years he studied first with Alfredo Gilles, and then with
Mariano Irigoyen, celebrated as the state's foremost educator. Irigoyen had
come to the Sierra as an employee of the company owned by Celso González
and his associates, but left business to teach in Guerrero. Later he earned re-
nown as a tough disciplinarian and the master of many later revolutionaries
from the district.[2] In addition, Abraham received informal instruction from
the example of his family's involvement in state and local affairs. Both his
parents had an avid interest in politics, and he overheard their discussions
with Guerrero's politicians about election tactics and economic rewards.

1. Almada, *Gobernadores*, pp. 454-55; for Jesús José Casavantes, ibid., pp. 290-95;
for Celso González, ibid., pp. 381-84; Alberto Casavantes González, "Arbol genealógico
de la familia del sr. d. Abraham González y Casavantes," *Boletín de la Sociedad Chihuahuense de Estudios Históricos* 11 (1964), between pp. 7 and 8; Moreno, *Hombres de la
revolución*, p. 62.
2. Joaquín Márquez Montiel, *Hombres célebres de Chihuahua* (Mexico: Editorial Jus,
1953), pp. 142-45.

Travel heightened the boy's appreciation of the world outside the Papigochi Valley. Visits to relatives elsewhere in the state, perhaps even in the United States, broadened his perspective and prepared him for a move to the state capital after completing primary school.

His parents had high hopes for their oldest son, and his marks in school soon brought him to the attention of his uncle serving in the state legislature. The possibility that Celso might use his political and economic influence in the boy's favor was realized after Abraham's mother died in 1878, leaving his father to care for eight children.[3] Celso became Abraham's patron and arranged for his preparatory education. Arriving in Chihuahua City in 1879, Abraham briefly attended the Instituto Científico y Literario, the state's only preparatory school, where he studied mathematics, metaphysics, and jurisprudence.[4] The sons of Chihuahua's most influential families were among his classmates there. Beyond the classroom he discovered the city. In many ways the capital was only a slightly larger version of Guerrero, but bursts of activity disrupted the measured life of this isolated, provincial town of twelve thousand persons. Itinerant peddlers periodically left for the mountains, to return months later with wagon loads of ore from the mines; a few mule drovers regularly shipped merchandise and minerals between the nearly inaccessible sierra villages and the state capital; merchants' caravans occasionally arrived from the United States with goods freighted south from St. Louis, San Antonio, or Santa Fe.[5] But the greatest diversion came from the rough-and-tumble politics when the legislature sat in full session. The young student must have felt a sense of excitement living in Chihuahua City and moving in the highest circles with his uncle.

Abraham received encouragement to seek education from the best possible institution,[6] and his uncle's financial interests and concern for education dictated the youth's decision to complete his secondary studies in the prestigious Escuela Nacional Preparatoria in Mexico City. After completing preparatory school, in 1883 he enrolled in Notre Dame University in South Bend, Indiana, for business training. For two years he studied commerce and philosophy, while gaining an enduring appreciation of the political system of the United States.

3. Matías C. García, "Rasgos Biográficos del sr. d. Abraham González," *El correo de Chihuahua* (Chihuahua City), September 21, 1911.

4. For information on the institute, see Lister and Lister, *Storehouse of Storms*, p. 94.

5. Leonidas L. Hamilton, *Hamilton's Mexican Handbook: A Complete Description of the Republic of Mexico . . . and a Commercial Directory of the Principal Business Men of Mexico* (Boston: D. Lothrop & Co., 1885), pp. 136-37, 139.

6. Almada, *Gobernadores*, pp. 336, 381, 403, 405, 412.

The sudden death of his father abruptly concluded Abraham's formal education in 1885.[7] González returned to Chihuahua to manage his inheritance and to begin his career. He did not have a college degree but was well educated for the time. His knowledge of English could prove useful in a state bordering on Texas; and although he was not wealthy, he did own agricultural lands near Guerrero. Besides, his uncle had valuable connections in the state capital. During Abraham's absence, Celso's political group had supported the successful reelection of Porfirio Díaz in 1884 and received the president's backing in state politics.[8] Abraham could look to the future with confidence.

González undoubtedly returned on the railroad by way of El Paso, then south to Chihuahua City on the newly completed Mexican Central, whose opening had been celebrated with fiestas in 1884. He found the city changed. This provincial capital boomed as a division point on the railroad, its growing population augmented by North Americans seeking economic opportunities and Asians who had come as construction workers and stayed to open small businesses. Using funds acquired from the railroad, the state government had begun construction of a long-proposed state office building. Streetcars moved through widened thoroughfares, causing a constant clatter punctuated by the periodic arrival of freight and passenger trains.[9]

Celso and his cohorts, known as the Papigochi Party, profited from the economic boom and controlled state affairs until 1892. The ascendance of his patron's political party along with the speculative atmosphere held González in the capital. He easily obtained positions as city traffic inspector and manager of the streetcar line, both thanks to Lauro Carrillo, interim governor and owner of the urban railroad concession. A few years later his uncle helped him to secure a more desirable position, and one that would better utilize his commercial training, as chief cashier of the Banco de Chihuahua, the oldest bank in the state. In all his business affairs González earned a reputation for competence and honesty, but by the 1890s his promising career proved ephemeral as rival politicans undermined the Guerrero faction's control of Chihuahua.[10]

7. *EPMT*, October 21, 1911; González to Madero, cited in José C. Valadés, *Imaginación y realidad de Francisco I. Madero*, 2 vols. (Mexico: Antigua Librería Robredo, 1960), 2: 22-23. The usually reliable Almada mistakenly reported (*Gobernadores*, p. 454) that González attended the University of Indiana and other authors have accepted his statement.

8. Almada, *Resumén*, p. 339.

9. Rosenzweig, *Porfiriato: Vida económica*, 7: 182-92; Creel, *Chihuahua*, p. 24; Lister and Lister, *Storehouse of Storms*, pp. 172-75.

10. Almada, *Gobernadores*, pp. 409, 455.

González found, as his political connections eroded, that the flourishing Terrazas-Creel clique threatened not only his prospects but also his livelihood. Enrique Creel masterminded a consolidation of the state's banking houses that climaxed with the absorption of the Banco de Chihuahua in 1896,[11] leaving González unemployed. Although he owned land in Guerrero Canton, González was not an hacendado. Any increase in his grazing property would require him to compete with the land companies operating in the region and with the monopoly of the cattle business held by the Terrazas family and a few large foreign-owned corporations. After the turn of the century, González made a brief venture into mining in the Aldama region, but again the competition of tax-exempt foreign companies blocked his success. His education in the United States, particularly his fluency in English, did provide minor jobs. He became the translator, then editor, for a small weekly newspaper, *El padre padilla*, and on occasion he worked as a translator for the United States consul in Chihuahua City.[12]

González obtained more permanent work when he joined an American cattle firm with landholdings in Chihuahua. He first became a representative of an El Paso company managed by Charles Newman and later handled local orders for a Kansas City, Missouri, company.[13] As a cattle agent, he bought and sold cattle, and introduced the first Hereford stock into the state. During this period he met Pancho Villa and purchased a few head of cattle from him without inquiring too closely into their origins before shipping them to the United States.[14] Traveling throughout the state, González must have been struck by the tremendous economic development in which he shared only modestly. Certainly by 1903 he recognized that his prospects had dissipated.

Reared in the sierra, Abraham had received a legacy of direct action to meet adversity. As a native son of Guerrero, he grew up in an atmosphere of politics, surrounded by men who turned easily to the gun when their aims were thwarted. Gabriel Casavantes had led the 1879 revolt and Celso González had been titular head of the 1887 outbreak. Abraham counted relatives among the rebels massacred when federal troops finally brought an end to the

11. Almada, *Revolución en Chihuahua*, 1: 85-87.

12. Almada, *Gobernadores*, p. 455. Evidence of González's service for the American consul is contained in Ellsworth to Secretary of State, November 30, 1907, NF, case 69/15-20.

13. *EPMT*, October 21, 1911; *Hearings, 1913*, testimony of Charles M. Newman, pp. 113-17.

14. Juan Gualberto Amaya, *Madero y los auténticos revoluciónarios de 1910 hasta la Decena Trágica y fín de General Pascual Orozco* (Mexico: n.p., 1946), pp. 17-18; Calzadíaz Barrera, *Hechos reales*, 1: 27.

Tomochic affair. His birthright included not only family, business, and political prospects, but also a proclivity to violence to achieve his goals.[15]

Frustrated by the obstacles that blocked his career, González began a flirtation with the PLM movement. He favored changes in the government and could support the PLM programs to better the lot of the laborers and the campesinos, to improve education, and to guarantee civil rights. He traveled widely as a cattle agent and seems to have distributed the PLM newspaper in the sierra. Yet he eschewed the increasingly revolutionary plans of the Liberals, although his brother, Santiago González Casavantes, sat in Liberal councils and acted as an adviser during the drafting of the Plan of 1906.[16] Abraham's association with the rebels was encouraged when others from the Guerrero District, such as José de la Luz Soto, joined the movement and was further reinforced when he struck up an acquaintance with Braulio Hernández, a local schoolteacher with radical notions. Nevertheless, González was no Liberal; he was a reformer, not a revolutionary.[17] The PLM failed in its invasion, but González recognized its legacy of resistance and would later utilize it.

II

After the brutal, if temporary, suppression of the PLM, Porfirio Díaz suddenly announced in a magazine interview published in March, 1908, that he would not seek a sixth reelection in 1910. His decision added to the consternation of his opponents, many of whom suspected a ruse to trick remaining challengers into the open, and inaugurated a period of intense political activity.[18]

While González and others like him in Chihuahua waited for some reaction to the dictator's announcement, outside the state independent politicians forced an advantage from Díaz's interview. One of them, Francisco I. Madero, a Coahuilan hacendado and critic of the dictatorial regime, investigated to his

15. Jordán, *Crónica*, chap. 27, passim; Moreno, *Hombres de la revolución*, 62; Lister and Lister, *Storehouse of Storms*, pp. 183-86.

16. González Ramírez, *Las ideas, la violencia*, p. 57, n. 52. For a copy of the Liberal Plan in English, see Cockcroft, *Precursors*, pp. 239-45.

17. [Ricardo Flores Magón] to José de la L. Soto, June 22, 1905, STC, box 26, folder 1; *Hearings, 1913*, testimony of Félipe R. Gutiérrez, p. 279; Valadés, *Madero*, 2: 27.

18. Díaz gave the interview to James Creelman, who published it in *Pearson's Magazine*, March, 1908; then it was widely reprinted in translation. See Juan Sánchez Azcona, *La etapa maderista de la revolución* (Mexico: Talleres Gráficos de la Nación, 1960), pp. 28-30.

satisfaction the credibility of the interview, then summoned friends to prepare for the 1910 elections.[19] Although broadcasting his views in letters to men of similar persuasion, he did not take immediate action because he feared an early campaign would exhaust its force before the election, still two years off.[20] Preferring to generate enthusiasm for his beliefs, he wrote *The Presidential Succession of 1910*, which circulated privately in the last months of 1908 before its general release January, 1909.

In the book Madero gave his interpretation of Latin American history and emphasized his reluctance to employ revolutionary methods to achieve political success. He called for a return to rule by law, an end to personalistic government, and the reestablishment of the Constitution of 1857, including its provisions for state sovereignty. Accomplishment of these goals, he argued, could be realized only through methods based on the experience of the United States. His antipathy for revolution resulted from his consideration of Latin America's past, his belief in democracy, and his shrewd understanding of the Díaz government. Latin America's history during the nineteenth century had been a dismal chronicle of wars, *caudillo* rule, stagnant economies, and diminished international significance. Madero reasoned that frequent coups d'etat prevented national progress and encouraged recourse to power rather than law and reliance on personality rather than ability. Progress made during long, stable regimes came to nothing if authority was transferred by bloody and destructive revolution.[21]

After explaining his opposition to dictatorship, Madero outlined procedures necessary to alter Mexico's retrograde heritage. He believed that the creation of a strong organization based on principles rather than personalities should be the first step in any political campaign. He hoped to form local clubs to place propaganda in newspapers and to participate in local elections. Recognizing the futility of disorganized regional movements, he proposed a

19. Madero to Manuel de León, March 15, 1908, Archivo de don Francisco I. Madero, Instituto Nacional de Antropología e Historia (microfilmed by El Centro de Documentación Histórica, reel 7) (hereafter cited as AM). Madero wrote that he had received several private *informes* that Díaz meant what he said in the Creelman interview. Reliable biographies of Madero include Valadés, *Madero*; Charles C. Cumberland, *Mexican Revolution: Genesis under Madero* (Austin: University of Texas Press, 1952); and Stanley R. Ross, *Francisco I. Madero: Apostle of Mexican Democracy* (New York: Columbia University Press, 1955).
20. Madero to Zefarino Valadés, September 28, 1908, AM, reel 7 (see similar letters throughout reels 7 and 8); Alfonso Taracena, *Madero, el héroe cívico* (Mexico: Ediciones Xóchitl, 1946), pp. 77-79.
21. Francisco I. Madero, *La sucesión presidential en 1910* (San Pedro, Coahuila, 1908), pp. 310-16; Valadés, *Madero*, 1: 171-73.

national committee (Comité Directivo para la República) to coordinate district groups, proselytize where no organizations existed, and convoke a convention to select candidates for national offices. A national campaign firmly rooted in the localities, he believed, could coalesce latent opposition at the same time that it put democratic principles into immediate practice.[22]

Madero expected his book to arouse interest throughout the country, but he did not anticipate the hundreds of requests for copies that he received early in 1909. From Chihuahua alone, he received orders for over 125 copies during January and February. Bulk shipments went to Chihuahua City and Parral, and several persons, including the future revolutionary Guillermo Baca and Governor Creel, received individual copies.[23]

Waiting only a brief time for the book to make its impact, Madero formed an organizational committee, the Centro Antirreeleccionista de México, in May, 1909, with Emilio Vázquez Gómez and other independents. In a manifesto the committee announced its intention to campaign for the presidency, and proposed a national convention to nominate candidates for the impending elections. It called on the people to make the centenary of independence the year in which administrative tyranny was overthrown by the election of new men and in which constitutional rights were reasserted by the use of the franchise.[24] The vote, not revolt, would animate all personal and states' rights outlined in the Constitution of 1857.

In an early move, the new party founded a newspaper, *El antirreeleccionista,* published first as a weekly and later as a daily. The executive committee installed locals in Mexico City and its environs, and during June and July wrote numerous letters designating party organizers throughout the republic that made possible a rapid expansion of affiliates.[25] The most dramatic of the Centro's propaganda programs were the campaign trips of Francisco Madero. A

22. Madero, *Sucesión presidencial,* pp. 316, 318, 329-30; Madero to Victoriano Agüeros, August 6, 1908, AM, reel 7.

23. Madero to Mercedes de Madero, December, 1909, in Isidro Fabela, ed., *Documentos históricos de la Revolución Mexicana: Revolución y régimen maderista,* 5 vols. (Mexico: Fondo de Cultura Economica, 1964; Editorial Jus, 1965), 1: 22 (hereafter cited as *DHRM*). Orders for the book are contained in AM, reel 8, passim. For examples from Chihuahua, see Madero to Marcial Bassoco, February 18, 1909; to Enrique C. Creel, February 20, 1909, to Baca, February 23, 1909, AM, reel 8.

24. "Manifesto a la nación," *DHRM,* 1: 43; Francisco I. Madero, "El partido nacional antirreeleccionista y la próxima lucha electoral: Su programa, sus trabajos," ibid., 1: 28-38. Despite the Creelman interview, in February, 1909, Díaz had become a candidate for reelection; see Ross, *Madero,* p. 69.

25. Cumberland, *Mexican Revolution,* p. 79; Roque Estrada, *La revolución y Francisco I. Madero: Primera, segunda, tercera etapas, 1911-1912* (Guadalajara: Imprenta Americana, 1912), p. 104.

vice-president of the organization and independently wealthy, he devoted himself to speaking engagements; in a ten-month period, from June, 1909, to April, 1910, he made three major and several minor tours of the country publicizing the party's goals and organizing adherents.[26] In addition, he maintained a massive correspondence encouraging the formation of Anti-reelection groups and sounding out potential regional leaders.

III

In Chihuahua City, Madero's overtures found a receptive audience that included Abraham González, Braulio Hernández, and Cástulo Herrera, as well as others who were disenchanted with oligarchical administration. They read his book as rapidly as copies became available and, meeting in a public plaza to avoid detection, discussed programs and principles and decided to form an opposition party.[27] Their apprehension about their political activity was dispelled by the formation of another independent group, the Club Electoral Ignacio Allende, while encouragement came when the national committee designated González as one of the party's state representatives.[28] González organized a provisional committee, which called a general meeting on July 11 in the O'Bannon Villa in Chihuahua City. Nearly two hundred people attended and, exercising the club's democratic principles, elected by secret ballot the group's officers, including González as treasurer. After the voting, provisional president Pascual Mejía read an act of foundation officially installing the club as an affiliate of the Anti-reelectionist party.[29]

González delivered a formal address on the purposes of the movement, opening with an exposition of the manner in which the government had violated the constitution: "The Díaz government prostituted the electoral provisions," he insisted, "by holding sham elections to maintain the façade of the Constitution." Porfirian politics demonstrated that voting rights could only be guaranteed by their exercise, not by their incorporation into legal docu-

26. Taracena, *Madero*, pp. 192-93. For accounts of the tours by Madero's companions, see Félix F. Palavicini, *Mi vida revolucionaria* (Mexico: Ediciones Botas, 1937), pp. 13-35, and Estrada, *La revolución*, pp. 141-232.

27. Valadés, *Madero*, 2: 24; Eulogio Salazar, Jr., "El protomartír del antirreeleccionismo," *El heraldo* (Chihuahua City), March 7, 1951; Moreno, *Hombres de la revolucion*, pp. 62-63.

28. The group was founded May 9, 1909, with the following officers: Francisco Solís, president; Miguel Sarabía, vice-president; and Polícarpo López, secretary. See *El correo*, May 15 and 16, 1909.

29. Ibid., July 14, 1909, and exchange of letters between González and Grégorio M. Prieto in ibid., June 11, 1910.

ments. The Anti-reelectionist party, he told his audience, intended to reawaken democratic procedures by offering alternatives to official candidates in elections. The independent slate would not be arbitrarily selected, but chosen by the vote of local delegates at a nominating convention. He called on those present to support the assertion that only free elections and time limits on public office holding could redeem the nation. "Chihuahuans," he concluded, ". . . I invite you to second our noble ideas and suggest that we adopt as the name for this association Club Antirreeleccionista 'Suffragio Efectivo y No Re-elección' " (the Effective Suffrage and No Reelection Antireelectionist Club). The crowd responded with tremendous applause and immediately endorsed his proposed name as their motto. They decided to call the organization the Centro Antirreeleccionista Benito Juárez in honor of the hero of nineteenth-century reform.[30]

Governor José María Sánchez took the precaution during the association's first meeting of ordering uniformed police to surround the Villa O'Bannon and of planting plainclothesmen in the crowd. Since the meeting was orderly, the police took no action, but four days later when the club sought a permit to stage its first public event, a demonstration before a monument dedicated to Benito Juárez on the anniversary of his death, the request was denied on the orders of the governor.[31] Following this initial setback, the club's activities were kept under official surveillance for several months but were not interfered with.

Although the national committee had appointed local organizers in Chihuahua, the directors remained uncertain that the group had been formed. Inefficiency and some duplication marked their massive campaign, and there was also an understandable lack of coordination between the committee in Mexico City and Madero, its roving spokesman. The confusion was clearly demonstrated in mid-July, when Madero wrote to Silvestre Terrazas, well known for his independent views, asking him to organize his friends in Chihuahua in support of the cause and offering to dispatch messengers from San Pedro, Coahuila, to discuss national programs. He must have been delighted

30. Ibid., July 14, 1909, includes the complete speech. Other members of the executive committee were Aureliano González (no relation to Abraham), president; Pascual Mejía, vice-president; José de la Luz Navarro, second vice-president; Rafael Martínez, secretary; Ignacio León Avila, J. P. Lomelín, and Tomás Silva, members of the executive committee. Among the members were Santiago González Casavantes, Braulio Hernández, and Cástulo Herrera. For a more complete roster, see Almada, *Revolución en Chihuahua*, 1: 153.

31. Francisco R. Almada, *Vida, proceso, muerte de Abraham González* (Mexico: Talleres Gráficos de la Nación, 1967), p. 22; *El correo*, July 14, 1909.

to learn that a local club had already been established. He responded immediately by writing Aureliano González, president of the Benito Juárez Club, asking him to correspond with the central body to coordinate activities with national plans.[32]

Among their first objectives, Chihuahua's Anti-reelectionists sought a newspaper to publicize their activities and to carry other propaganda. That consideration influenced the members when they elected Silvestre Terrazas, editor of *El correo de Chihuahua*, to the executive committee. Terrazas declined the position, however, fearing that his participation would prejudice his reputation as an independent journalist, perhaps even predispose the state government to close his newspaper. Nevertheless, he carried regular reports of club activities and announcements of its meetings and sold Madero's book at his editorial offices.[33] To achieve the club's propaganda purposes González founded *El grito del pueblo*, which he edited and distributed from the club's offices.[34] The cost of publishing a newspaper created a financial problem that the members resolved by assessing monthly dues. González stressed that nobody would be excluded from membership because they could not pay the levy, but added that the dues of fifty centavos were urgently needed for operating expenses.[35]

The members hoped to promote Anti-reelectionist programs through the formation of branch clubs across Chihuahua. Almost simultaneously with the institution of the Benito Juárez group, independent Mexicans organized similar clubs in the state's other large towns, Juárez and Hidalgo de Parral.[36] The Chihuahua City group planned organizations for each of the district capitals and sent agents to proselytize throughout the state. The executive body, following the pattern of the national committee, posted commissions to representatives in villages who enlisted followers and also handled arrangements for

32. Madero to Silvestre Terrazas, July 15, 1909, and Madero to Aurelio *(sic)* González, July 20, 1909, AM, reel 9. Silvestre, poor relation of the Luis Terrazas family, was a journalist first for a Catholic newspaper, then his own *El correo*. His views generally followed those of advanced Catholic social reform until 1906, when they became more pointedly antiadministration, especially anti-Creel. See Sandels, "Silvestre Terrazas and the Old Regime in Chihuahua," *The Americas* 28 (1971): 192-93.

33. Sandels, "Silvestre Terrazas, the Press," pp. 199-201; advertisement in *El correo*, August 19, 1909. Governor Creel had already closed the editorial offices for a brief time in early 1909.

34. Esteban B. Calderón, "El Maderismo en Chihuahua," *El nacional* (Mexico City), November 20, 1931.

35. *El correo*, August 4, 1909. Dues equaled twenty-five cents.

36. For information on the Parral club, see Madero to Pablo Olivas Prieto, July 23, 1909, AM, reel 9; *El correo*, July 13, 1909; Amaya, *Los auténticos revolucionarios*, pp. 17-18. For Juárez, see *El correo*, July 29, 1909.

the arrival of club representatives.[37] Agents capitalized on the latent hostility toward the Terrazas-Díaz regime by revitalizing the former organizations of the Liberal party to establish a system of sympathetic groups. González traveled widely, encountering particular success in the western cordillera, where he knew the people and played on their resentment toward state authorities. Although general dissatisfaction and fragments of the clandestine PLM movement assisted the Anti-reelectionists, the statewide network resulted more from the promotional activities and friendships of the party members, especially González.[38] By January, 1910, energetic recruitment had won the state group enough adherents to carry out an active club program.

Programs of the weekly meetings of the Benito Juárez Club emphasized Madero's democratic precepts in regard to free elections and rotation of public officials. As an immediate goal, the members attempted to educate the electorate in its civil rights and obligations as well as to encourage participation in local elections. Throughout the fall of 1909 they studied state and national electoral laws, discussed the political systems of democracies throughout the world, and encouraged further home study by selling low-cost editions of the electoral laws and state and national constitutions.[39]

Calling on other independent civic groups to unite by presenting a common slate of candidates, the Benito Juárez Club took a step toward fusion by meeting jointly with the Ignacio Allende club in October. The combined group of over five hundred persons voted by secret ballot to choose candidates for the November elections. Members of both clubs' executive committees dominated the lists; Abraham González was nominated as a candidate for substitute member of the city council.

The clubs campaigned vigorously, but their efforts had little impact. Official candidates won nearly every office, although the challengers did manage a few neighborhood positions. Following announcement of the official results, *El correo* published its tabulation of ballots, giving a narrow victory to the independent candidates. The Anti-reelectionists protested to the state legislature that open fraud had marred the election. They found especially irritating the vague terms of the laws which virtually precluded successful protest

37. Aureliano González to Albino Frías, September 1909, STC, box 28, folder Albino Frías, is an example of the type of correspondence used by the Benito Juárez Club.

38. Almada, *Revolución en Chihuahua,* 1: 153; Rafael Martínez, Carlos M. Samper, and José P. Lomelín, *La revolución y sus hombres (apuntes para la historia contemporánea)* (Mexico: Talleres Tipográficos de "El tiempo," 1912), p. xix. An account of González's trip to recruit in Guerrero City was reported in *El correo,* September 21, 1909.

39. See particularly accounts of meetings in *El correo,* August 3 and 5, October 12, and November 9, 1909. The club sold the constitutions and the electoral laws for twenty-five centavos a copy.

against illegal polling practices, and their petition carefully exposed the un-democratic aspects of the electoral process and proposed remedies to prevent a recurrence of irregularities. They called for a precise definition of fraud with specific penalties. Since the legislature had recessed, the protest was received by the permanent delegation, which replied that reform would require amendment of the state constitution and suggested that the petition be resubmitted in June, 1910, after the deputies reconvened.[40]

In the fall of 1909 the Anti-reelectionists clearly intended to function as a loyal opposition. They demonstrated their moderate philosophy in their weekly sessions, electoral campaigns, and reliance on petitions to obtain redress of grievances. As late as December, 1909, they voted a solemn protest against governmental suppression of Anti-reelection clubs in Yucatán and called for national petitions against the policy. An even clearer example of their unshaken moderation was the publication of a public salute to Porfirio Díaz as he crossed Chihuahua by train to meet President William H. Taft at the Juárez-El Paso border.[41]

Officials of Chihuahua's state government ignored the Anti-reelectionists as an insignificant challenge to their authority. Satisfied that the nascent party could be snuffed out easily if necessary, the Terrazas-Creel machine occasionally harried its members but made no concerted efforts to crush it during 1909. The government disrupted the club's public demonstrations, prevented its meetings in public halls, and, members charged, made some illegal arrests and assessed outrageous fines during municipal elections.[42] On the other hand, when the group obtained a meeting place in a private home, it held weekly meetings without interference, and its business and newspaper office was allowed to remain open without molestation. The state's leniency reflected complacency born of the effective manner in which it had suppressed other challenges to the established order. Thus through a favorable combination of active promotion and governmental smugness, the Anti-reelectionists flourished in Chihuahua.

IV

Madero's organization did not fare as well in the rest of the nation. During the summer of 1909, many of Díaz's supporters opposed the official candidate for the vice-presidency and turned to a porfirian administrator and mili-

40. Ibid., October 12 and 28, November 3, December 1, 24, 25, and 28, 1909.
41. The salute was approved by majority vote at the meeting of October 3; see ibid., October 5, 1909.
42. Ibid., July 25, October 12 and 28, 1909.

tary officer, Bernardo Reyes, who attracted many independents as well; *reyismo* boomed as a political movement.[43] Madero's party ran a poor third behind the reelectionists, who favored the dictator, and the group supporting Reyes. Since some of its members crossed over to the *revista* party, during the fall of 1909 there was seldom a quorum at the meetings of the Anti-reelectionist national committee. Only Madero's zeal held the Anti-reelectionists together during those trying months. He responded to the decline of the Centro's fortunes by forging ahead with plans for a national nominating convention in the spring of 1910. Working with other members, he set April 15 as the date for the convention and outlined a procedure for choosing delegates. He also undertook another political tour to strengthen the resolve of party members and to solicit the support of independents. Although he had just recovered from a debilitating illness, he made a brief journey to Oaxaca as a prelude to a swing around the Northwest. From December, 1909, to January, 1910, he made a full circle from Querétaro, through Jalisco, Sinaloa, Sonora, Chihuahua, and back to Querétaro.[44]

As Madero tried to repair the national organization, the Chihuahua City club was strengthened by the acquisition of a dynamic leader whose enthusiasm matched that of the national spokesman. Aureliano González resigned as president of the Benito Juárez Club, and its members, meeting on December 26, 1909, elected Abraham González as his successor. In his acceptance speech, the new president said that he felt greater satisfaction than if he had been elected state governor. "Election by a group of free men . . . ," he explained, "is a thousand times more honorable than selection by an autocrat after sham elections." He then called for the club to work with renewed vigor for the eventual triumph of their principles.[45] González's first job was to make preparations for Madero's arrival on his campaign tour. The expected date of his visit had been advanced because of persistent rumors that henchmen of the Sonora authorities would attempt to assassinate him.[46]

43. Eberhardt Victor Niemeyer, Jr., *El General Bernardo Reyes*, Biblioteca de Nuevo León (Monterrey, Mexico: Universidad de Nuevo León, 1966), pp. 143-79; Anthony T. Bryan, "The Career of General Bernardo Reyes: Continuity and Change in Mexican Politics, 1905-1913" (Master's thesis, University of Nebraska, 1967), pp. 125, 127-52.

44. Cumberland, *Mexican Revolution*, pp. 87-89; Estrada, *La revolución*, pp. 101, 136-38, 141-68.

45. *El correo*, December 31, 1909. The reasons for Aureliano González's resignation are obscure. Perhaps his position as secretary of the Associated Press of Mexico absorbed most of his time as that group struggled to obtain freedom of the press and to provide funds for legal support of jailed journalists.

46. For an account of the tour in Sonora and the assassination threats, see Estrada, *La revolución*, pp. 154-57, and Alfonso Taracena, *Mí vida en el vértigo de la Revolución Mexicana. Anales sintéticos, 1900-1930*, 2d ed. (Mexico: Ediciones Botas, 1936), p. 85.

In early January, 1910, González, accompanied by others from the Chihuahua City group, went to Juárez to meet Madero, arriving by train from Nogales. González and Madero had corresponded about party matters but had never met before. The Anti-reelectionists held a small reception on Madero's arrival on January 14, then the delegation made a leisurely trip to Chihuahua City. The state government made no deliberate effort to forestall the *maderista* campaign there, although it took the precaution of mobilizing units of the rurales in the event trouble should erupt during public demonstrations. The city officials, on the other hand, threatened to arrest the leaders of the Benito Juárez Club if the meetings became disruptive. The organizers had invited Anti-reelectionists from across the state to Chihuahua City and they expected a large number to come. Fearing that a single huge demonstration might provoke city or state officials, González arranged for Madero to speak at several meetings dispersed through the town's electoral districts.[47]

A crowd of a thousand people met Madero and his entourage at the railroad station on the morning of January 16. Braulio Hernández, an intimate of González, introduced Madero. Speaking from the station platform, Madero and his companion, Roque Estrada, preached on the need for free elections and rotation of public officials. Then the party, escorted by González and Hernández as well as other members of the Benito Juárez Club, made the round of neighborhood rallies.[48] The strategy of dispersed meetings worked effectively. The day passed without incident and Madero departed the following morning for another day of engagements in Hidalgo del Parral before leaving Chihuahua.[49]

Assessments of the tour through the state varied. Roque Estrada, Madero's co-speaker, felt encouraged by what he reported as middle-class crowds. Chihuahua's shopkeepers and professional men gave the movement greater respectability and wider support than if it were based solely on the students and the workers who backed Madero in other regions. In contrast, Enrique C. Creel, congratulating himself on the way his government had handled the "radicals," reported to Vice-President Ramón Corral that the rallies were complete fiascoes, attended only by "the curious, who [queue-up] for an exhibition of a rare animal or some company of clowns." González wrote to Madero that his appearance had attracted great interest throughout the state. The local leader capitalized on the general excitement by publishing a souvenir edition of Madero's and Estrada's speeches to publicize the tenets of the

47. Valadés, *Madero*, 2: 27.
48. *El Correo*, January 15, 16, and 18, 1910.
49. An account of Madero's reception in Parral is contained in González to Madero, January 18, 1910, "Archivo de Madero," *LO* (LA), December 17, 1933.

party and to aid recruitment. The program succeeded: by February, 1910, the club claimed thirteen hundred members in Chihuahua.[50]

Madero's trip through the North had accomplished more than he had dared hope. Leaders recruited as a result of it, such as Manuel Bonilla in Sinaloa, founded new local units of the party, and others, including Benjamín Hill and José María Maytorena in Sonora, reorganized existing *reyista* groups to support the Anti-reelectionists.[51] Furthermore, as a direct outgrowth of the campaign in Chihuahua, the Benito Juárez Club discussed the possibility of nominating Madero as a presidential candidate for the 1910 elections. The tour had altered his position from spokesman to acknowledged leader of the opposition political party.

V

Serious discussion of possible party nominees began in Chihuahua City's club on January 20, 1910, and with little thought to alternatives the group selected Madero as their candidate for the presidency. In reporting the decision, González explained that before the tour the members had informally considered a number of persons, but Madero's visit had made him a unanimous selection. They also debated possible running mates for Madero but failed to reach a decision. González apparently persuaded his fellows to allow their presidential choice to indicate his preference for vice-president. He wrote Madero that if he planned to imitate "the system of American politics," he should be aware of "the fact that in the United States the candidate for president has great influence in the selection of the vice-president." "Besides," González continued, "in our cause there is no other person who has had your advantage, by virtue of your trips through various states of the country, of dealing personally with our supporters." He asked Madero to put aside modest reticence and to indicate confidentially whom he desired as a second on the party ticket.[52]

Awaiting a reply, González arranged a series of joint meetings with the Ignacio Allende Club in Chihuahua City. The two organizations met weekly for discussions about common support of the nominees. Finally, on February

50. Estrada, *La revolución*, p. 167: Creel to Corral, January 25, 1910, "Archivo de Corral," *LO* (LA), October 3, 1937; González to Madero, January 17, 1910, and January 18, 1910, "Archivo de Madero," ibid., December 17, 1933; *El correo*, February 23, 1910.

51. Manuel González Ramírez, ed., *Manifiestos políticos (1892-1912)* (Mexico: Fondo de Cultura Económica, 1957), pp. 73-77.

52. González to Madero, January 21, 1910, "Archivo de Madero," *LO* (LA), December 17, 1933.

13, 1910, the combined membership voted by more than a two-thirds majority to endorse Madero's candidacy at the national convention.[53]

The combined parties waited for nearly two months before learning Madero's choice for a running mate. During the interval Madero had carefully weighed various possibilities and sounded out several prospects, probably beginning with Toribio Esquivel Obregón of Guanajuato. Finally in mid-March he recommended Francisco Vázquez Gómez, brother of the president of the national executive committee and formerly the personal physician of Porfirio Díaz. On March 20, the Chihuahua City group voted to support his suggestion, and Madero in turn used their endorsement to persuade Vázquez Gómez to join the lists of the Anti-reelectionists even though he had been committed to Bernardo Reyes.[54] With instructions to nominate a Madero-Vázquez ticket, González was chosen to head Chihuahua's delegation to the party's national convention in Mexico City.[55]

More than one hundred delegates assembled on April 15, 1910, in Mexico City for the opening of the Anti-reelectionist caucus, and by the last session that number had nearly doubled. The general excitement had a touch of apprehension as the government prevented some representatives from attending and planted spies among the participants. In a more menacing gesture, Vice-President Corral issued a warrant for Madero's arrest, forcing him into hiding for the first day of the convention, but the meeting began on schedule nevertheless. José María Pino Suárez was chosen as convention president by acclamation at the first session, and Abraham González was selected for the executive committee as second vice president.[56] In the afternoon the conferees took up the selection of the party's presidential candidate. González nominated Madero in the name of the Chihuahua delegation. After some discussion his proposal was approved. The next day the convention turned to the vice-presidency. Toribio Esquivel Obregón made a determined bid for the position, but in the final balloting Madero's choice, Francisco Vázquez Gómez, prevailed.[57]

53. *El correo*, February 17, 1910.
54. Francisco Vázquez Gómez, *Memorias políticas, 1909-1913* (Mexico: Imprenta Mundial, 1931), 23-24.
55. *El correo*, March 24, 1910.
56. This account of the convention is based primarily on the minutes of the sessions recorded by the secretary, Roque Estrada, and transcribed in *La revolución*, pp. 199-238. For surveillance reports on the delegates, see the letters from Francisco Chávez and Francisco A. Beltrán in "Archivo de Corral," *LO* (LA), October 31 and November 7, 1937.
57. Almada, *Gobernadores*, p. 455; Estrada, *La revolución*, pp. 201, 230-32. The nominees and their votes were: Madero, 159; Esquivel Obregón, 23; Fernando Iglesias Calderón, 3.

Having agreed on their slate, the members drew up a campaign platform. They accepted an eclectic statement which reflected the ideas that Madero had publicized for over a year and that would appeal to a wide audience. In addition to calling for electoral reform, they sought to reestablish the Constitution of 1857 with its provisions for confederated government and limited tenure of public officials. They also demanded some moderate reform legislation aimed at improving public education, encouraging agriculture, bettering army life, and ameliorating labor conditions.[58]

After the convention adjourned April 17, the delegates returned to their homes to campaign for the June elections of national and local officials. As the Anti-reelectionist canvass reached a new intensity, the government increased its harassment by dispersing rallies and arresting party members. Official suppression climaxed in early June, when state police in Monterrey arrested Madero. He was held in jail until after the elections to disqualify his candidacy.[59]

Chihuahua's Anti-reelectionists campaigned vigorously for the national candidates as well as for a full slate of state congressional and administrative nominees. González dedicated himself completely to the cause. Utilizing the pages of *El grito del pueblo* and contributing to other newspapers, he wrote reams of propaganda. In a one-man effort to reach all the voters, he crisscrossed the state exhorting the electorate. To mobilize a disenfranchised but powerful segment of the population, he sponsored the formation of a women's chapter of the party in Chihuahua City and spoke at its first meeting, telling the audience that they had all the obligations but none of the privileges of citizenship. His crusade prompted Juan Sánchez Azcona, a member of the national executive committee, to recall that González was the party's most ardent partisan in the entire North.[60]

But González's efforts proved futile as the state government took extraordinary measures to control the polls, prevent disruption of the voting, and ensure the selection of porfirian electors in the popular balloting portion of the two-step indirect elections. The governor placed federal troops on alert and called district officials to the capital to give them precise instructions for

58. Estrada, *La revolución*, pp. 230-32.

59. Cumberland, *Mexican Revolution*, pp. 110-13; Henry Lane Wilson, U.S. ambassador, Mexico City, to Secretary of State, June 9, 1910, Records of the Department of State relating to the Internal Affairs of Mexico, 1910-1929, 8183/323, National Archives microfilm publication (microcopy no. 274), 1910-1914 (hereafter cited as RDS); Philip C. Hanna, U.S. consul general, Monterey, to Secretary of State, June 8, 1910, 8183/322.

60. "Marzo 7 de 1913," *El universal* (Mexico City), March 7, 1936.

the regulation of voting with an indication of expected results.[61] As expected, Díaz and Corral won sweeping victories in the popular elections and their selection by the electoral ballots in July was a foregone conclusion. In Chihuahua, the reelectionists kept all contested positions and elected a substantial majority of the presidential electors. The next month the electoral college gave Díaz and Corral 351 votes and Madero and Vázquez Gómez only 25.[62] Legitimate political opposition to the porfirian government had failed; for the Anti-reelectionists there now remained no recourse but revolution.

61. Almada, *Vida González*, pp. 25-29. The indirect electoral system called for popular balloting in June, followed in July by the voting of the electoral college composed of district electors. A letter describing steps taken to control the elections from Chihuahua's governor to Creel is reprinted in Almada, *Revolución en Chihuahua*, 1: 156-58.

62. Wilson to Secretary of State, June 27, 1910, RDS, 8183/332; Wilson to Secretary of State, July 14, 1910, RDS, 8183/337.

3

Rebel Gunrunner

Madero opposed violence; he had initiated the Anti-reelectionist movement not so much to oust Díaz but as a method of transition to a responsive administration without disrupting the peace and economic growth fostered during the dictatorship. If rebellion were required for each change of government, Madero believed, Mexico would never progress, never develop. Yet as early as December, 1909, during his campaign in Sonora, he recognized that implementation of the party's programs might require insurrection, although he evaded the prospect and made no preparations for it. At the nominating convention some delegates had informally discussed the possibility of revolt, but opinion was widely divided. After Madero's arrest in June, 1910, and his release on bail, he cautiously sounded out his aides and learned that the party membership was split between those loyal to him who felt compelled to revolt, and those allied with Francisco Vázquez Gómez who decried armed resistance to the government. Receiving enough affirmative support to take action, Madero called his lieutenants together for a strategy meeting in San Luis Potosí. In July, several Anti-reelectionist leaders, including Abraham González and Gustavo Madero, considered overall preparations and immediate tactics. In their discussions, a plan was evolved to convert the party into an insurrectory movement and to seek an alliance with the exiled PLM.[1]

Madero planned to delegate authority to local leaders, and he compiled a list of persons whom he trusted to be informed of the impending revolution.[2] González directed communications in the North and immediately dispatched messengers to cities and regions where earlier political tours had revealed widespread support for the cause. Among the most active couriers was José de la Luz Soto, a member of the Benito Juárez Club, who traveled throughout the states of the Pacific North, from Jalisco to Sonora.[3] Wary of using documents to identify themselves, De la Luz Soto and others carried small photographs of Anti-reelectionist leaders and passed oral messages to their contacts.[4]

Hoping to recruit a rebel force that included experienced veterans of the 1906 and 1908 invasions as well as eager converts from the 1910 elections, Madero appealed for unity with the PLM. He closed his eyes to the PLM's precepts and said he could see little difference between the democratic aims of his followers and the socialistic goals of the Liberals. Ricardo Flores Magón could, however, and he said so in a seething editorial that bitterly recalled his three years in American jails while the Anti-reelectionists eclipsed his party. He refused to cooperate with the latecomers to the struggle against Díaz and dryly remarked that if Madero were intent on revolt he should enlist in the PLM.[5]

Unruffled by Flores Magón's response, Madero completed his preparations, then with Roque Estrada jumped bail and made his way through northern Mexico into exile in Texas disguised as a railroad mechanic. Shortly after his arrival, Madero received congratulations by telegram from the Benito Juárez Club on his safe journey.[6] In San Antonio he joined other members of the party's executive committee—although Gustavo Madero and Francisco and Emilio Vázquez Gómez were conspicuously absent—and together they began work as a revolutionary junta.[7]

1. Valadés, *Madero*, 2: 14-15, 66-70; Federico González Garza, *La Revolución Mexicana: Mi contribución político-literaria* (Mexico: A. del Bosque, 1936), p. 247.

2. Madero to Filómeno Mata, August 10, 1910, AM, reel 9.

3. Pedro González-Blanco, *De Porfirio Díaz a Carranza* (Madrid: Imprenta Helenica, 1916), pp. 66-67; José G. Zuno, *Historia de la revolución en el estado de Jalisco* (Mexico: Talleres Gráficos de la Nación, 1964), p. 55; Valadés, *Madero*, 2: 57.

4. This seems to be a logical interpretation of the exchange of photographs discussed in Madero to González, August 27 and October 1, 1910, AM, reel 10.

5. Valadés, *Madero*, 2: 69-70; Eugenio Martínez Núñez, *La vida heróica de Praxédis G. Guerrero* (Mexico: n.p., 1960), p. 221.

6. González to Madero, October 10, 1910, AM, reel 8.

7. Cumberland, *Mexican Revolution*, pp. 117-21. Madero badgered Francisco Vázquez Gómez to come to San Antonio or to aid the conspirators in the capital city; see Madero to Vázquez Gómez, October 25, 1910, AM, reel 19.

Madero's flight from Mexico caused repercussions in many parts of the country. Repression was intensified and apprehension spread among the Anti-reelectionists. Many potential rebels feared the government had discovered their intentions, but in Chihuahua the administration's seemingly haughty complacency continued. Early in the summer, following the presidential elections, crowds spontaneously voiced their dissatisfaction with the outcome, and the governor, with surprising speed, arrested many of the protestors. Demonstrators, including some *maderistas*, filled jails in Chihuahua, Guerrero, Casas Grandes, and Parral, but the government aimed only at putting down the riots, not at proscribing the Anti-reelectionist party. After this flurry of police action, officials turned their attention away from the incipient revolutionaries to arrangements for a spectacular celebration of the centennial of national independence.[8]

This distraction allowed members of the Benito Juárez Club to operate publicly. They kept their offices open and continued publication of *El grito del pueblo*. While officials maintained routine surveillance, González directed the conspiracy in his state, recruited followers, collected arms and funds, and relayed information from the exiled leaders to followers in the interior. The man who had faithfully worked for change through constitutional processes plunged "up to his eyes in the forthcoming revolution."[9]

I

After his meeting with Madero in July, González and the Benito Juárez Club began preparations for the revolution. The executive committee redefined its objectives and men like Braulio Hernández, Aureliano González, José P. Lomelín, Tomás Silva, and Pascual Mejía followed the club's president in his transition from political rival to rebel. Only the club secretary, Luis Rojas, hesitated, and Madero counseled González to allay Rojas's anxieties and bring him into the cabal.[10] With Rojas reassured and with dependable backing in the capital, González next moved to unite local clubs into a statewide revolutionary organization. He traveled widely to inform members of the revised plans. While the approaching centennial celebration created a hubbub in Chihuahua City, district leaders and prospective commanders arrived to confer on tactics, and González designated military officers who included Guillermo

8. Calzadíaz Barrera, *Hechos reales*, 1: 33-37.
9. Ira J. Bush, *Gringo Doctor* (Caldwell, Idaho: Caxton, 1939), p. 157.
10. Madero to González, August 5, 1910, AM, reel 8; Calzadíaz Barrera, *Hechos reales*, 1: 26-28; Moreno, *Hombres de la revolución*, p. 64. J. P. Lomelín, the rebel, should not be confused with Antonio V. Lomelí, Mexican consul in El Paso.

Baca in Parral, Toribio Ortega in Cuchillo Parado, José de la Luz Blanco in Temosáchic, and Cástulo Herrera in the Caretas-San Andrés region.[11] In addition, González enlisted two exceptional men as guerrilla leaders, bringing Pascual Orozco, Jr., and Pancho Villa into the revolutionary conspiracy.

Tall and resolute, Orozco had refused to follow his father as a shopkeeper in the mountain village of San Isidro. He preferred the independence, danger, hardship, and profits of an *arriero*, a muleteer. Driving his mules and supervising men had fostered in him the habit of command; protecting ore shipments from bandits and wandering the cordillera in all kinds of weather had bred self-reliance and taught him practical geography. He became self-assured and successful. He had taken little interest in the presidential campaign, although his father-in-law and other relatives joined the Anti-reelectionists. Then he encountered the restrictiveness of the porfirian regime when a competitor became a paid agent of the governor and, with political backing, cut into his freight business. In October, Orozco rode to the state capital, talked with the conspirators, and decided to join the cause. After a second meeting at the end of the month, González decided Orozco possessed the qualifications of a guerrilla leader and commissioned him as the rebel commander for the Guerrero district. Revenge against his business rival, Joaquín Chávez, and insurrection against the government appealed to Orozco's direct personality; he devoted himself to the movement.[12]

If muleskinning sharpened Orozco's abilities as a potential military leader, his career lacked the excitement which marked the profession of Pancho Villa. Despite a try or two at making a legitimate livelihood, Villa was a bandit chieftain and as a matter of survival learned to live off the land and to employ tactics of sudden strikes with quick dispersal. Living outside the law, he hated the oppressive regime. He was reckless enough to enlist in the revolution and tough and wily enough to succeed. In October, González, who had first met Villa while buying and selling cattle in the sierra region, arranged a clandestine meeting with him a few blocks from the railyards in one of the capital's poorer neighborhoods. He suggested to Villa the possibility of escaping punishment for his crimes and the opportunity of becoming a respected citizen if the revolution succeeded. Perhaps persuaded by these entreaties, but more likely tempted by the adventure, Villa accepted with a flourish, according to popular tradition, announcing he had no other wish than to be named a colonel and to die for his country. González sent him into the mountains as a

11. Meyer, *Mexican Rebel*, p. 14, note 16.
12. Ibid., pp. 17-18; Amaya, *Los auténticos revolucionarios*, pp. 103-4.

captain, promising a promotion when he had enlisted a company of three hundred men. [13]

The rebels had little trouble recruiting an army. As a result of the work of the PLM and the Anti-reelectionist clubs there existed a substantial group of men opposed to the government. Potential followers were found among the people distressed by declining opportunities and increasing competition. Small stockmen, sharecroppers, railroad workers, itinerant farm hands, lumberjacks, clerks, miners, and peddlers had escaped complete domination by the expanding haciendas and the growing foreign companies, but they anxiously saw threats from both. Laborers came into contact with their counterparts from north of the border—imported to the mines, lumber camps, and railyards—and the Mexicans soon wanted equality with them. A depression forced contraction of work in the mountains, especially when the Sierra Madre Land and Lumber Company passed into receivership. Workmen went three months without pay before the shutdown and it took over a year before the courts could arrange for the sale of the property. Even then, the executor, Judge Albert B. Fall, would only promise that sometime in the future he would pay fifty cents on every dollar of wages. Even worse, there had been a succession of three bad harvests, with the likelihood that 1910 would be no better; families faced the prospect of giving up their independence for the unhappy but certain security of hacienda life. It was an anxious time, and the rebels found many recruits among those troubled by poor crops, underemployment, and job discrimination. These were men of some means, as evidenced when they appeared with their own horses and armed with a bewildering variety of rifles, although they had little ammunition. Villa, in fact, would accept only those who owned guns and animals. [14]

As enlistment gained momentum, González established communications

13. There are numerous accounts of Villa's enlistment in the rebel movement, and virtually every author points out the importance of González in the recruitment. This account is based on Octavio Magaña Cerda, "Historia documental de la revolución," *El universal*, June 11, 1950, which is the recollections of Santiago González Casavantes, Abraham's brother. Tales of varying reliability reach a low point in the apocryphal anecdote by Giuseppe Garibaldi that he recruited Villa for the rebels. See his *Toast to Rebellion* (Indianapolis: Bobbs-Merrill, 1935), pp. 262-64.

14. Clark W. Reynolds, *The Mexican Economy: Twentieth-Century Structure and Growth* (New Haven: Yale University Press, 1970), pp. 15-26, 73-74, 137. Moisés González Navarro, "Mexico: The Lop-sided Revolution," in *Obstacles to Change in Latin America*, edited by Claudio Velíz (London: Oxford University Press, 1965), pp. 207-8, describes land acquisition and attendant labor systems. Marion Letcher, U.S. consul, Chihuahua City, to Secretary of State, October 17, 1913, RDS, 812.00/9483; *Hearings, 1913*, testimony of José Cordova, p. 505; *EPMT*, December 7, 1910. For the correspondence on the bankruptcy case, see NF, case file 14164.

with the revolutionary leaders in San Antonio to coordinate his actions with their plans. His close friend and adviser, Braulio Hernández, shuttled between the juntas in exile and in Chihuahua, carrying reports to Madero and funds to González for ammunition and supplies. The exiles operated on a slim margin. Hernández seldom received more than a few dollars; and on one occasion when authorized to transfer a fortune of eighteen hundred dollars to Chihuahua, he had to wait until Alfonso Madero pawned a valuable ring to obtain the funds. As soon as the rebel program, the Plan de San Luis Potosí, was prepared, he brought copies to González for circulation to other rebel chieftains in Chihuahua and deeper in Mexico.[15]

With the aid of the junta, Madero had written the San Luis Plan as a statement of their immediate goals and the precepts that would guide them. In Mexican fashion, they cast their intentions as a legalistic pronouncement to the people, dated October 5, the last day of Madero's residence in Mexico, to avoid international complications. The document reviewed the legal efforts of the Anti-reelectionists to reform the government, declared the summer elections void, named Madero provisional president, and made vague promises to aid those who had lost their lands and to improve conditions in Mexico following the revolution. The plan outlined military procedures and called for a national uprising on November 20. Because the document included the date, it circulated only among conspirators held in highest confidence until November 15, when it was released generally to the rebels.[16]

Knowledge of the San Luis Plan with its date for revolution gave impetus to González's acquisition of arms and ammunition. Because of Chihuahua's contiguous border with Texas, he only needed to arrange shipment to his subordinates in Mexico of material legally purchased in the United States. In early October he sent his brother Santiago and José P. Lomelín to establish a junta in El Paso. They purchased guns and ammunition, smuggled them into Chihuahua, and provided a supplemental communications link with San Antonio. González gave them the Benito Juárez Club's treasury, but Madero furnished most of their scant war chest. The exiled leader deposited money in a special account in the First National Bank of El Paso for Lomelín and oc-

15. U.S., Senate, Committee on Foreign Relations, 66th Cong., 2d sess., 1920, *Investigation of Mexican Affairs*, 2 vols. (Washington: GPO, 1920), 2: 2518-20, testimony of Braulio Hernández (hereafter cited as Fall Committee); Amado Aguirre, *Mís memorias de campañas—apuntes para la historia* (n.p., n.d.), p. 6.

16. Cumberland, *Mexican Revolution*, pp. 118-21; Almada, *Revolución en Chihuahua*, 1: 161. A copy and translation of the San Luis Plan are included in *Hearings, 1913*, pp. 724-35.

casionally cabled small additional amounts to the agents.[17] Santiago coordinated the delivery system by slipping Lomelín's purchases south for distribution to regional leaders. The junta also passed messages between Madero and González. Often the provisional president telegraphed instructions to Lomelín, who sent them by messenger to González. As the revolution approached, Madero called Lomelín to San Antonio to give him oral instructions on tactics, stressing the importance of disrupting the telegraph and railroad lines between Chihuahua City and Torreón.[18] Poor communications and supply shortages plagued the revolutionaries throughout Mexico, but González's efforts provided Chihuahua's rebels with sufficient equipment to maintain the struggle during the first crucial weeks when other guerrilla bands collapsed without guns or guidance.

The Anti-reelectionists attempted to maintain secrecy, but the government kept well informed of their preparations. Villa's enlistment attracted attention and allowed the police to penetrate the rebel organization. They dropped felony charges against one of Pancho's friends, Claro Reza, when he agreed to become an informer. Later through Villa's backing he joined the revolutionary council in the capital city. From the reports made by Reza and other spies, the police soon accumulated a thick file on González, Villa, and others, but they only tightened surveillance, keeping lists of the names of all those who visited the rebel offices or associated with the conspirators. When Villa learned of Reza's duplicity, he confronted his former *compañero* in broad daylight in the center of town and ruthlessly gunned him down, then galloped away to the hills. But even Reza's murder did not alter the deliberate police policy.[19]

As the revolutionaries became increasingly apprehensive of official scrutiny and excitement mounted with the approach of the insurrection, sudden demonstrations broke out in Chihuahua City. A Mexican youth, who had confessed to a murder in Rock Springs, Texas, had been dragged from his cell and burned to death at the stake by enraged ranchers. Riots swept Mexico as reports reached the country of the atrocity and of a Texas jury's inability to identify the lynchers. In Chihuahua a mob gathered in the plaza, then marched through the streets until dispersed by rurales. Small groups continued to

17. Madero to J. P. Lomelín, November 6; bank deposit, November 12; Lomelín to Madero, November 12, 1910, AM, reel 18.
18. Madero to Lomelín, October 17 and 30, November 6, 1910, AM, reel 18; Calderón, "Maderismo en Chihuahua," p. 10; Calzadíaz Barrera, *Hechos reales*, 1:39.
19. Calzadíaz Barrera, *Hechos reales*, 1: 26-28. The police file on the rebels has now disappeared, although Almada used it in 1947; see *Vida González*, p. 34.

roam the city, throwing rocks at the passing carriages and the front gates of North Americans and cursing the foreigners.[20]

The Rock Springs incident briefly diverted attention while González called district leaders to Chihuahua and informed them of the exact day of the uprising. After meeting on the night of November 17, the rebels sneaked away from the city with copies of the San Luis Plan and military instructions.[21] Meanwhile, state officials became unnerved; fearing that the riots portended the revolution, they made a preemptive roundup of the movement's leaders. In Chihuahua City police raided the offices of the Benito Juárez Club, where they confiscated records and arrested Aureliano González, Tomás Silva, and Pascual Mejía. Throughout the state, the government struck against the rebels. In Guerrero City, the commander of the army garrison ordered the jailing of known conspirators and succeeded in capturing Juan José González and four other suspects. At the bullring in Juárez, the police arrested forty persons, known sympathizers of Madero, on drunk charges. The sweep seemed successful. United States Consul Leo Keena confidently reported that, despite persistent rumors, no revolt would happen in Chihuahua.[22]

The raids did not surprise the Anti-reelectionists. They expected official repression and probably had confederates among the police who relayed news of the impending arrests.[23] Those arraigned were propagandists and organizers. Guerrilla leaders escaped because they had left for the field immediately after the November 17 meeting. González had departed at once for Presidio, Texas, where he met Lomelín and they prepared to make an assault on Ojinaga, Chihuahua, just across the river.[24] Suppression came too late; the revolutionary army González had built was ready for the national insurrection.

II

Madero intended to lead the revolution in his native Coahuila and sent

20. Frederick C. Turner, *The Dynamic of Mexican Nationalism* (Chapel Hill: University of North Carolina Press, 1968), pp. 216-17; *EPMT*, November 15, 1910.

21. Calzadíaz Barrera, *Hechos reales*, 1: 40; Valadés, *Madero*, 2: 84.

22. Almada, *Revolución en Chihuahua*, 1: 169; Adrian Aguirre Benavides, *Madero el inmaculado: Historia de la revolución de 1910* (Mexico: Editorial Diana, 1962), p. 172; Leo J. Keena, U.S. consul, Chihuahua City, to Secretary of State, November 18, 1910, RDS, 812.00/387.

23. Villa claimed he had a friend, José, who was a member of the *rurales* and provided him with information; see Martin Luis Guzmán, *Memorias de Pancho Villa* (Mexico: Compañía General de Ediciones, 1968), pp. 42-43.

24. García, "Rasgos biográficos," p. 3; Sánchez to Creel, November 27, 1910, AREM, L-E 613.

money for arms and horses to the state's rebels. After wading the river and riding to a prearranged site, he found only a fraction of the anticipated force and none of the weapons. His personal military effort had failed, but he demonstrated that he sought a viable organization, not personal glory. Despite the discouragement of his fiasco, he provided a legitimate structure for the revolution by appointing provisional governors, many with military responsibility, from "national territory on the banks of the Rio Grande."[25] His action created the impression that the revolution was a revolt of resident Mexicans, not the effort of exiled pretenders, and also reduced the chance of prosecution under United States neutrality laws. Disappointed, but not despondent, he returned to Texas with a flimsy alternative of embarking from New Orleans, in the porfirian fashion of 1876, for one of Mexico's ports.[26]

The general call to arms went unanswered. Even in Chihuahua where the best-organized conspiracy existed, the uprising sputtered. In sporadic actions Toribio Ortega pronounced against the government in Cuchillo Parado, José de la Luz Blanco declared for the revolution in Tomasáchic, Pancho Villa and others rose in arms near San Andrés, Guillermo Baca attacked Parral, and Pascual Orozco struck in San Isidro. The rebels tore up part of the Mexican Northwestern Railroad and Orozco demonstrated his talent by winning his first encounters,[27] but the dispersed strikes achieved little.

Lacking the daring and skill of Orozco, González suffered a setback in his initial foray. Named provisional governor and colonel in command of the Chihuahua-Durango military zone,[28] he intended to occupy a port of entry on the international frontier to serve as a Mexican headquarters for the rebel junta, provide an entrance for war material from the United States, and possibly supply income from customs receipts. Juárez offered the most attractive target, but the preemptive police raids had destroyed the rebel apparatus there and forced a chance in strategy. Ojinaga then became the target. With an assault set for November 20, González, Lomelín, and twenty-seven riflemen crossed into Mexico and a guide directed them to a rendezvous near the

25. Decrees 4-12, November 20, 1910, AM, reel 18, include designations of provisional governors for most states.

26. Cumberland, *Mexican Revolution*, pp. 124-25.

27. Almada, *Revolución en Chihuahua*, 1: 170; Meyer, *Mexican Rebel*, pp. 19-20; reports on the Parral battle are contained in Keena to Secretary of State, November 23, 1910, RDS, 812.00/466; Keena to Hanna, November 24, 1910, National Archives, Post Records of Embassies and Consulates, Record Group 84, Correspondence of the Consulate General, Monterrey, Mexico, C8.6d, pp. 151-52 (hereafter cited as PR).

28. A decree naming González was not found in the Madero correspondence, but he was reported to be using the title in Antonio Brava, Mexican consul, Nogales, to Creel, December 17, 1910, AREM, L-E 620; see also Almada, *Gobernadores*, p. 456.

small pueblo. The exiles came well armed, but the rebels who met them lacked ammunition and many had no weapons. González dreaded defeat at the hands of the federal garrison and decided only to threaten battle by bivouacking just outside the village. For three weeks the irregulars probed and skirmished in this isolated northeastern corner of Chihuahua, waiting for González to complete the transfer of arms and supplies from Shafter and Presidio, Texas.[29] Certainly not an inspired military leader, he at least sensed two guerrilla principles: avoid defeat, and remain in arms.

Reports of roving rebel bands, attacks on district towns and a pitched battle in Parral shocked the residents of Chihuahua City. Coming soon after protests against the Rock Springs incident and the police raids on the Antireelectionists' offices, the outbreaks inspired rumors of an imminent attack. Apprehension mounted as Silvestre Terrazas's newspaper reported military encounters and published the San Luis Plan. The alarmed governor, José M. Sánchez, ordered Terrazas jailed and *El correo* closed,[30] and tried to calm the people by preparing defenses. After a general meeting with the governor, businessmen and civic leaders enlisted in volunteer military companies and subscribed to an emergency war fund.[31] The anticipated siege never came, but the townspeople remained tense and Sánchez worried about how to end the fighting.

National leaders in Mexico City belittled the rebel threat along the border. Following the disjointed fighting of November 20, the revolution faltered and its leaders returned to exile. The movement dwindled to small groups in remote Chihuahua by the end of the month.[32] Under the sure hand of the minister of foreign relations, Enrique Creel, the government expected to crush the remnants of the revolt by destroying the juntas in the United States. Creel, who had directed the defense against the Flores Magón rebellion, prepared to handle Madero in a similar way. He repeatedly ordered his ambassador in Washington to protest violations of neutrality and to insist on action by the Justice Department. Mexican consuls, following instructions, paid informers and hired detectives to create an intelligence system, and Creel

29. González-Blanco, *Díaz a Carranza*, pp. 67-68.

30. *El correo*, November 19, 20, 1911; Sandels, "Silvestre Terrazas, the Press," pp. 209-11.

31. Keena to Secretary of State, November 21, RDS, 812.00/441; November 21, RDS, 812.00/442; December 8, 1910, RDS, 812.00/510.

32. Wilson to Secretary of State, November 26, 1910, RDS, 812.00/484; Sánchez to Creel, November 20, 1910, AREM, L-E 614.

again called on the Thomas Furlong Agency of St. Louis to obtain evidence of the exiles' conspiracy.[33]

The Díaz cabinet confidently expected to smash the revolution, and Madero, despairing at the same prospect, again decided to leave San Antonio. Discouragement paralyzed other members of the junta. Only word of Orozco's victories held them together. From sketchy reports they learned that Orozco had captured several villages, held Guerrero City under siege, and had routed a federal relief force. The rebels likewise suffered from lack of regular intelligence. When Orozco failed to receive messages from the rebel leaders in Texas, he wrote Ricardo Flores Magón requesting reinforcements and asking about González.[34]

González had lost touch with Orozco's forces, but he did not sulk in exile. He desperately hoped to win a victory at Ojinaga. Purchasing arms and horses, he sent them across the Rio Grande to the insurgent camp. He also summoned other rebel bands to cooperate in the assault, and soon troops under José de la Luz Soto and Toribio Ortega posted pickets a few miles from the border town. The federal army too prepared for the upcoming battle, sending fresh men from the south equipped with field guns. By mid-December, González had assembled seven hundred men to engage six hundred regulars.[35] The rebel chief, after pointing out the disparity in numbers, demanded that the garrison commander surrender the city. The officer, Alberto Dorantes, responded by conscripting all the men in the town and attacking the rebels. The two armies met on December 15 just outside Ojinaga at the Venegas rancho. The federals used their mountain guns to advantage and forced the rebels into retreat. As González pulled back his men, he rationalized that the isolated town would not be of value to the cause. Perhaps thinking that his men were too valuable to throw against artillery, he rationalized that victory would only mean having to maintain an occupation force in the town.[36] A week later the armies fought again at El Mulato, and the federals convinced many rebels that they

33. Francísco León de la Barra, Mexican ambassador, U.S., to Secretary of State, November 28, 1910, RDS, 812.00/497; Creel to de la Barra, December 28, 1910, AREM, L-E 620; Furlong to Creel, November 17, 1910, AREM, L-E 612. Scattered through this file series are the reports of various detectives.
34. González Garza, *La Revolución Mexicana*, p. 251; Almada, *Revolución en Chihuahua*, 1: 187.
35. Ellsworth to Secretary of State, December 10, 1910, RDS, 812.00/568; *EPMT*, December 9, 16, 1910.
36. Ellsworth to Secretary of State, December 11, 1910, RDS, 812.00/569; Guillermo Porras to Secretary of Foreign Relations, December 17, 1910, AREM, L-E 620; Alberto Terrazas to Creel, December 26, 1910, AREM, L-E 620; García, "Rasgos Biográficos," p. 2; *EPMT*, December 11 and 18, 1910.

should avoid pitched battles. González dispersed his troops with orders to continue guerrilla raids. He retired to El Paso, disabused of his military abilities, to concentrate on supplying arms to the rebels and reestablishing communications with scattered units in the state.

III

After his unsuccessful military venture, González decided he could best fulfill his military-administrative obligations by directing the revolutionary movement from El Paso. His tenure as a field commander served as a hard measure of his talents. The campaign had not failed for want of men, supplies, or organization—those he had provided—but he lacked the subtle ability to inspire his men, to force a slight advantage and then capitalize on it. Still, he came to El Paso convinced that the movement would succeed, and his confidence revived a junta that had languished during the first weeks of the insurrection. His enthusiasm inspired Santiago González, Alberto Fuentes, and Cástulo Herrera, and dispelled their gloomy pessimism. For victory, he believed the rebels only needed well-armed men of steel determination. He threw himself into the effort to provide organization, provisions, and recruits, but recognized that he alone could not rouse his countrymen. He called on Madero to enter Mexico in a dramatic gesture that would evoke admiration, perhaps even comparison to the heroic Juárez, who had fought his way out of a corner in Chihuahua in the 1860s to reclaim the nation.

In late December, González sent Hernández to urge Madero to assume personal command of the rebels in Chihuahua. Hernández, Madero, and Federico González Garza met for discussions in which Hernández pleaded for Madero to assume leadership in the field. He insisted that the provisional president must return to Mexico and strengthened his argument by repeating the rumor that the United States Department of Justice had authorized Madero's arrest. González Garza disputed the proposal and abused Hernández for his presumptuousness. Hesitant to make a second crossing, Madero found ample rationalization in González Garza's oratory to reject the entreaties. Even the timely arrival of González in San Antonio could not alter his decision.[37]

Dismayed but undaunted by Madero's refusal, González returned to El Paso to accomplish his goals. Well aware of surveillance by agents of both Mexico and the United States, he disarmed observers by operating openly, even seeking out publicity for his activities. He rented downtown offices in

37. Estrada, *La revolución*, pp. 364-66.

the Caples Building for his provisional government of Chihuahua and gave regular interviews to the growing press corps that gathered to hear reports of the progress of the revolution. González was well known in the border business community, and he capitalized on the friendship of his acquaintances while affecting a scrupulously legal position. Appealing to the political sentiments of Americans, he arranged to publish a letter in the *El Paso Morning Times* explaining that the rebels only wanted to establish "fair taxation, diffusion of public instruction . . . ; in short . . . popular government, based on the law." He made clear that the revolution was confined to Mexico and declared that the exiles had conformed to the laws of the United States. In a conversation with an agent from the federal Bureau of Investigation, he offered the information that he had retained legal counsel to prevent any violations of United States regulations. He stressed the same point in another interview, saying, "My business here has been entirely regular."[38]

Behind the screen of his pretender government, González directed a masterful campaign to provision rebel forces. To facilitate the transfer of equipment and the command of the war, he strengthened communications with the fighting units. He dispatched the former foreman of his Guerrero ranch to locate the guerrillas in the western mountains,[39] and soon created a network that relayed reliable reports of military engagements and channeled supplies to the combatants. He enlisted Mexican freight dock workers in the railyards and sympathetic brakemen on freight trains to convey supplies to isolated spots along the right of way for smuggling into the war zone. During December he purchased at least two consignments of thirty thousand cartridges from the Shelton and Payne Company, then shipped them west on the Southern Pacific Railroad to be hauled across the chaparral wastes from southern New Mexico into western Chihuahua.[40] Smaller loads of equipment he often carried into Mexico himself. His continual crossing of the international frontier enraged the Foreign Relations Minister, and the Mexican ambassador repeatedly demanded that the United States government interdict these obvious violations of neutrality.[41]

The conspirators purchased guns and ammunition in towns throughout

38. *EPMT*, January 9, 1911; J. Herbert Cole to Chief, Bureau of Investigation, January 5, 1911, RDS, 812.00/628.

39. Edgcumb Pinchon, *Viva Villa: A Recovery of the Real Pancho Villa* (New York: Grosset & Dunlap, 1933), p. 145.

40. De la Barra to Secretary of Foreign Relations, February 28, 1911, AREM, L-E 635.

41. Creel to De la Barra, December 28, 1911, AREM, L-E 620; memorandum, R. A. Esteva Ruíz to Secretary of Foreign Relations, January 4, 1911, AREM, L-E 623. For a discussion of U.S. enforcement of neutrality legislation, see below, pp. 55-57.

West Texas and shipped them to a collection center. Goods obtained from hardware stores and sportsmen's shops in the Big Bend region were sent by train to Toyah, a whistle stop on the Texas-Pacific line, then by wagon to a ranch owned by a Mexican-American near the town of Alpine, a station on the Southern Pacific. Moving supplies to El Paso for illegal shipment to Mexico became a routine exercise. With carbines and shells camouflaged in tool chests, González would dress as a mechanic and board the Southern Pacific for the rebel supply depot in El Paso.

The junta also enlisted sympathizers who came to the border to join the revolution. Word circulated through the Mexican community that prospective volunteers should get in touch with González at his office or by mail at a special post office box. The rebels sought out expatriate Mexicans, particularly in Texas, playing on their sentiments with the promise of a better life after the revolutionary victory. Other agents recruited in major cities such as Denver, Oakland, Kansas City, and Chicago.[42]

With extensive news coverage, the rebellion soon attracted international attention and a motley group of adventurers turned up in El Paso. Speaking for most of them, one journalist later rhapsodized, "Never was there such a colorful, romantic, noble and foolish period."[43] Among those lured to west Texas was the scion of a famed revolutionary family, Giuseppe Garibaldi, who had fought for the liberation of Greece and Venezuela and for the suppression of the Boers. He hunted out González and tried to enroll in the cause, but the rebel chief demurred, hesitant to let foreigners fight in a national independence movement. After a few days of consideration, he relented. The brash young volunteer swaggered around El Paso, awaiting an opportune moment to slip over the border and join the troops.[44] Others, less experienced but no less eager, enlisted and soon the garish rabble included Tom Mix and Sam Dreban, "the fighting Jew." Captain Oscar Creighton, "the dynamite Devil," formed a foreign legion to engage the federal army.[45]

González worked hard to impress the Americans and to fend off the persistent private detectives and government agents. He encouraged curious report-

42. Foster [Furlong] to Creel, January 16, 1911, AREM, 1-E 624; A. J. Ortíz, Mexican consul, Tucson, to Secretary of Foreign Relations, January 19, 1911, AREM, L-E 625; Carlos Pereyra, Mexican consul, San Antonio, to Secretary of Foreign Relations, February 10, 1911, AREM, L-E 629; *EPMT*, January 24, 1911.

43. Timothy G. Turner, *Bullets, Bottles and Gardenias* (Dallas: Southwest Press, 1935), p. 23.

44. Garibaldi, *Toast to Rebellion*, pp. 220-26.

45. Foster [Furlong] to Creel, February 3, 1911, AREM, L-E 629; Mary Thurber, " 'Soldier of Fortune' Who Fought with Madero Returns to El Paso," *EPMT*, March 29, 1955; Haldeen Braddy, *Cock of the Walk: Qui-qui-ri-quí: The Legend of Pancho Villa* (Albuquerque: University of New Mexico Press, 1955), p. 97.

ers to join the rebels in the field, hoping to secure sympathetic coverage of their campaigns. The desire for a correspondent became so strong that the rebels tried unsuccessfully to bribe the editor of the *San Antonio Light* into sending one of his men into Chihuahua. With Timothy Turner, the reporter assigned to cover the revolution for the *El Paso Herald*, González had a warm friendship; he permitted Turner to attend junta meetings in exchange for favorable headlines.

Turner and González obtained a lawyer for the rebels by persuading C. F. Z. Caracristi to accept an appointment as diplomatic agent and legal counsel. Caracristi, a man of influential friends and suspicious business, was an old hand at shadowy affairs in Mexico. An occasional mining engineer, sometime business associate of Creel, self-styled Austrian prince, he traded in conspiracies for personal gain.[46] He did provide valuable service by compromising the Mexican consul in El Paso, Antonio Lomelí, in early 1911. Lomelí bartered regular information on federal troop movements in Chihuahua and a copy of the government's message code for three thousand dollars in installments of three hundred dollars a week.[47] Others even more disreputable than Caracristi offered their dubious assistance, but they were rejected. For the most part, the rebels preferred to recruit Mexicans. They suborned Enrique Ornelas, the consul in San Antonio, and without his knowledge also enticed four employees of his consulate into their ranks.[48]

The rebels' success in creating a clandestine intelligence apparatus was counterbalanced by the system of spies and informers working for the Mexican and United States governments. Luther Ellsworth, consul at Ciudad Porfirio Díaz, directed border vigilance with methodical thoroughness. While the rebels recruited minor bureaucrats and diplomatic employees, Ellsworth countered by enlisting five Mexican informers, who joined the Madero organization in San Antonio and provided regular reports of the junta's activities.

46. Turner, *Bullets*, pp. 23-24. Information on Caracristi is contained in *EPMT*, November 25, 1909; Lewis A. Martin, U.S. consul, Chihuahua City, to Secretary of State, October 9, 1908, NF, case 15970; W. D. Pearce to Department of State, June 6, 1909, NF, case 5967/55; Ellsworth to Secretary of State, March 2, 1911, RDS, 812.00/887; Wilson to Secretary of State, April 30, 1912, RDS, 812.00/3810.

47. Antonio V. Lomelí, Su Expediente Personal, H/131/178, Deposition of C. F. Z. Caracristi before J. B. Baker, Notary Public, Webb County, Texas, June 11, 1913, AREM, L-E 1189.

48. Exchange of letters, J. R. Hunter, Border Secret Service, to Madero, November 1, 1910; Madero to Hunter, November 17, 1910, AM, reel 18. Hunter claimed to have negotiated with Bernardo Reyes, then offered his surveillance and gunrunning services to Madero, who refused. See Attorney General to Secretary of State, December 5, 1910, RDS, 812.00/535; Franklin Macregla to Secretary of State, February 7, 1911, RDS, 812.00/759.

As González carried out his program of supply, the month and a half of fighting sifted out the rebels. Some returned home, able neither to understand their failure to win a quick victory nor to withstand the rigors of irregular campaigning.[49] Larger numbers volunteered, and the troops, especially Orozco's, grew almost daily with enlistments. Time annealed the irregular rebel forces into tough units. Orozco's command captured Guerrero City in early December and soon controlled the entire district.

National officials decided that the *maderista* uprising, at least in Chihuahua, was rooted in local politics. The dictator put increasing pressure on Governor Sánchez to suppress the *bandits* in his state. The governor, desperate to comply with Díaz's orders, received José M. Gardena, a leading resident of the state capital, who suggested that a peace commission go to Guerrero City. He reasoned that the rebels must be unaware that the revolution had failed in the rest of Mexico: once Orozco's men learned they stood alone, they would negotiate an end to the fighting. With the governor's approval, Gardena and four associates went to the rebel camp. Before talks could begin, scouts reported that a federal army was advancing on their position. The rebel commander reacted immediately to the double-cross, sending the envoys scurrying back to Chihuahua City.[50] As they departed, Orozco told them that his men would stack their arms only when they could vote in "fair elections. We want to elect a new president and all state officers from the governor down to the *mozo* who cleans the patio of the statehouse."[51]

On learning that the peace initiative had failed, Díaz denounced the effort and forced the governor to resign. He named Alberto Terrazas as Sánchez's successor and made it clear that he would not commit more soldiers to the state. Furthermore, he suggested that Terrazas recruit civilians, even resort to conscription if necessary, to form special militia companies. When the story circulated in Chihuahua City, members of the lower classes became terrified at the prospect of fighting the rebels, and many left the city for the insurgent lines or the border. Terrazas also had reservations about drafting troops, fearing that arming such men would be tantamount to giving guns to the enemy. As the crisis deepened, he finally called for volunteers, but his appeal received a mute response. In little more than a month Díaz dismissed Terrazas and recalled Miguel Ahumada, who had ruled Chihuahua from 1892 to 1903, to pacify the state.[52]

49. Ellsworth to Secretary of State, July 31, 1910, NF, case 4028/394; Sánchez to Creel, November 31, 1910, AREM, L-E 614.

50. *EPMT*, December 5, 1910. Other members of the committee included Amador González, Luis de la Garza, and Eduardo and Fernando González.

51. Ibid., December 7, 1911.

52. Ibid., December 26, 1910; January 6 and 12, 1911; Almada, *Vida González*, p. 49.

Confusion in the government and the success of rebel armies encouraged the exiles. González made numerous trips to confer with the junta in San Antonio. He usually returned with guns and ammunition to drop at points along the railroad for distribution in northern Chihuahua.[53] His conversations with Madero had two principal themes: the provisional president's duty to join the men in arms and the desperate need for funds. Madero furnished most of the money, but González badgered him for more because he was closer to the field and knew the need for equipment. He also searched for other sources of money. With their military success, the rebels began to collect the discarded gear of the federal army. González noted that they had begun with .30-.30s and .44-caliber Winchesters, but by January they had captured over a thousand Mausers from government troops. The insurgents also forced loans from businessmen in occupied communities. González instructed his officers to continue the practice, but to take into consideration the circumstances of those pressed and also to divide the funds. He suggested that officers keep enough for field expenses, and send the remainder to the junta. In El Paso, González approached his acquaintances, trying to trade on the prospect of a rebel victory. He managed some short-term loans from arms suppliers; Shelton and Payne, for example, often dropped part of their sales commission. As inspiring as the capture of Guerrero Canton was to the rebels, sympathetic American businessmen demanded a major victory before risking their capital.[54] The need for money and the prospect of American loans encouraged González to look covetously at Juárez.

An attack on the border city would require a larger force, and González began to parley with representatives of the Liberal party. No formal agreement had been reached before the revolution; the two parties simply drifted into a working arrangement during the last months of 1910. The Liberals received orders to revolt simultaneously with the *maderistas*, but not to make common cause. In Chihuahua they rose in rebellion at the end of November, 1910. One group declared against the government in Bachiniva, but they could not sustain operations and soon joined Pascual Orozco's command. Praxédes Guerrero, a prominent Liberal officer, invaded Chihuahua in December and attacked the village of Janos. He was killed during the battle, and the survivors of the raid enlisted with José Salazar. Small Liberal bands fought independently through December and January, but their efforts were negligi-

53. Creel to Consul, El Paso, January 20, 1911, AREM, L-E 677; Foster [Furlong] to Creel, January 25, 28, 1911, AREM, L-E 626; Lomelí to Secretary of Foreign Relations, January 19, 1911, AREM, L-E 624.
54. *EPMT*, January 5, 1911; Almada, *Vida González*, p. 37; *Hearings, 1913*, testimony of Lawrence F. Converse, p. 104.

ble and they operated exclusively in the Galeana district in the northwestern corner of the state.[55] Despite its reduced numbers and lack of military success in Chihuahua, the PLM maintained a separate revolutionary identity in the war zone in matters of recruiting and supply procurement.[56] On the other hand, the Anti-reelectionists believed that the duplication of revolutionary apparatus in the United States increased the possibility of attracting unfavorable notice from Justice Department agents and unnecessarily divided the opponents of the dictator.

Representatives of the two rebel parties agreed to meet in El Paso during January. Lázaro Gutiérrez de Lara, representing the PLM, traveled from Los Angeles to meet González, the negotiator for the Anti-reelectionists. Gutiérrez de Lara and González met several times, often at the bandstand in the central plaza, assuming that being seen in public would allay suspicion. Their talks centered on joint action against the dictatorship, and resulted in an agreement on common military activities but no formal pact.[57] González must have felt keen disappointment when Ricardo Flores Magón repudiated any association with the Anti-reelectionists and increased his newspaper's propaganda efforts against them. Flores Magón's rigid adherence to his anarchistic ideology and his army's success in Baja California made him unwilling to compromise, but his vitriolic attacks on other rebels, his unbending nature, and the growing number of foreigners in the PLM force alienated several Liberals. Gutiérrez de Lara, Antonio I. Villarreal, and José María Leyva renounced their allegiance to the PLM and joined the *maderistas.*[58]

During January, 1911, the progress of the rebellion moved Madero to greater optimism about its chances of success. He assumed more authority over his organization and called for stricter secrecy from junta members. To reduce the possibility of prosecution for violation of neutrality legislation, he ordered Emilio Vázquez Gómez, recently arrived in exile, to refrain from public comment on the party's political and military policies. Sensing the dangers of his office—possible assassination by Mexican thugs or arrest and extradition by United States marshals—Madero decided to select a provisional vice-president. After a discussion with his staff, he wrote a letter explaining his reasons for designating a second in command, then offered the position to

55. Lowell L. Blaisdell, *The Desert Revolution: Baja California, 1911* (Madison: University of Wisconsin Press, 1962), pp. 18-19; Almada, *Revolución en Chihuahua,* 1: 176, 179.

56. Foster [Furlong] to Creel, January 20, 1911, AREM, L-E 624.

57. Lomelí to Secretary of Foreign Relations, January 18, 1911, AREM, L-E 624, and January 18, 1911, AREM, L-E 677; reports of Mexican agent Louis G. Gill to Secretary of Foreign Relations, January 19 and 23, 1911, AREM, L-E 623.

58. Ross, *Madero,* p. 145.

González. Madero told González the choice was made in recognition of his talents, "the manner in which you organized the campaign in the state of Chihuahua, your tact, your perseverance, your intelligence, your sincerity."[59] González accepted the appointment.

Because of the intense pressure applied by spies who had forced him to sneak out of San Antonio and go into hiding in Dallas, Madero decided to join González in El Paso, then at a proper time slip into Mexico. Before traveling to El Paso, he cut his beard as a disguise. Madero soon experienced at first hand the shoestring finances of the junta. Trying to keep his presence secret, he lived with other exiles at the house of Hernández's wife. Occasionally he chipped in something for the larder, but for the most part he only stretched the meager funds. With money in short supply, the rebels could not pay the rent on their offices in the Caples Building, and when they left for the front, Raúl Madero had to leave Señora de Hernández an IOU for his washing. Remembering the hardship and perhaps the unpaid laundry bill, Hernández later declared, "The truth of God is that the revolution was fought with the abnegation and hunger of the Mexicans."[60]

In January, 1911, González called for an attack against Juárez. He needed a victory to offset the publicity given the followers of Flores Magón, who had just captured Mexicali and planned to occupy all of Baja California, and he sent word to Orozco to bring his men down from the mountains. Orozco feinted an advance on the state capital with finesse, then marched to Samalayuca, twenty-five miles south of the border. As his army approached the town, he called on the junta for fresh recruits, provisions enough to undertake a siege, and care for the wounded.[61]

González frantically tried to supply all the army's needs. Late one evening he went to the home of Dr. Ira Bush, who also had an office in the Caples Building, and asked him to treat the wounded in Samalayuca. Bush agreed to go as a Red Cross volunteer and the following morning attempted to cross the border, but U.S. Army sentries prevented his departure until he obtained permission from the Mexican commander in Juárez. After a long delay, the officer approved the request and Bush made a quick dash to the rebel camp, where he cared for the wounded. Once Orozco's army reached the outskirts of Juárez, Bush returned to El Paso to meet González again. This time the provisional governor offered him the position of chief surgeon of the rebel army with the rank of colonel. Bush accepted and immediately returned to

59. Sánchez Azcona, "Marzo 7 de 1913," 15, reprints the letter as does Valadés, *Madero*, 2: 100.
60. *Hearings, 1913*, testimony of Hernández, p. 120.
61. Meyer, *Mexican Rebel*, pp. 23-25; Blaisdell, *Desert Revolution*, pp. 38-40.

the field. He transported the seriously injured soldiers along back roads, then across the Rio Grande to a makeshift hospital in the Mexican district of El Paso, called Little Chihuahua. For the remaining months of the revolution, he operated the hospital, relying on volunteer nurses and funds provided by the rebel governor.[62] González did not have the same success in supplying arms and reinforcements. He managed to send Orozco only twenty-five men and three mules loaded with weapons. Although he worked incessantly to obtain guns and volunteers, his efforts made little headway as the United States government tightened its enforcement of neutrality and Madero decided to assume more responsibility for the revolution.

Madero's military leadership divided the ranks and frustrated the capture of Juárez. He appointed a general staff of José de la Luz Soto, Eduardo Hay, Giuseppe Garibaldi, Rafael Aguilar, Manuel García Vigil, and Octavio Morales, and sent them to command the rebel forces. Their arrival upset the veteran troopers. Many refused to submit to the new officers, and Orozco was particularly irritated by the selection of untried superiors, but other units agreed to join Madero's appointed staff, splitting the army at an inopportune time. Madero also set the date for the attack on Juárez to coincide with the anniversary of the adoption of the Constitution of 1857 and on a convenient day for his crossing into Mexico. The interval until the appointed day allowed the federal army to reinforce its garrison. The news that more regulars were moving toward the city, the lack of ammunition for a siege, and the division among the men convinced Orozco he should withdraw.

When the army retreated, Madero decided to postpone his return to Mexico until the rebels won a victory. His advisers, led by González, urged him to assume command at once to heal the injured feelings among his officers and repair the dissension among the soldiers, some of whom were returning home. González insisted that the disintegration of the movement could be prevented only by Madero.[63] The clinching argument came from a report that the United States Justice Department had instructed federal marshals to swear out warrants for the arrest of both Madero and González.[64] Justice agents had obtained incontrovertible evidence of violation of neutrality laws on February 12, 1911, when they arrested Martín Casillas, armed with a Winchester and 150 cartridges he had purchased in El Paso and carrying dispatches for

62. Bush, *Gringo Doctor*, pp. 167-71; Lomelí to Secretary of Foreign Relations, February 22, 1911, AREM, L-E 637.

63. Almada, *Revolución en Chihuahua*, 1: 189, 195-96; Meyer, *Mexican Rebel*, p. 26.

64. Wickersham to Secretary of State, January 26, 1911, RDS, 812.00/673; J. A. Fowler, special agent, to Secretary of State, January 27, 1911, RDS, 812.00/679.

the guerrillas in the field.[65] The letters incriminated the provisional president and vice-president.

News of the American plans reached the rebels from their confederate, Lomelí, and persuaded the members of the junta to return to Mexico. González's service in exile thus came to an abrupt end, although he had probably intended to remain in El Paso for a time. Madero left his personal secretary, Federico González Garza, in charge of the junta. González's efforts had been successful. A correspondent, disenchanted with his assignment on the border, unknowingly paid tribute to González when he wrote, "Nothing has been accomplished by the insurgent forces outside the columns of the El Paso press." A United States Army officer also commended the rebel leader when he reported that the people sending arms, ammunition, and horses across the border "have a perfect system of espionage."[66] González made final arrangements for his departure, borrowed thirty dollars from a friend for expenses, and with Madero slipped out of El Paso and across the Rio Grande into Chihuahua in the predawn hours of February 14, 1911.[67]

65. *EPMT*, February 13, 1911; González to Commanders in the Field, contained in Lomelí to Secretary of Foreign Relations, February 24, 1911, AREM, L-E 639.

66. Reporter for the *New York Herald* cited in Clendenen, *Blood on the Border*, p. 129; Capt. R. W. Hoyt to the Adjutant General, January 13, 1911, RDS, 812.00/652.

67. *Hearings, 1913*, testimony of Hernández, p. 120; Amaya, *Los auténticos revolucionarios*, p. 134.

4

Insurgent Governor

Before fleeing to Chihuahua, González had directed the junta in El Paso for more than two months without interference from the United States government. Earlier the Mexican Liberals had been hounded from Saint Louis to Montreal then back to Los Angeles and eventually jailed, but González appeared in public, chatted with secret servicemen, and gave interviews to journalists. The difference resulted from a change in the enforcement of neutrality legislation. Often misunderstood, the law's most important provision prohibited instigating revolution from the United States against a friendly nation. What constituted inciting a revolution remained open to interpretation. The Theodore Roosevelt administration had taken a strong view and harried the PLM. Local peace officers pursued the exiles and often used convenient pretexts to return political exiles to Mexico. Stories that rural policemen shot down extradited prisoners, rumors that Mexican consuls bribed local sheriffs to aid in the chase, and newspaper accounts that reported the tortuous efforts to convict Flores Magón of a crime bred popular curiosity that the then powerful Socialist party of the United States tried to excite into indignation. The House of Representatives heard accounts of alleged persecution of political refugees from the Honorable William B. Wilson of Pennsylvania, who

55

demanded a congressional investigation and offered a list of persons who would testify that federal agents throughout the Southwest had improperly aided the Mexican espionage system.[1] His attack on the cavalier way the Mexican government operated in the United States helped to force a more cautious policy regarding the *maderista* rebels.

A change in the enforcement of the neutrality laws also followed the transition in the White House from the stick-waving Roosevelt to the gavel-swinging Taft, who, because of his legal training and judicial experience, adopted a more restrained policy.[2] The Mexican ambassador presented three rebel activities as violations of American statutes: the distribution from United States soil of propaganda against the Díaz government, the sale of war goods to the insurgents, and the shipment of arms and ammunition across the border. The president's cabinet was divided on the proper handling of these practices; consequently, confusion developed among the federal officers enforcing the law along the border. Finally Secretary of State Philander Knox tried to clarify the issue. He informed the Mexican minister on December 1, 1910, that the Constitution of the United States guaranteed freedom of speech to citizens and to resident foreigners and that the sale and delivery of materiel remained legal commerce since the Mexican government did not recognize the rebels as belligerents. In an obiter dictum, he added that even if the rebels received belligerency status, the laws required only the confiscation of captured supplies, not the suspension of the traffic. The neutrality laws merely set penalties for arming and initiating a military invasion from the United States. Other cabinet members did not see the issue in the same light, however, and the attorney general continued his department's surveillance of the rebels in exile and prepared to arrest their leaders.[3]

The attitude of Americans along the border also helped to alter neutrality enforcement. Many sympathized with the rebels. Madero, González, and others were seen as reformers, not the wild-eyed extremists that the newspapers portrayed the Liberals and Flores Magón as being. Besides good will, these Americans often gave aid to the exiles, informing them of the activities of secret servicemen.[4] Moreover, Texans, especially, resented the policy of the Mexican government. Porfirian administrators demanded that the United

1. Ivie E. Cadenhead, Jr., "The American Socialists and the Mexican Revolution of 1910," *Southwestern Social Science Quarterly* 43 (1962): 103-11; *EPMT*, June 9, 1910.

2. Harold E. Holcombe, "United States Arms Control and the Mexican Revolution, 1910-1924" (Ph.D. dissertation, University of Alabama, 1968), p. 22; chap. 2, passim.

3. This discussion is based on Edward J. Berbusse, "Neutrality-Diplomacy of the United States and Mexico, 1910-1911," *The Americas* 12 (1956): 265-83.

4. Ellsworth to Secretary of State, December 3, 1911, RDS, 812.00/549.

States prevent the shipment of arms and ammunition, yet the law officers were all gathered on the northern bank of the Rio Grande. The Mexicans did little to police their side of the frontier; instead they spent their energies petitioning the United States. Many Americans inquired how neutral a policy could be that made marshals the agents of a foreign government. A Texas newspaper editor described the situation: *"The American side of the Border is a solid living mass of troops, marshals, and officers of every description. The Mexican side of the same border is one vast blank spot*—nary a darned officer in sight." "What," he wanted to know, "is the Mexican government doing to put down these disturbances . . .? " Going a step further, the attorney general reported in a memorandum that the efforts to remain neutral had "begun to encroach on good sense."[5]

Secret agents and spies who flocked to the border spent more time checking on each other than on the rebels. Men from the Furlong Agency watched the federal officers to learn what information the government had collected, and the government kept appraised of the Furlong agents. The State Department, the attorney general's office, and the Customs Bureau each maintained independent, often competing, surveillance operations. With a herd of secret servicemen milling around the suspected rebels, Consul Ellsworth, who tried to coordinate border espionage, cried out in despair that nothing could be accomplished until the number of agents was reduced.[6] In El Paso the scene anticipated the Keystone Kops; rebels, agents, detectives, and informers gathered to watch each other. The Sheldon Hotel sheltered much of the cloak-and-dagger enterprise. At one point, Madero family members, Consul Ellsworth, Mexican informants, U.S. Army officers, Justice Department spies, and a number of newspaper reporters all took lodging there.[7] Suspicion, mistrust, rumored conspiracy, and alleged and actual double agents made it impossible to compile evidence that the attorney general could use to demand the arrest of Madero and González. Reports from various intelligence sources contradicted one another, making it impossible to determine where Madero was, where the rebel headquarters was, and what the rebels were doing. Only the capture of armed rebels crossing the border, in particular Martín Casillas, provided the undeniable evidence on which to issue warrants. That court order brought González to another phase of his career when he returned to Chihuahua.

5. Attorney General's Memorandum, March 2, 1911, RDS, 812.00/780, includes quotes from the Eagle Pass *Texas News and Guide*, n.d. [1910].
6. Ellsworth to Secretary of State, March 7, 1911, RDS, 812.00/924.
7. Turner, *Bullets*, p. 24; Bush, *Gringo Doctor*, p. 179.

I

With the end of his duties as recruiting officer and gunrunner in exile, González returned to Chihuahua as governor, vice-president, and colonel in the army of an insurgent state. He had revealed little military talent in his adventures near Ojinaga and displayed no desire to repeat the experience. Discounting his rank, even refusing to wear army insignia, he dressed like a sportsman in riding breeches, shirt and starched collar, tie, bush jacket, and campaign hat. Only a tricolor ribbon on his lapel marked him as a rebel.[8] Eschewing battlefield command, he worked in the months before the rebel victory to give roots to his provisional government. Conquered territory was not merely occupied by the rebels, but was first reorganized, then governed by González. His actions altered the challenge to the dictatorship: after March, 1911, the porfirian government no longer confronted roving bands of guerrillas, but a separatist state with both civil and military authority in the greatest part of its area.

While González established civil government, Madero, with the same stubbornness that had earlier marked his refusal to leave the United States, decided to command the army. He insisted that the general staff coordinate rebel forces and also decided on military objectives. His stiff-necked commands were efforts to unify the insurgents, but his first actions only divided them. Already resentful toward their newly appointed staff officers, Orozco and other veterans in late February protested the promotion of Garibaldi to lieutenant colonel and the high rank given to other foreigners. Some officers drew an analogy between the rebel promotions and Díaz's xenophilia. Stung by the comparison with porfirian policies, Madero retorted that Garibaldi followed the example of such famous volunteers to the cause of liberty as Lafayette and Miranda.[9] González, who had inspired the Italian's promotion, aided Madero in successfully, if temporarily, glossing over the incident.

While his army seemed to be crumbling from dissension, Madero recognized the growing strength of the Liberals. At the end of January they had captured Mexicali, a port of entry on the California border, and other *magonista* troops had invaded Chihuahua. Shortly after his return to Mexico,

8. Valadés, *Madero*, 2: 110.

9. Madero to Manuel García Vigil, Roque González Garza, Octavia Morelos, and Antonio Ruíz, February 28, 1911, in Armando de María y Campos, ed., *Las memorias y las mejores cartas de Francisco I. Madero* (Mexico: Libro-Mex, Editores, 1956), pp. 132-33 (hereafter cited as *Cartas*).

Madero encountered a Liberal unit which refused to recognize him; he ordered the men disarmed. Other Liberals roamed in small bands throughout the
state.[10] Internal disputes among the Anti-reelectionists and the presence of
insurrectionist rivals convinced Madero he had to win a major battle. He
wanted to offset the PLM success; provide the rebels with a site for their provisional government; and at the same time demonstrate the mettle of his staff,
the capabilities of the foreign legion, and his own ability to command. He
selected Casas Grandes in northwestern Chihuahua as his target. Directing the
preparations, he ordered Orozco to Galeana to wait in reserve. On the eve of
the battle, González, who had fought before, tried to dissuade his chief from
leading the attack, arguing that the president was not required to risk his life.
Madero petulantly snapped that in the event of his death González had already been named vice-president.[11]

Madero's army advanced on March 6 against the small but well-armed federal force defending Casas Grandes. The foreign legion was ordered to cut
telegraph and railroad lines, but somehow during the confusion the orders
were delayed and the wires were never cut. When the volunteers arrived to
tear up the rails of the Mexican Northwestern Railroad, they met an advancing relief column. The reinforcements scattered the foreign legion, then
caught them in a crossfire.[12] The battle ended in diaster for the rebels. Madero was wounded, a number of insurgents were killed, and a few of their soldiers and a great deal of their equipment was captured. The defeated warriors,
followed by the wounded and the stragglers, regrouped with Orozco's men.
Chastened, Madero decided to relinquish field command and to devise strategy only in consultation with his officers.

Laying new plans for their campaign, Madero, González, and Orozco decided to split their forces. The larger column, under Orozco, with Madero and
most of his entourage, would move northeast along the railroad to make another attempt to take Juárez. The smaller unit, commanded by Marcelo
Caraveo, would escort González and Pascual Orozco, Sr., to Guerrero Canton,
where they would establish civil government for the sierra region. Before the
army divided, it moved to Bustillos to recuperate.[13]

While the men rested on a hacienda owned by one of his uncles, Madero

10. Blaisdell, *Desert Revolution*, pp. 39-40; Almada, *Revolución en Chihuahua*, 1:
197.

11. Valadés, *Madero*, 2: 123; Ellsworth to Secretary of State, February 13, 1911,
RDS, 812.00/819; Meyer, *Mexican Rebel*, p. 27.

12. Almada, *Vida González*, p. 39.

13. Valadés, *Madero*, 2: 140; Meyer, *Mexican Rebel*, pp. 27-28.

organized a provisional national government. The San Luís Plan alluded to an insurgent state by declaring the elections of 1910 void and naming Madero interim president until elections could reconstitute a legitimate administration. From the first day of the rebellion, the rebels had taken steps toward civil government: Madero had named provisional governors on November 20, 1910. Orozco, after occupying villages in the Sierra Madre, presided over elections of new municipal presidents and district chiefs in San Andrés, Bustillos, Temósachic, and Santa Isabel. Besides establishing an outfitting center in El Paso, González had formed a state government in exile. Madero sanctioned those steps taken to demonstrate that the rebels were not engaged in a barracks revolt, but planned to establish a new government that would revitalize the governmental institutions and invigorate the national constitution. His creation of an insurgent state within national boundaries anticipated the tactics of later social revolutionaries as he tried to involve the entire population of rebel-held areas in the revolution, whether they served in his army or not. Finally, by providing a civil regime he intended to begin such conventional functions as the collection of taxes.[14]

Madero and González established a government in Bustillos and issued executive orders in the name of the Mexican people, calling for the replacement of porfirian officials, outlining military conduct to be followed in the war zone, and reiterating the programs of the rebels. In his most important circular, Madero issued a statement on election and the franchise. Every citizen had the inviolable right to vote; interference with that right robbed man of one of his most precious possessions. To steal a man's vote by prohibiting him from exercising it was a crime, and offenders were to be punished as thieves. Public officials guilty of this outrage were to be dismissed from office. Madero also replaced the indirect system of elections with direct balloting for national officers. He attempted to eliminate the prerogatives of official candidates by forbidding electioneering by local authorities. He dictated that all candidates had to declare themselves two months before election day and that the tabulation of ballots had to be supervised by representatives of all parties.[15]

To assist the people of rebel-held areas, Madero prohibited the collection

14. *EPMT*, December 2, 1911; Robert W. McColl, "The Insurgent State: Territorial Bases of Revolution," *Annals of the Association of American Geographers* 59 (1969): 613-31.

15. For copies of the decrees, see Correspondencia del Presidente Francisco I. Madero, Mayo a Junio, 1911, caja 1, items 2341-49, Archivo Madero, Biblioteca Nacional (hereafter cited as BNAM); the election decree, March 18, 1911, is also contained in Fowler to Secretary of State, April 15, 1911, RDS, 812.00/1372.

of head taxes from workers and farmers because, he said, they could barely scratch out a living without paying those exactions. Responding to the suspension of constitutional guarantees by the Díaz government, Madero said that the government's action was like that of Maximilian and would lead to the execution of political prisoners. If that resulted, he warned, the rebels would hold the bureaucrats responsible. The insurgents wanted to centralize their control of the revolutionary bands beginning to appear throughout the nation, but Madero and González could hope to communicate instructions to their followers only in the neighboring states of Coahuila and Sonora.[16]

In mid-April the rebels pulled out of Bustillos. As they split up, González and his escort marched southward to consolidate the regions under rebel control. Once his column arrived in the Papigochi River Valley, he confirmed in office the administrators elected under Orozco's supervision and appointed new officials for other villages. He installed civil officials in San Buenaventura, Cruces, Namiquipa, Bachiniva, and Guerrero City. In the government seats of these mountain cantons, he continued the office of *jefatura política* and saw that it was filled by men sympathetic to his cause, appointing Miguel Rascón in Guerrero and Rafael Becerra in Andrés del Río, and confirming Francisco R. Jiménez in Rayon.[17]

Bandits, taking advantage of the revolution to declare themselves revolutionaries, had made forced loans or sacked ranches and businesses in the district. In response, González instructed the new officials to issue guarantees immediately to people and their property. He emphasized that protection should be extended to both Mexicans and foreigners. Local leaders followed his commands by appointing a rebel constabulary to enforce order, and the insurgent police soon restored peace, eliminated banditry, and provided a secure environment for the continuation of business. Certain problems demanded González's personal attention. Following Madero's example of concern for the rebel soldiers, he attempted to aid the families of the men in the field,[18] but he could not offer them financial help because he still faced the incessant cash crisis of the revolution.

16. Almada, *Vida González*, p. 41.
17. Amaya, *Los auténticos revolucionarios*, p. 140; Almada, *Revolución en Chihuahua*, 1: 201; Letcher to Secretary of State, April 6, 1911, RDS, 812.00/1318. Amaya is stridently anti-González, and his charge that Caraveo rather than González accomplished the civil organization reflects his bias.
18. Statement of Daniel C. Sutton of the Boston-Mexico Development Co., March 24, 1911, in Cole to Chief, Bureau of Investigation, RDS, 812.00/1152; W. H. Paul, manager, Dolores Mines Co., to Letcher, January 20, 1912, enclosure 12 in Letcher to Wilson, January 23, 1912, PR, Monterrey, Correspondence CO, 1912, class 8, 800; *EPMT*, April 17, 1911.

González hoped that by regularizing civil government he might establish a sound economic base. He tapped the major sources of funds in the region by ordering that all taxes be paid to insurgent officials. His agents collected levies from Mexicans and, more importantly, from foreign-owned cattle ranches, mines, and lumber camps as well. Company managers paid the taxes because the rebels controlled the region and gave guarantees. The governor soon extended his fiscal administration and charged customs on exports from the state. Those cattle shipments that did not pass through Juárez were easy to locate and assess. Several North American stockmen operating in Chihuahua wanted to move their herds north before the fighting intensified, and González collected duties from trail bosses before allowing them to cross into the United States. His friendship with the El Paso business community and his willingness to scale down assessments to a reasonable level while issuing safe-passage papers induced the owners to pay. Mexican herds, such as those of Luis Terrazas, were confiscated on occasion for the war effort, then marketed in the United States.[19]

González extended his administration as federal authority diminished throughout Chihuahua. Following rebel victories during April the federal army with civil officers in their wake retreated to garrison towns. By the middle of the month they controlled only Chihuahua City, Santa Rosalía, Parral, and ports of entry along the border. In six of the state's twelve cantons González installed rebel sympathizers, and in the other districts where the rebels were not strong enough to establish their government, none existed.[20] There was a growing belief that the rebels would succeed. Revolutionary military success had not destroyed the federal army, but the creation of civil government promised permanence for their movement. Even in distant Mexico City, the United States ambassador observed that "a new order of things is to be ushered in." That the revolution's principles of political and electoral reform "would be put into trial," he found, "no one doubts."[21]

Combined with the conviction that the rebels would win at least a partial victory, there was a strong desire to end the fighting. Civilian hardships and desertions contributed to the collapse of the Díaz regime in Chihuahua. As early as February, reports from towns throughout the state emphasized food shortages and business decline. Newspapers in March carried stories of hunger,

19. Ellsworth to Secretary of State, April 25, 1911, RDS, 812.00/1550; Garibaldi, *Toast to Rebellion*, p. 279.

20. Letcher to Secretary of State, April 6, 1911, RDS, 812.00/1318; April 21, 1911, RDS, 812.00/1577.

21. Wilson to Secretary of State, April 26, 1911, RDS, 812.00/1543.

inflated prices, and the exile of professional men.[22] Most people appeared apathetic toward the government's efforts to defeat the rebels, and sizable numbers demonstrated a preference for the rebels. In Juárez, the American consul estimated that nine out of ten residents favored the revolution, while his counterpart in Chihuahua City reported that the government could count on no more than 5 percent of the townspeople. By the end of March these consular observers no longer questioned a change in the porfirian regime; it only remained to be determined how thorough the alterations would be.[23] That was not decided until the Battle of Juárez.

II

As González organized an insurgent government in western Chihuahua, the rebel column led by Orozco and Madero moved north toward Juárez. By mid-April the troops threatened the city and Madero demanded its surrender. The federal commander refused.[24] The arrival of peace emissaries from Porfirio Díaz delayed the battle. Agreeing to an armistice on April 20, 1911, Madero called together his advisers so they could hear the dictator's overtures. Rebel chiefs from around the state soon arrived in the camp outside Juárez. After two days of hard travel from Guerrero, partially by train, González arrived on April 28, only to learn that Madero was inclined to accept the dictator's offer.[25] Díaz's representatives conceded most of the reforms demanded in the San Luis Plan, including the resignation of the vice-president, but they proposed to maintain Díaz in the presidency. Madero's advisers, particularly Francisco Vázquez Gómez and González, counseled him to reject the offer until the government agreed to the abdication of the president too and the appointment of several rebel governors. Vázquez Gómez and other negotiators had demanded these concessions in earlier informal discussions.[26] While the talks continued, Mexican and American sightseers flocked to the rebel headquarters. The curious took pictures and crowded around Madero, and the

22. Ellsworth to Secretary of State, February 6, 1911, RDS, 812.00/806; Turner, *Mexican Nationalism*, pp. 145, 147.

23. Leonard to Secretary of State, March 19, 1911, RDS, 812.00/993; Edwards to Secretary of State, March 21, 1911, RDS, 812.00/1063.

24. Meyer, *Mexican Rebel*, pp. 28-29.

25. Madero to Mercedes G. de Madero, April 25, 1911, in *Cartas*, p. 136; González to González Garza, April 26, 1911, BNAM, 5/2297.

26. Amaya, *Los auténticos revolucionarios*, pp. 171-72; Meyer, *Mexican Rebel*, p. 29.

press reported, "The one man who shared the honors with Madero was Governor Abraham González, who is universally admired and liked."[27] For several days, Madero and González seemed to do little but pose before kodaks and shake hands with a throng of well-wishers.

After discussions with his associates, Madero rejected the peace offer, although the government's representatives continued to plead for acceptance of their proposals in the name of Mexican nationalism. Pointing out that President Taft had mobilized troops along the border, they argued that battles along the frontier would aggravate the situation. If North Americans were killed or wounded, it might precipitate intervention. They recalled that divisions among Mexican leaders in 1846 had allowed the United States to plunder Mexican territory.[28] But the force of this argument was destroyed by the good relations the revolutionaries maintained with influential persons in El Paso. González's success in fostering good will among the Texans was revealed when Juan Hart, a member of El Paso society, invited Madero and his advisers to sneak across the border and attend a banquet in their honor. Hart's motives went beyond simply paying tribute to a friend on the verge of success. El Paso shook with rumors about the rebel demands, and a local newspaper reporter turned up to interview González after the dinner. The provisional governor quickly tried to allay the anxiety of border residents who held property in Mexico. He discounted stories that the rebels would institute a Mexican homestead act using land from expropriated estates, then went on to say: ". . . the principal issues involved are local self-government, a guarantee of the autonomy of the states, free speech, a free press, and the sovereignty of the people. This secured, then the national congress, selected by the people, can enact laws to overcome any injustice that has grown out of class legislation." To provide a convincing note, the journalist added that González "has the reputation of being an exceptionally able man, and also very conservative."[29]

The rebels could afford to dally with peace negotiations as their prospects increased during the armistice. Because the ceasefire applied only to the district around Juárez, the rebels kept up their military activities and soon controlled railroads and telegraph lines throughout the state. González played only a minor role in negotiations, but continued to handle many of the bothersome but necessary administrative details. He vigorously enforced the rebel customs, collecting taxes on cattle herds shipped out of the state. His agents

27. *EPMT*, May 1, 1911.
28. Amaya, *Los auténticos revolucionarios*, p. 175.
29. Ernest O. Schuster, *Pancho Villa's Shadow* (New York: Exposition Press, 1947), pp. 69-73; *EPMT*, May 2, 1911.

charged all the traffic would bear, and in one arbitrary assessment they demanded five dollars a head. The North American owners went to see González, whom they knew, and persuaded him to reduce the tax to a dollar and a half a head. With his concurrence, they paid only three thousand dollars for their cattle to leave Mexico. At their meeting, González took the opportunity to importune the owners for a loan of twenty-five thousand dollars but they refused to grant it. Another stockman paid two thousand dollars for his herd to enter the United States, and also refused to lend the rebels money even at 40 percent interest. Although it was rumored that Z. T. White provided the rebels with five thousand dollars, there is no evidence to support the allegation.[30] With the funds he did have, González purchased cartridges in El Paso. Some he stockpiled for the expected battle of Juárez, but he sent most of them into the field. He dispatched one shipment of more than twenty thousand rounds to the sierra for distribution to the garrisons as Chínipas, Santa Isabel, and San Andrés and for the troops commanded by José de la Luz Soto.[31] His duties became increasingly important because the rebel provisional administration was the only government in the state outside of Chihuahua City and Juárez.[32]

When the armistice ended on May 6, 1911, Madero decided to break off negotiations and move his men away from Juárez. His decision was based on the advice of González, González Garza, and others who recognized that time favored the rebels. As long as they maintained their army in the North, the burden of ending the revolt fell on the federal government. Madero also feared that in an attack on Juárez stray bullets might fall into El Paso and provoke American intervention. But while Madero wanted to retreat, his military officers opposed waiting for Díaz's government to collapse. They itched for a fight.

In defiance of Madero's command, the troops opened an assault on Juárez, probably at the orders of Orozco with the connivance of Villa.[33] For three days the federal forces held on. The city echoed to the constant rattle of rifles, the periodic thump of artillery shells,[34] and the more frequent explo-

30. *Hearings, 1913*, testimony of Charles Newman, p. 35; testimony of Charles K. Warren, pp. 798-99.

31. González to Albino Frías, April 20, 1911, STC, box 28, folder Albino Frías.

32. Ellsworth to Secretary of State, April 29, 1911, RDS, 812.00/1614.

33. Meyer, *Mexican Rebel*, pp. 29-30; Amaya, *Los auténticos revolucionarios*, pp. 179-80.

34. While in El Paso, González had inspired the theft of an old Civil War cannon, known as the "Blue Whistler," that stood in the plaza in front of the town's city hall. The cannon was smuggled by Dr. Bush and his friends into Mexico, where it was used in the Battle of Juárez. After the revolution, González returned it to El Paso with a guard of honor. See Bush, *Gringo Doctor*, pp. 181-84, 188.

sion of dynamite hurled by the attackers. The rebels began destroying the town, house by house, holding the defenders in a tightening circle. The United States Army was alerted, while curious El Paso residents flocked to the river's edge and perched along upper stories of business buildings to admire the bloody spectacle. A few spectators were killed and others wounded by ricocheting bullets, but United States officials did nothing. Finally on May 10 the federals capitulated.

Success ruined the superficial unity of the victorious army. Disenchantment with civilian leaders had grown since Madero first sent a general staff to take command; it heightened when the provisional president assumed command to attack Casas Grandes; and it climaxed with the order to retreat from Juárez. The participation of foreign volunteers aggravated the tension, especially when Garibaldi received the sword of the surrendering federal commander. A final rub came with Madero's organization of a provisional cabinet after the victory. As in choosing a general staff, he excluded military officers despite their obvious contributions and turned to those men who had spent most of the revolution in the United States.[35] Admirable as his plan to institute a civilian regime may have been, the appointment of Venustiano Carranza as war minister enraged several of the officers. Carranza, a civilian who had taken no part in the military campaigns, had also served in various offices in the porfirian administration before joining the rebels. Many of the soldiers, believing that they had won a hollow victory, proposed to confront the provisional president.

Orozco and Villa went to Madero and demanded the resignation of the cabinet and the trial of the captured federal commander as a war criminal. The meeting turned into an acrimonious exchange between the short, stubborn civilian and his taller, bitter officers. González physically separated the antagonists and calmed their tempers to reduce the shouting match to a reasonable discussion of differences. When some order returned, Madero expounded his right to make independent selections to his cabinet and emphasized the importance of exorcising militarism from the government. He resolved the issue of the federal commander by ordering Garibaldi to escort him across the border to be interned by United States authorities. The mediation of González calmed Villa and persuaded Madero and Orozco to reach an

---

35. Members of the cabinet were Francisco Vázquez Gómez, minister of foreign relations; Gustavo A. Madero, minister of hacienda (finance); Venustiano Carranza, minister of war; Federico González Garza, minister of gobernación (internal affairs); José María Pino Suárez, minister of justice; Juan Sánchez Azcona, secretary to the president. See Valadés, *Madero*, 2: 167.

accord that prevented an immediate break, but it did not satisfy Orozco's demands or mollify his hostility.[36]

While the army officers tried to figure out what they had won, González provided civil government for the city. On the afternoon the federal army surrendered, he told a reporter that "as soon as the men get a little needed rest we will start to give Juárez its first real civil government."[37] By his first orders after he established headquarters in the building formerly occupied by the district prefect he posted guards to curtail the looting that had begun during the fighting, commissioned city police, closed saloons, and halted the sale of alcoholic beverages. The army was detailed to bury the dead in common graves and to place the wounded in hospitals under the supervision of Dr. Bush. These sanitary measures had particular urgency because typhus had broken out in the city during the battle. Bush set up medical facilities in the Juárez hospital and in two hotels whose owners had fled to El Paso. González provided him with two hundred federal prisoners, who cleaned up the city to prevent further spread of disease. He named José Guadalupe González as the temporary administrator of the city and appointed José de la Luz Blanco as prefect of the Juárez district. The town council resumed its activities with new members, also appointed by González, who were rebel sympathizers from the region.[38]

In an attempt to renew the city's economic life, González sent permission to the authorities of the Mexican Central and the Mexican Northwestern railroads to begin repairing their tracks and telegraph lines. Work was started immediately and progressed so rapidly railroad officials predicted the resumption of daytime passenger service and regular freight runs between Juárez and Chihuahua City by the end of May.[39] The governor sent Garibaldi to El Paso to negotiate the reopening of the international bridges, although he made it clear that the saloons would remain closed and that he would not permit gambling in the city. Within a few days the international traffic resumed. Informing the residents of his government's intention to make restitution for losses suffered during the battle or by looting, he requested that the citizens, particularly merchants, provide inventories of goods and personal property

36. Meyer, *Mexican Rebel*, pp. 32-37; Estrada, *La revolución*, p. 476; Ramón Puente, "La verdadera historia de Pancho Villa," *Excélsior*, March 30, 1931.

37. *EPMT*, May 12, 1911.

38. Almada, *Vida González*, pp. 45-46; Bush, *Gringo Doctor*, pp. 210-11.

39. *EPMT*, May 14, 1911; Schuster, *Villa's Shadow*, 82-83; C. R. Hudson, vice-president of Mexican National Railroad, May 29, 1911, enclosed in Wilson to Secretary of State, June 1, 1911, RDS, 812.77/98. No night passenger service was anticipated by the railroads for some time because of the Liberal bands still operating in the state.

lost. He admitted that it might be some time before funds would be available for payment, but he guaranteed compensation.[40] On May 18, after a week of intensive work, González decided he had the situation in hand and planned a celebration. He arranged a banquet in the Juárez casino and invited several prominent El Pasoans and the rebel command to a party that lasted until dawn.[41]

González's celebration occurred a few days prematurely. Representatives of the rebels and the dictator had not yet reached a satisfactory agreement on peace terms, but as a result of the rebel capture of Juárez they finally worked out a method of turning over government to the victors. The final agreement was codified in the Treaties of Juárez of May 21, 1911, a modest document that required the resignation of the president and vice-president, new presidential elections, indemnification for revolutionary destruction, and a general amnesty. Although not included as a written provision of the treaty, oral assurances were given to Madero that he might nominate some cabinet members in the caretaker government that would supervise the new elections as well as designate some state governors to rule during the transitional period.[42] President Díaz accepted the treaty and resigned four days later, handing the government over to a caretaker administration with Francisco León de la Barra as provisional president. The revolution had achieved its goal of removing Díaz from the presidency, but its realization of a more responsive government was not so clear-cut. Since the state legislatures could not be ordered to accept provisional governors, the weak point in the treaty was the problem of getting Madero's appointees into office. Nevertheless, Madero was satisfied; for him the revolution had ended and he could return to reformist policies.

While the rebels waited for the treaties to go into effect, the El Paso business community held a celebration with Madero and González as guests of honor. González attended the testimonial banquet as he waited for the state legislature to validate his appointment as governor, and he accepted an invitation to take a brief holiday in New Mexico as the guest of Juan Hart. With a party that included most of the El Paso Chamber of Commerce, González and Villa took the train for Cloudcroft. Along the route Mexican expatriates saluted the rebel chiefs in recognition of their efforts in the struggle against Díaz. After a few days' rest, they returned and prepared to travel to Chihuahua City.[43]

40. Edwards to Secretary of State, May 11, 1911, RDS, 812.00/1732; *EPMT* May 13, 1911; Garibaldi, *Toast to Rebellion*, pp. 296-97.
41. Schuster, *Villa's Shadow*, p. 84.
42. Cumberland, *Mexican Revolution*, p. 150.
43. *EPMT*, June 1, 5, 1911; Schuster, *Villa's Shadow*, pp. 88-89.

In the state capital González would face problems more complex than those of the revolution. He would confront the aspirations of those who believed that the revolution meant more than simply the resignation of Díaz. He would encounter wily porfirian politicans who maneuvered to reassert their authority. In Juárez he had sampled the impending difficulties when he began the discharge of rebel troops, negotiated with Liberal forces still in the field, and had been forced to wait, hat in hand, for the state legislature to approve his appointment.[44]

González had contributed decisively to the success of the *maderista* revolution. His role did not include brilliant military command, but his recruits, Orozco and Villa, had provided that. By organizing the Anti-reelectionist forces before the insurrection, by outfitting the men in the field, and by creating an insurgent state government he enhanced the victory achieved in May. The direction of his government seemed sure. Many positive actions had been taken during the last months of the fighting which indicated that his civilian government would break cleanly with the past. But there were seeds of disharmony and omens of a troubled future. Two actions by Madero seemed particularly ominous: first, the effort to subordinate Orozco to the general staff dismissed his contributions too facilely; second, the appointment of González to a variety of civil and military positions appeared to be a continuation of policies of the previous regime.[45] Both of these decisions contributed to discontent that would make it difficult for González to sustain his authority. González's skill in organization and allegiance to his chief would be his major assets in the trials he faced as governor.

44. See below, pp. 91-92.
45. Amaya, *Los auténticos revolucionarios*, pp. 133-34.

5

Governor of Chihuahua: Politics

Francisco Madero had appointed provisional state governors early in the revolution, but their installation following the rebel victory proved difficult. Rivals contended for the office in states that had strong Anti-reelectionist parties; in other states, no candidates acceptable to the rebels appeared. State constitutions, which Madero desired to respect, specified diverse methods for the selection of provisional governors and in many instances directed the legislators to name an alternate if the executive resigned. In these cases, the Anti-reelectionists confronted a recalcitrant body elected under porfirian auspices. The Díaz dictatorship collapsed as an administrative instrument after the Battle of Juárez, but Chihuahua's politicians did not intend to surrender as easily or as completely as the national government.

I

The members of the porfirian administration in Chihuahua found encouragement for their intransigence in events in the state. The federal army had not received orders to lay down their arms, and one force, commanded by General Lauro Villar, attacked the town of Cuchillo Parado six days after the declarations of peace.[1] The Liberal party refused to accept the victory of Madero's army. From his headquarters in Los Angeles, California, Flores Magón issued the May 24 Manifesto exhorting his followers to reject the peace treaties, and small PLM bands continued their rebellion in Chihuahua throughout the summer of 1911.[2] The possibility of either federal resistance and the schism between the insurrectionists heartened Governor Miguel Ahumada and he delayed his resignation.

The permanent delegation called the legislature into special session on May 18 to deal with the political crisis resulting from the rebel victory at Juárez and to urge the governor to remain in office. The deputies strengthened Ahumada's position by granting him extraordinary authority in finance, military affairs, and police matters. In a five-day session they gave the governor a vote of confidence and expressed the hope that he would continue to rule Chihuahua.[3] They made no mention of González, but their actions indicated that they planned to avoid naming him provisional governor.

Madero would not accept the delaying tactics of the Chihuahua legislature or of its counterparts in Sonora and Coahuila. He determined to remain on the border until his appointees had obtained their offices as governors of these states. When the deputies in Saltillo failed to appoint Carranza, Madero ordered troops to march toward the city in an open show of force, then had a direct telephone connection installed between the legislative chambers and his office in Juárez. He also sent troops south from Juárez to intimidate the legislators in Chihuahua's capital.[4] Ahumada could withstand the pressure only until May 31, when he offered his resignation to the permanent commission.[5]

The deputies reconvened on June 2 for their regular session. Working under the shadow of rebel troops just north of the city and with the information that the legislatures of Coahuila and Sonora had appointed rebel governors, they considered Ahumada's resignation. Madero's insistence persuaded them; and they took solace in the announcement by interim president Francisco León de la Barra that special elections would be held in October to seat democratically elected state officials.[6] The legislators now saw that they

1. Cumberland, *Mexican Revolution*, pp. 154-55.
2. Almada, *Revolución en Chihuahua*, 1: 257-60.
3. *El periódico oficial del estado de Chihuahua*, vol. 31, extra edition to no. 39 (May 16, 1911), p. 1, and no. 41 (May 25, 1911), pp. 1-3 (hereafter cited as *PO*).
4. *EPMT*, May 26, 31, 1911; minutes of the session of the Coahuila legislature for May 27, 1911, in *El Periódico Oficial del Estado de Coahuila*, vol. 19, no. 51 (July 26, 1911), p. 2.
5. *El correo*, June 1, 1911.
6. *PO*, vol. 31, no. 45 (June 4, 1911), p. 1, and no. 48 (June 15, 1911), pp. 1-2; *EPMT*, June 1, 1911.

might use the precepts of the Anti-reelectionists to their own ends. After some deliberation, they allowed Ahumada to vacate the governor's office and selected González as interim governor with only one negative vote.[7] Their decision represented an apparent respect for the popularity of the Anti-reelectionists, but actually they tried to prevent the candidacy of the state's most prominent rebel in the fall elections.

The legislators recognized that Madero had repeatedly expressed the belief that rotation of public officials and free elections offered the only safeguards of a democratic society. The San Luis Plan, in an exacting statement, prohibited reelection of the president, the vice-president, the state governors, and the municipal presidents. Madero had already resigned as provisional president following the peace agreements so he would be eligible to campaign for office.[8] The deputies confidently expected that González would follow Madero's example. They presented the new governor with a devilish dilemma: remain in office and be ineligible for election or resign and allow the legislature to select someone who would control the election machinery.

For the moment the Anti-reelectionists ignored the political intrigue; González had been named governor. The Benito Juárez Club, suppressed since November, reappeared, and its members announced they would arrange a gala reception for the new governor on his arrival. They invited public contributions for the celebration. González had been expected at the opening of the legislative session and when he did not appear, there were rumors that he would come by train on June 4. The failure of the railroad to return to normal schedules, however, and González's efforts to discharge rebel troops postponed his arrival until a week after his appointment to office.[9]

Traveling in a special train with several officers and a bodyguard of rebel soldiers, González reached the state capital on June 9. The long delay had heightened anticipation. Admirers, undeterred by a sudden cloudburst, lined the tracks for several miles outside the city and a large crowd swarmed around the depot. A federal army band played and the people cheered as the provisional governor stepped onto the platform to meet the welcoming committee. Alberto Talavera of the Benito Juárez Club greeted the governor, whose response was lost in shouts and band music. With tears of joy in his eyes, González embraced representatives of his former enemies, the federal army and the reelection party, to demonstrate that he meant his administra-

7. *PO*, vol. 31, no. 45 (June 2, 1911), p. 1; no. 46 (June 8, 1911), p. 3.
8. Ross, *Madero*, p. 172.
9. *El correo*, June 3, 4, 10, 1911; *EPMT*, June 7, 1911; Almada, *Vida González*, p. 49.

tion to be one of reconciliation. Then he led the crowd to the statue of Benito Juárez in the plaza in front of the governor's office, where he delivered a short discourse expressing his allegiance to the goals of the revolution. Following the speech, the committee escorted him to the Hotel Palacio for a champagne reception.[10]

The next morning Manuel Rubio, president of the legislature, administered the oath of office and declared June 11 a holiday in honor of the new governor. After meeting the deputies and introducing his escort of rebel officers, González delivered a "Manifesto to the People of Chihuahua" in which he called on those who had rallied to overthrow tyranny to redouble their efforts to rebuild the state and to reconcile its people. Having won their political rights, he cautioned, Mexicans must now use them. He advised the citizens to organize political parties and campaign earnestly with the assurance that his government would not interfere. The dignitaries then retired to a reception salon in the capitol where González received well-wishers throughout the day. While delegations such as the chamber of commerce offered their support to the governor, the Twentieth Battalion band kept up a steady drone of background music.[11]

The Benito Juárez Club called an extraordinary session on June 11, and over two thousand people gathered in the Teatro de los Héroes for the governor's appearance at the session. After the cheers of welcome had quieted, González made the surprise announcement to the members and guests that he had come to submit his resignation to the club. He explained that his participation in the group's partisan activities would prejudice his duties as governor. The crowd roared its approval, and Hernández, González's secretary general, followed with his resignation. Colonel Antonio I. Villarreal took the rostrum and harangued the audience on the principles of the revolution and the lingering threat from Bernardo Reyes and other reactionaries. In the afternoon the city celebrated. The fiesta began with an afternoon band concert, followed by an exhibition baseball game between the rival "Mexico" and "Chihuahua" teams, and concluded with a bullfight arranged for the enjoyment of the governor and the townspeople.[12]

While the city feted the governor and his advisers, the main contingent of the army commanded by Pascual Orozco remained bivouacked thirty miles to the north at El Saúz.[13] Rumors linked the officer's desert exile to his argu-

10. *El correo*, June 10, 1911.
11. *PO*, vol. 31, no. 48 (June 15, 1911), pp. 8-10; also in *El correo*, June 11, 1911.
12. *El correo*, June 11 and 12, 1911.
13. Amaya, *Los auténticos revolucionarios*, p. 216.

ment with Madero in Juárez, conjuring up the demon of military revolt against the new civilian authorities. To forestall such idle talk, Orozco sent a message to Silvestre Terrazas for publication in *El correo*. His statement explained that the rebel army remained under orders and would not enter the city until directed to do so by the commander of the second military zone, Abraham González. In the same newspaper, the governor commended Orozco's remarks, but he did not order the troops to come to the capital until June 21.[14] He wanted to make clear that his assumption of power did not depend on military occupation.

After González ordered the rebel army to Chihuahua City, he sent a unit of federal troops to meet them at the outskirts of the city. The two groups of soldiers then entered together in a symbolic display of reconciliation between federal and rebel armies. As the men paraded through the streets, the crowds cheered, with their loudest shouts for Orozco. The public reception for the military hero of the revolution surpassed even that given to González.[15] The march ended at the governor's palace, where the commanders of the rebel and federal armies joined González on a balcony to speak to the crowd. After an exchange of greetings, González repeated his conciliatory message by referring to the "alliance of the .30-.30 with the Mauser" that reunited all Mexicans as brothers. One of the rebel colonels extolled the achievements of the rebel army and concluded that their military duties would exclude the soldiers from candidacy in the upcoming elections.[16] He was a better soldier than prophet.

II

Anticipation of free gubernatorial elections slated for late summer dominated political speculation and partisan maneuvering in the first weeks of the revolutionary government. The interim governor had encouraged politicking in his inaugural address, but his own candidacy for the governorship remained uncertain. While González's friends waited to see if he would seek nomination, the gubernatorial campaign became a puzzle of contradictory motives. Of those who wanted a rebel candidate, many looked first to González, who apparently would have to resign before running for the office. Others considered alternative men of revolutionary sentiments and found two, Silvestre

14. *El correo*, June 13 and 14, 1911.
15. Letcher to Secretary of State, June 22, 1911, RDS, 812.00/2179.
16. *El correo*, June 22, 1911. The quotation is from *PO*, vol. 31, no. 52 (June 29, 1911), p. 1.

Terrazas, the rebel journalist, and Pascual Orozco, the military hero. The deposed Terrazas-Creel ring saw an opportunity to confound the rebels and perhaps divide them in the elections. González wanted a full term as governor but hesitated to resign because he feared allowing the legislature to choose another interim governor without some assurance he would be a rebel sympathizer. Pascual Orozco, Jr., "fell victim to the great temptation of the military hero"[17] and sought the office, encouraged by Pascual, Sr., who believed he could advance his son's career.

At the end of May, a group in Juárez made plans to work for a four-year term for González, and about the same time a Guerrero City club was organized to promote his election.[18] During the first weeks of June, Anti-reelectionists and independents in the state capital pondered other candidates. A delegation from the new Chihuahua Democratic Club sounded out editor Terrazas, but he declined, saying he preferred a career as an independent newspaperman.[19] Representatives of Anti-reelectionist clubs and spokesmen for the old regime visited Orozco at his camp in El Saúz to urge his candidacy. Silvestre Terrazas and Orozco talked on the afternoon of June 19, but the editor refused to reveal the subject of their discussions when he returned to the Chihuahua City.[20] At a meeting of the Benito Juárez Club two days before the general and his army entered Chihuahua City, Rodolfo Ugalde nominated Orozco for governor. Because the motion came from a spokesman of the trolley workers' mutual society, it caused a heated discussion that ended without a decision.[21]

Orozco promised to be an attractive candidate even if González did resign his interim office. Some former rebels compared the two men and found the general more capable and more likely to "guarantee the liberties won" at Juárez.[22] Certainly he had demonstrated ability during the revolution. The old guard recognized not only that he was popular with the people, but also that he had reason for dissatisfaction with Madero and González. On several occasions his career had been shoved aside by Madero. Following the peace agreements, when the rebel leader found places for most of his aides, he made

17. Meyer, *Mexican Rebel*, p. 30.
18. *El correo*, June 6, 1911; *EPMT*, May 29, 1911.
19. *El correo*, June 23, 1911.
20. Almada, *Vida González*, p. 65.
21. *El correo*, June 20, 1911. Ugalde's employer was Martín Falomír, a porfirist deputy in the state legislature. Because the workingmen were striking the streetcar company, I discount the possibility that Falomír put Ugalde up to the nomination.
22. Servando I. Esquivel to Silvestre Terrazas, June 20, 1911, STC, box 20, folder E miscellany.

Orozco the commander of Chihuahua's rural constabulary with the less-than-handsome salary of eight pesos a day. González also irked Orozco. The interim governor had supported Madero unquestioningly and received many honors which the military man must have considered uncalled for. The reception Orozco received when González at last summoned him to the state capital strengthened the feeling that he had been badly dealt with by the leaders of the rebellion. These attitudes were encouraged to persuade Orozco to run for the governorship.[23]

As the city celebrated Orozco's arrival with dinners and tributes, his old friends and some new acquaintances escorted him to exclusive spots—the casino, the Tivolí de Nombre Díos, the gun club—and to private homes. As the moment's hero was squired about the state capital, Terrazas suddenly announced to the readers of *El correo* that the henchmen of the old regime planned to bribe Orozco and offer him as an independent candidate for the governorship. The editor warned that even with Luis Terrazas and Enrique C. Creel out of the state, their machine, guided by Juan Terrazas, hoped to use the Orozco candidacy to split the revolutionaries, thus frustrating their reform program. But he added that the general had too much insight, too much experience to be duped.

The Chihuahua Independent Club was organized to support Orozco. It began as a group representing those who believed that he was the most able man for the office, but it soon came under the direction of the old regime. The club tried to push Orozco into an active campaign by distributing handbills throughout the city on June 26 announcing his candidacy. The reaction came immediately. The editor of *El correo* rebuked Orozco for rejecting the advice published the day before and called on him to reconsider. Terrazas pointed out that since the general could not meet the age requirement (thirty years) for the office, he would be ineligible to run anyway and his campaign could only confuse his friends and console his enemies. Other Anti-reelectionists discussed what course of action to follow and on June 28 delegations visited Orozco. Representing a number of political organizations, a spokesman from the Benito Juárez Club confronted him and argued that he should renounce his candidacy because it imperiled the Anti-reelectionists' chance of political success. Orozco calmly assured the delegation that he had not accepted the gubernatorial candidacy, trenchantly added that no interest

23. Meyer, *Mexican Rebel*, p. 39; Amaya, *Los auténticos revolucionarios*, pp. 260-63. Orozco did receive a bonus of fifty thousand pesos during the mustering out of troops which made the salary of 8 pesos a day easier to live on. See below, p. 93.

had money enough to buy him, then, suddenly coy, suggested that if the people chose him, he would run for governor.

As the civilians left, a representation from the rebel army appeared before their commander. The officers insisted that the Chihuahua Independent Club was the cat's-paw of the old regime, and said that if Orozco did not disengage himself from politics, the army would withdraw recognition of him as its chief. Again Orozco told his petitioners that he had accepted no nomination, but if chosen by the people he would serve. The following day a circular appeared in the city affirming that Orozco had dropped his candidacy for the good of the state, and an intimate, Colonel Juan Dozal, repeated in a newspaper interview Orozco's denial that he was a candidate. While the general made it clear that he had not been taken in by the oligarchs, his statements to the civil and military delegations also made it evident that he would accept nomination by the Anti-reelectionists. The Benito Juárez Club was discussing its choice, and Orozco angled for their endorsement.[24]

In an effort to head off Orozco's candidacy, González announced that he would resign as interim governor during the first week of July.[25] The Benito Juárez Club on July 2 selected its candidate for governor. Both González and Orozco were nominated, and the former won a decisive victory, getting 371 of 375 votes; Orozco received a solitary ballot. The club members then proposed a fusion of all the civic groups in the city, and two days later members of the Benito Juárez Club, the Motherland and Liberty Club, the Ignacio Allende Electoral Club, the Workers' Democratic Club, and the Miguel Hidalgo Democratic Club formed a city-wide party in support of González. The coalition dispatched a circular to all political organizations in the state asking them to join in the formation of a state party, the Anti-reelectionist Democratic party, and to hold a nominating convention to select a common candidate for governor.[26] González endorsed these actions and repeated his intention to resign his post.

While the Anti-reelectionists launched their campaign for González, they turned their propaganda against Orozco. They made every effort to prove his alliance with the old guard through guilt by association,[27] but Orozco remained silent. In a friendly letter Madero took the opportunity to commend Orozco's break with the Chihuahua Independent Club and to point out the dangers of splitting the movement at the very moment of its success. For

24. *El correo*, June 25-30, 1911; *EPMT*, July 2, 1911.
25. *EPMT*, June 20, 1911.
26. *El correo*, July 3 and 5, 1911.
27. Meyer, *Mexican Rebel*, p. 40.

good measure, he repeated the observation that the general was not old enough to meet the age requirement.[28] At the same time, Orozco received encouragement to remain a potential candidate from two sources. First, González delayed his resignation because he doubted the legislature would appoint the rebels' choice as interim governor. Second, Orozco's father urged his son to make a campaign. Orozco leaked word that he might become a candidate if González continued to violate the San Luis Plan and remarked ominously in an interview that if the governor persisted in breaking the promises of the revolution, he would never be allowed to take office. The Terrazas-Creel people in the state also incited rumors that Orozco might still become a candidate. Recognizing that he offered the best chance to frustrate revolutionary goals in Chihuahua, they ignored the possibility of offering a candidate of their own. When a man of obvious porfirian links, Félipe Seíjas, announced in Juárez that he was running for the office, he received no support from the Terrazas people.[29]

But the electoral tension dissipated even more quickly than it had built up. On July 10 Madero explained in a newspaper interview that under no circumstances would a provisional governor campaign for the office. He explained that the resignations of some interim appointees, especially those in Yucatán and Chihuahua, had been delayed by difficulties of finding acceptable substitutes, but those problems had been overcome. With Madero's word that González would resign, Juan Terrazas gave up his campaign for Orozco and on July 11 returned to Mexico City.[30] The following morning a circular appeared in the capital city that reported Orozco's unequivocal withdrawal from the contest. Discussing Orozco's declaration that night, Luis Terrazas, Jr., vented his frustration by cursing the general and the rebel army as a "pack of thieves." His outburst was overheard, and young Terrazas was jailed for several hours before he was released because of his legislative immunity. Within the week the city celebrated the thirtieth anniversary of Benito Juárez's death. At a private dinner party González and Orozco reconciled their differences and Orozco promised his support to the gubernatorial candidate.[31]

Except for Terrazas's drunken outburst, the old regime remained silent on the realignment of the rebels. An unofficial spokesman for the former regime

28. Madero to Orozco, July 5, 1911, AM, reel 18.
29. *EPMT*, July 9, 1911. The newspaper reported that Selíjas "has stated that he was always an insurrecto sympathizer, but the fact that he kept the knowledge to himself during the time his country needed his services is alone considered enough to plunge him into political oblivion." See *EPMT*, July 10, 1911.
30. Ibid., July 8, 10, and 12, 1911.
31. *El correo*, July 12, 1911; *EPMT*, July 15 and 21, 1911.

appeared, however, in the pulpit of the state capital's cathedral when Father
Juan B. Riske began attacking the rebels and their programs. His sermons
soon became tirades against the revolution, oral assaults on the rebel leaders.
Incensed, rebel adherents held a public rally and called on the federal government to expel the priest as an undesirable person. Since Riske was an immi-
grant Turk, it was expected that the government would simply order his
deportation. When no word arrived from Mexico City, threats against the
priest finally forced him out of his parish and on July 28 he left for exile in
El Paso.[32] Beyond the diatribes of the priest, the campaign proceeded during
July without interference from the oligarchs.

The formation of Anti-reelectionist clubs spread rapidly throughout the
state. Reports appeared almost daily in *El correo* of locals established to
endorse the election of González for governor and the candidacy of Madero
and Vázquez Gómez for president and vice-president.[33] Like their predeces-
sors before the revolution, these groups held discussions as a method of political education. A favorite topic was González's responsibility to resign at the
end of the month. In one debate in Juárez, the members of the Diez de Mayo
Club discounted the governor's duty to step down, arguing that if he did it
might act as a precedent for future officials to leave office shortly before the
end of their terms to run for reelection.[34]

At the end of July, González made final preparations to launch his campaign. He arranged to capitalize on his reconciliation with Orozco. On the
morning of the twenty-fourth, the two rebel leaders met in an open-air rally,
and after they exchanged *abrazos*, the governor announced that all danger of
a split between the rebels had passed.[35]

González also thought he had perfected a scheme to compel the legislature
to select his choice as interim governor. As part of a general effort to free
political prisoners, he took under consideration the incarceration of three
former employees of the Banco Minero serving long sentences for robbing
that Terrazas-owned bank in 1908. His request that a grand jury reopen the
case was a popular move because many believed that the prisoners had been
convicted to cover up the connivance if not the participation of some members of the Terrazas family, especially Luis Terrazas, Jr., who was widely
suspected of involvement in the robbery. At González's urging the grand jury
asked the permanent delegation of the legislature to suspend that body's

32. *EPMT*, July 16, 18, and 28, 1911.
33. *El correo*, July, 1911, passim.
34. *EPMT*, July 16, 1911.
35. Ibid., July 26, 1911.

immunity since the younger Terrazas and two other suspects were deputies.[36] González then called the legislature into special session and submitted his resignation. Using the inquiry into the robbery and the prospect of lack of immunity from court proceedings as a lever, he expected to have his candidate, Aureliano González, named as substitute governor in return for abandoning criminal investigations. But his ploy failed. The deputies would not suspend their immunity, and they proposed to name Dr. Canuto Elías, a respected neutral, as governor.[37] González's bargaining power was further weakened when news circulated that Enrique Creel had petitioned Madero to intercede in the robbery case. Unwilling to trust the elections to a governor who was not firmly committed to the rebel cause, González reconsidered his resignation.

Anti-reelectionists around the state also had grave doubts about what action the porfirian legislature might take. They launched a campaign to prevent the governor from leaving office. De la Luz Soto led the attempts to persuade González not to allow the deputies the opportunity of naming a successor. Letters to newspapers and petitions from various Anti-reelectionist clubs poured into the governor's office asking him to remain in office and assuring him of their conviction that he was an honest, honorable man who would not be guilty of trying to maintain himself in office for an unwarranted period of time.[38] Influenced by his political friends and rebel comrades and by the failure of his effort to intimidate the deputies, González reversed his decision and withdrew his resignation on August 8.[39]

It was an unfortunate choice. His action was rash and left his government vulnerable to attacks by opponents of the revolution. In subsequent months, charges that Madero and González had discarded the San Luis Plan would garner supporters for their opposition, among them General Orozco, who had withdrawn his candidacy in the belief that the interim governor would resign his office.

The campaign for governor climaxed on August 10 with a convention in the capital city. Nearly 150 delegates attended the opening session and unanimously named González as the Anti-reelectionist Democratic party's nominee for governor. They also indicated their desire to maintain the national ticket of Madero and Vázquez Gómez but refused to endorse a slate of candidates

36. For a discussion of the case, see below, p. 110-111, and Sandels, "Silvestre Terrazas, the Press," pp. 136-55.

37. *EPMT*, July 31 and August 1, 1911.

38. José de la L. Soto to Col. D. Albino Frías, August 4, 1911, STC, box 28, folder Albino Frías.

39. *EPMT*, August 3, 7, and 8, 1911.

for the legislative and judicial elections, since they had not previously discussed those posts with their local clubs. Some charged that González had tried to impose a list of deputies on the convention and complained at the pressure he applied.[40]

Orozco remained quiet about the events taking place in the capital. Rumors linked him with efforts to encourage the presidential aspirations of Bernardo Reyes, later with the possibility of a *reyista* revolt, but these stories were the work of gossips and without foundation in fact.[41] Orozco seemed chastened by his experience of the previous month and ignored the opportunity of protesting when he heard complaints that the governor used his office to create a personal political machine to ensure his election.

Certainly González had a great many patronage appointments to distribute when he assumed the governorship in June,[42] but he based his selection of officials on a man's demonstrated loyalty to the revolution. His goal was the replacement of the porfirian bureaucracy, not the development of a personal political following. Among the men named to offices were several veterans closely allied with Orozco. The charge that González planned to create a personalistic organization cannot be substantiated; the absence of fraud and manipulation in the elections further destroys the validity of that contention.

The elections for governor and other state officers fell on August 20, 1911. The day passed quietly. The provisional governor did not face serious opposition either on the ballot or in the streets.[43] When the legislature reconvened on September 10 to validate the results, they approved 48,474 votes for González, 341 for Orozco even though he had withdrawn, and a sprinkling for other candidates. The deputies also verified the elections of the state judges and representatives to the state legislature.[44] González announced with mixed emotions that the defeat of a few candidates who had received the support of the Anti-reelectionist party proved the democratic nature of the elections,[45] although a majority of the winners had been active revolutionaries.

40. *El correo*, August 11, 1911; Letcher to Secretary of State, August 19, 1911, RDS, 812.00/306.

41. Meyer, *Mexican Rebel*, pp. 42-43.

42. Luis Vargas Piñera, "El gobierno maquinó la sublevación de Pascual Orozco contra Madero," *Excélsior*, September 4, 1938.

43. Letcher to Secretary of State, August 20, 1911, RDS, 812.00/2396.

44. *PO*, vol. 31, no. 76 (September 21, 1911), pp. 5-10. Other gubernatorial candidates and the number of votes they received were Guillermo Baca, 150; Aureliano González, 39; Silvestre Terrazas, 12; and Luis Terrazas, 2.

For the names of the judges and deputies chosen in the election, see ibid.

45. "Informe del Gobernador Interino Constitucional Abraham González," *PO*, vol. 31, no. 75 (September 17, 1911), pp. 2-8.

A great crowd congregated in the capital city for the inauguration of González and the newly elected officials on October 4. Many former soldiers and officers of the insurrectionary army attended the ceremony. Following his installation, González received his former comrades in arms in the *salón rojo* of the governor's palace and spent the rest of the day celebrating his victory.[46]

III

Politicking did not end with González's nomination. Elections for municipal officers and the presidency followed the special state balloting. González tried to remain aloof from local elections. He announced that he would support no candidate for public position and warned the *jefes políticos* not to interfere in the canvass. Because of the tendency for local officials to influence voters, he instructed all prefects to resign if they were candidates for municipal posts.[47] González's only concern was that the local elections be democratic; in other respects he wanted to remain a disinterested spectator.

Controversy over the election of the president and vice-president, however, forced González to take an active role in the national campaign. The revolution had been fought with the intention that Madero would become president, and he had resigned his provisional office after the signing of the Treaties of Juárez to avoid compromising the San Luis Plan. From the end of May until his election in October he worked to ensure his election and that of a compatible slate of adherents, but before he began to campaign vigorously, he wanted to purge the Anti-reelectionist party of divisive persons. He was particularly anxious to remove Francisco Vázquez Gómez as the vice-presidential candidate.[48] With that in mind, Madero dissolved the prerevolutionary party in July and formed a new organization, the Constitutional Progressive party. He adamantly declared that the San Luis Plan and the party platform of 1910 remained as the guides for the new party, which he intended to create primarily to exclude former supporters who had wavered in their allegiance. Francisco Vázquez Gómez was the most prominent opponent of the new party. While he and others decided to continue the national Anti-reelectionist organization,[49] Madero called for a national convention of his party.

46. *El correo*, October 5, 1911, p. 1; Calzadíaz Barrera, *Hechos reales*, 1: 85-86.
47. *PO*, vol. 31, no. 83 (October 15, 1911), p. 1; no. 90 (November 9, 1911), p. 4.
48. The following account, unless otherwise noted, is based on Cumberland, *Mexican Revolution*, pp. 161-71.
49. *La actualidad*, vol. 1, no. 76 (1911), in *DHRM*, 2: 46-68.

The Constitutional Progressive party held its nominating convention in Mexico City on August 27. Madero was unanimously chosen for the presidential candidacy and the platform of the party was readily accepted. The only controversy occurred over the question of the vice-presidential candidate. Madero and his advisers supported José María Pino Suárez of Yucatán, but several delegates demanded that the party retain the Anti-reelectionist slate proposed before the revolution. Madero's choice prevailed; a clear majority voted for Pino. The backers of Vázquez Gómez threatened to split the party and at one point Antonio Díaz Soto y Gama recommended reconsideration of the question, but his resolution was rejected and the decision stood.[50]

Madero wanted to organize his government with men who were loyal to him, and Vázquez Gómez was suspect. After Madero's arrest in June, 1910, Vázquez Gómez had demonstrated a willingness to depart from the goals of the party by suggesting compromise with Díaz. Both of the Vázquez Gómez brothers had dallied in Mexico City in the early weeks of the revolution, and once Francisco arrived in the United States there were constant hints of his duplicity or conspiracy with representatives of the dictator.[51] During the protracted peace negotiations before the Battle of Juárez, Madero received numerous warnings—some unsolicited, some from rebel agents—that Vázquez Gómez might compromise the rebel position for either political or financial consideration.[52] Whether or not Vázquez Gómez had conspired against the revolutionaries for his personal gain, he certainly had demonstrated that he would act independently. Madero believed the continuity and efficiency of his government would depend on loyalty and discipline from his aides and administrators. That sentiment dictated that he drop Vázquez Gómez and choose a more loyal subordinate.

The Anti-reelectionists of Chihuahua felt a strong sentimental identification with the ticket of 1910. The Chihuahua City clubs had not only been among the first to propose the candidacy of Madero, but they had also delayed their decision on a vice-presidential nominee until Madero informed González of his choice for a running mate. The delegates from the state party had nominated the slate at the national convention in April, 1910; the national candidates were Chihuahua's candidates.

Throughout Mexico there was discontent with the substitution of Pino Suárez for Vázquez Gómez. Hostility varied from slight murmuring to open

50. Reports of the sessions of the convention are contained in *La actualidad*, vol. 1, nos. 91 and 92 (1911), in *DHRM*, 2: 100-29.
51. Cumberland, *Mexican Revolution*, pp. 113-15, 120, 134-35.
52. See "American Sympathizer" to Madero, n.d., BNAM, 5/2245, and Caracristi to General Madero, April 22, 1911, BNAM, 5/2258.

declarations against the deputies at the convention. Chihuahua's Anti-reelectionists tenaciously opposed the Pino candidacy. The state sent representatives from over seventy clubs to the convention; Chihuahua City's delegation had eight members with fifty votes. All the Chihuahua men were pledged to support the slate that was a heritage of the revolution, Madero and Vázquez Gómez,[53] but in the final vote most of them went over to Madero's choice.

A reaction began in Chihuahua when one of the representatives who had stood firm for Vázquez Gómez wrote from Mexico City to *El correo* to report on the convention. Anti-reelectionists met in a protest rally in Chihuahua City and censured their representatives for changing their votes to Pino. Then the angry members drafted a letter of protest to the executive committee of the national convention condemning the actions of the Chihuahua delegation for disregarding its instructions.[54] When the delegates returned home, an abusive crowd demanded an explanation of events at the meeting. Dissatisfied with accounts of the convention sessions, a majority of the members of the local party voted to suspend the delegates and withdrew recognition from the national party to campaign for a Madero-Vázquez Gómez ticket.[55]

Madero called on loyal partymen to discipline the Anti-reelectionists. The reaction against Pino's candidacy was particularly strong in the North, so he wrote two of his governors, Carranza and González, asking them to reunite the party. He told González to stress the need for unity on the entire party ticket, including Pino Suárez.[56] González favored the original slate but tried to gain support for Madero's choice. His activities were opposed by two prominent state Anti-reelectionists, his close friend and the secretary general of Chihuahua, Braulio Hernández, who worked publicly for Vázquez Gómez over González's protestations, and Silvestre Terrazas, who considered Pino's nomination an imposition on the Anti-reelectionists and used his newspaper to fight his election. Terrazas argued editorially against Pino and reprinted a number of newspaper stories alleging brutal acts by Pino as provisional governor of Yucatán.[57]

The strong inclination toward Vázquez Gómez could not be countered easily. Nevertheless, González persuaded some members of the Benito Juárez

53. Almada, *Revolución en Chihuahua*, 1: 246-47; *El correo*, September 5, 1911; *La actualidad*, vol. 1, no. 90 (1911), in *DHRM*, 2: 94.

54. *El correo*, September 6, 1911.

55. Ibid., September 9, 1911.

56. Madero to Carranza, September 7, 1911, *Cartas*, p. 191; Madero to González, September 7, 1911, ibid., p. 192.

57. Almada, *Revolución en Chihuahua*, 1: 246-47; Sandels, "Silvestre Terrazas, The Press," p. 219.

Club to drop their support of him. They turned not to Pino Suárez, however, but to a compromise selection, Fernando Iglesias Calderón.[58] The Anti-reelectionist club in Juárez proposed González as a compromise, but he urged that he receive no consideration because his candidacy would only contribute to divisions within the party.[59] The search for another candidate may have been an attempt to prevent Pino Suárez from receiving a majority of ballots with the hope that his nomination would be reconsidered. Madero ended that possibility when he announced that Pino Suárez needed only a plurality, not a majority of votes to win the election.[60]

The national elections were held in October, 1911. They were based on the previous system of indirect ballot. Popular voting took place on October 1, followed by balloting of the district electoral colleges October 15. In Chihuahua, Madero won an overwhelming victory, with only one electoral vote cast against him. After the outbursts against Pino Suárez, it must have been pleasing to Madero when he won 54 percent of the vote, but Vázquez Gómez also received a number of votes and defeated Pino Suárez in two of the three precincts in Chihuahua City. The final tally gave Pino Suárez 227 electoral votes to Vázquez Gómez's 165.[61] Similar results were recorded throughout Mexico.

Madero visited González before his inauguration as president. González traveled to Torreón to receive Madero and the two returned by train to Chihuahua City. Madero was given a tremendous reception on his arrival in the state capital. Twenty-five hundred people followed him from the railroad

---

58. Almada, *Revolución en Chihuahua*, 1: 246.
59. *El correo*, September 11, 1911.
60. "Statement of Francisco Madero," *DHRM*, 2: 224-25.
61. Cástulo Herrera, a dedicated member of the Benito Juárez Club, received one vote for the office of president. The breakdown of the secondary balloting for president and vice-president was as follows:

1st District (Chihuahua):
    President: Madero, 91; Herrera, 1
    Vice-President: Vázquez Gómez, 54; Iglesias Calderón, 23; Pino Suárez, 14; de la
    Barra, 1

2d District (Chihuahua):
    President: Madero, 68
    Vice-President: Vázquez Gómez, 50; Pino Suárez, 18

3d District (Chihuahua):
    President: Madero, 31
    Vice-President: Pino Suárez, 20; Vázquez Gómez, 11

4th District (Juárez):
    President: Madero, 101
    Vice-President: Pino Suárez, 68; Vázquez Gómez, 33

station to the government palace. Speaking from the balcony, Madero defended his selection of Pino Suárez as vice-president. Partway through his discourse the crowd began chanting, "Pino no! Pino no!" Madero lost his temper and told the people they should boo him too if they booed Pino Suárez. The crowd responded with "Madero sí, Pino no!" The chanting continued until Madero and González withdrew inside the building.[62]

The crowd's reaction to Madero's speech offered a rough referendum on the politics of the new administration. Madero's campaign had followed the San Luis Plan exactly along the path to the presidency. His popularity survived decisions to alter his prerevolutionary political organization but could not mollify the hostility to his elimination of Vázquez Gómez from the party's ticket. Moreover, the president-elect had been less demanding of his lieutenants than of himself in carrying out the rebel slogan of no reelection.

In Chihuahua, Governor González had experienced a period of intense politics as the specter of a schism over the candidacy of Orozco marred the first months of the provisional government. Although no open break occurred, Orozco's already bruised sentiments had been further injured by charges that he had been suborned by the Terrazas interests. González's revolutionary integrity slipped because of his unfortunate decision not to resign before campaigning for the governorship. He was also caught in the middle of the reaction against Madero's choice of a running mate.

Deposing Vázquez Gómez to install Pino Suárez as vice-president had damaged the unity of the Anti-reelectionist party in Chihuahua. González could not work within the state convention or local party because he had resigned from the Benito Juárez Club. His attempt to negotiate a compromise on the vice-presidential issue, which otherwise would have been made inside the party, was made publicly, strengthening the contention that the rebels

---

5th District (Parral):
    President: Madero, 89
    Vice-President: Pino Suárez, 86; Vázquez Gómez, 3

6th District (Batopilas):
    President: Madero, 35
    Vice-President: Pino Suárez, 21; Vázquez Gómez, 14

Total ballots for Chihuahua:
    President: Madero, 415; Herrera, 1
    Vice-President: Pino Suárez, 227; Vázquez Gómez, 165; Iglesias Calderón, 23; de la Barra, 1

Source: Almada, *Revolución en Chihuahua*, 1:248.

62. *El correo*, October 31, 1911.

intended to build an official party to exclude other contestants for office. The national elections thus accentuated rebel factionalism in Chihuahua, and the break between González and Hernández on the issue of the vice-president soon became permanent.

The governor's political efforts suggested that his chief concern was loyalty to Madero. In some instances, his overemphasis on supporting the rebel leader led González to make bad decisions which laid both himself and the Anti-reelectionists open to charges that they had discarded the San Luis Plan. Madero and his closest advisers had made the twin dicta of effective suffrage and no reelection the fundamental issues of the revolution, yet the first election for governor in Chihuahua violated those canons. González's poor judgment, probably resulting from his lack of experience and eagerness to maintain his authority, caused a deterioration of his popularity. Moreover, his lackluster politics irritated many and alienated other previous backers; it won him no friends. Yet in his administrative work in the months from June to November he demonstrated a natural ability. His capacity for administration was matched only by his zeal to realize reforms in Chihuahua.

6

Governor of Chihuahua: Administration

Using the extraordinary powers of the porfirian governorship, González tried to redeem the promise of the revolution in Chihuahua between June and November, 1911. A reformer, similar to the Progressives in the United States, he wanted to revitalize business and politics by breaking the Terrazas-Creel monopoly. He drew on the statements of the Anti-reelectionist party and his experience as a frustrated competitor against the oligarchy to envision opportunities for the talented of all classes and a tax system in which the wealthy shared in paying the cost of government. In such a society, he believed, the government would become responsive to its citizens.

His decrees reflected deliberate plans that he believed consistent with Anti-reelectionist ideas. The best-known statement of the *maderista* movement, the San Luis Plan, did little more than justify rebellion against the dictatorship. Yet a specific program that included provisions for modest reform did exist. Delegates had convened in April, 1910, to nominate Madero and to write a platform.[1] Their statement reaffirmed a belief in the Constitution of 1857, called for effective suffrage and no reelection, and listed steps for the

---

1. See the Appendix, p. 163, for a translation of the Anti-reelectionist party platform. The original version can be found in Estrada, *La revolución*, pp. 220-22.

general improvement of society. The Anti-reelectionists proposed an upgrading and expansion of public instruction, freedom of the press, comprehensive legislation to improve the lot of the Mexican worker and the small farmer, including the Indian. The authors of the platform sought development of natural resources with equal opportunity for exploitation by all citizens. González had served as one of the vice-presidents of the convention; he knew the principles of the program and his actions as governor revealed that he intended to put them into effect in Chihuahua. The San Luis Plan had offered a program to get the Anti-reelectionists into power. Once they achieved authority, González adopted the more positive tenets of the party's campaign statement.

Radicals in the state pressed reform on the governor. Several revolutionary veterans were former members of the PLM who had enlisted with the Madero forces. After the victory at least one of them, Lázaro Gutiérrez de Lara, came to Chihuahua City to organize unions and to obtain for the workers the rights outlined in the Liberal Plan.[2] The sporadic gubernatorial campaign of Orozco also forced the state government to intensify its reform efforts.

The first handbill announcing Orozco's candidacy had outlined his general goals and emphasized the following points in particular: expansion of primary education, establishment of equality before the law, restriction of monopolies, freedom of commerce, protection of workers, equal distribution of state resources, freedom of the press, freedom of municipal governments, and protection of legally obtained property.[3] Anxious to preserve Orozco's support for his new regime, González allowed the general to serve as the conscience of his administration. Orozco and the Liberals worried the governor to make him move further and faster in his program.

Because the governor began his administration in Juárez before the legislature approved his ad interim position, an outline of his plans circulated among the members of Chihuahua's porfirian government and high society. On his trip from the border to the capital, González's special train met the regular passenger train carrying his predecessor. The trains stopped so Ahumada could salute González and inform him of the situation in the state capital. As they parted, Ahumada added the half-humorous aside "I left you the [governor's] chair there and I hope that you aren't going to smash it." The remark alluded not only to González's portly size, but more importantly to

2. Almada, *Revolución en Chihuahua*, 1: 112; Dearing to Secretary of State, September 5, 1911, RDS, 812.00/2346.
3. *Revista chihuahuense*, June 20, 1911, reprinted in Almada, *Vida González*, pp. 209-12.

his plans to remake society through his policies of pacification, economic reform, and moral uplift.[4]

I

Pacification meant a return to civilian life and a reconciliation between the rebels and their former enemies. González planned to accommodate all but the leaders of the former government, and later in his administration he promised Luis Terrazas and other porfirian henchmen that their civil rights would be protected if they returned to Chihuahua. The governor first had to bring an end to fighting in the state. The Liberals, not content with the overthrow of Díaz, continued raids in remote regions, trying to incite an open rebellion against the new administration.[5]

Before he left Juárez, González commissioned José María Leyva, a former *magonista* turned *maderista*, and Jesús González Monroy as peace envoys. They went to Mexicali, where they successfully mustered out Liberals, giving each ten dollars severance pay, then moved on to Tijuana to interview the main contingent of PLM troops. There they talked for the rest of the summer. Flores Magón warned his men against negotiating with the "deserter" Leyva and pointed out that the delegation represented only a provisional governor of one state. The PLM soldiers tried to take advantage of the peace envoys by demanding back wages, one-hundred-dollar bonuses, and other concessions that they could not offer; and Madero undercut their efforts when he sent representatives to Los Angeles to bargain with the Liberal forces. The negotiations dragged on without success. Finally, United States marshals ended the problem when they arrested Flores Magón and several of his advisers for violations of neutrality legislation.[6]

While his mediators talked with the Liberal party soldiers, González dispatched loyal troops to disperse PLM forces in Chihuahua who refused to be discharged. After several skirmishes during the summer, they drove most of the Liberals across the border, where United States officials briefly interned many of them. Because González wanted to forestall a resumption of raids, he sent Abraham Molina to Juárez as an agent to defend the border. Sporadic fighting continued to vex the government, but the PLM bands constituted

4. Almada, *Vida González*, p. 49. A physical description of the governor is contained in Garibaldi, *Toast to Rebellion*, p. 222.

5. Almada, *Revolución en Chihuahua*, 1: 261.

6. The commission was dated June 6, 1911, Ciudad Juárez. It is reprinted in José María Levya, *Aportaciones a la historia de la revolución* (Mexico: n.p., 1938), p. 7. See also Blaisdell, *Desert Revolution*, p. 180; Almada, *Revolución en Chihuahua*, 1: 265-67.

little more than a nuisance. González, like the porfirian governors before him, was soon frustrated in trying to capture Liberals who skipped back and forth across the border. Finally he authorized Molina to use three companies of infantry in plainclothes to patrol the frontier. With reinforcements, and coordinating his efforts with those of United States intelligence officers, Molina soon reduced the problem. Their systematic pressure on the Liberal stragglers succeeded and González publicly reported in September that the threat had ended.[7]

González began the job of demobilizing his own rebel forces in Juárez. After sending units under Orozco to El Saúz, Villa to San Andrés, and Félix Terrazas to Casas Grandes, the governor discharged about seven hundred veterans no longer needed by Soto to keep order in the border city. The men received fifty pesos mustering-out pay and passes on the railroad to their homes. Hernández paid the soldiers with checks drawn on the Banco Nacional, which held the customs receipts captured when Juárez fell. Generally the men cashed their checks in El Paso, where they shopped for clothing, especially shoes and underwear before boarding the train for their villages.[8]

González interrupted the demobilization to go to Chihuahua City on June 9 to take office. Even in his assumption of power he illustrated his intention to rule as a civilian administrator by arriving in the capital with only an escort of soldiers. His refusal to wear military insignia or uniform suggested that he was a newly elected politician taking office rather than a conqueror claiming victory.

In Chihuahua City, González found that porfirian officials had already taken steps toward demilitarizing society. A decree of May 27, 1911, issued by the interim president dictated a general amnesty and ordered the release of all prisoners of war held in state prisons. Chihuahua's officials had freed most of their prisoners and provided them with railroad passes home. POW's captured in the Battle of Casas Grandes, including fourteen North Americans and two Germans, remained in jail on the technicality that they were federal rather than state prisoners. When González took office, he tried to secure their release but had to obtain a declaration from a federal judge before he could pardon them. He freed them on June 12, 1911.[9]

Madero directed that each of the veterans remaining to be discharged re-

7. Special Agent L. E. Ross to Department of Justice, September 7, 1911, RDS, 812.00/2354; *EPMT*, August 7, 1911; *PO*, vol. 31, no. 75 (September 17, 1911), p. 3.

8. *EPMT*, June 7 and 8, 1911; *Hearings, 1913*, testimony of Tullius M. Wingo, p. 132; Calzadíaz Barrera, *Hechos reales*, 1: 81.

9. *PO*, vol. 31, no. 46 (June 8, 1911), p. 33; Letcher to Secretary of State, June 6, RDS, 812.00/2054; June 12, 1911, RDS, 812.00/2108; *EPMT*, June 14, 1911.

ceive fifty pesos and passage home, with a premium of twenty-five pesos for every rifle surrendered to the government. Many junior officers received the same mustering-out pay as the troopers, but a few got a bonus of one hundred pesos. Commanders Orozco and Villa received fifty thousand and ten thousand pesos respectively. Most of the rebels were mustered out in Chihuahua City on June 24, within days of their arrival in the city. During June and July sixteen hundred men were disarmed and discharged to civilian life in the state capital. Others were released from the army in Juárez, Casas Grandes, Camargo City, Jímenez, Hidalgo del Parral, and Chínipas.[10]

After the large demobilizations, the governor retired the rest of the men in a leisurely manner. In late July troops were still being mustered out in Ojinaga, and in August there were reports of rebels still remaining in arms in some areas of Chihuahua. The troops discharged later in the summer received less pay than the others. None of them got more than twenty-five pesos and many received as little as a peso and a half, although González promised to petition for the full fifty pesos for them.[11]

The paltry compensation did not satisfy most of the rebels. Many had taken up arms in November, 1910, and remained in the ranks until June or July, 1911. Fifty pesos could hardly give them a new start in civilian life. After the June discharges, one group voiced its dissatisfaction to Villa, who approached the governor with a proposal to grant land to the veterans. González listened sympathetically, but replied that the men must have patience until the creation of governmental machinery for such action.[12] For many veterans a return to mufti meant going home "without a second shirt" to poverty and unemployment.[13]

A circular from the Ministry of War made the discharges seem particularly ironic. In mid-July the minister directed the governor to conscript men for the federal army. González retorted that a major cause of the revolution had been abuse of the military draft; he refused to comply. Since the rebels had fought for the establishment of a volunteer army, he added that when the army published its terms for enlistment, he would announce military opportunities.[14]

Not all the rebels received discharges. Madero appointed Orozco com-

10. Almada, *Revolución en Chihuahua*, 1: 240; Almada, *Vida González*, pp. 54-55, and document 6, pp. 178-79.

11. Fred M. Dearing, U.S., secretary of legation, Mexico City, to Secretary of State, September 5, 1911, RDS, 812.00/2346; *EPMT*, July 31, 1911.

12. Calzadíaz Barrera, *Hechos reales*, 1: 82-83.

13. Almada, *Vida González*, p. 55.

14. *EPMT*, July 17, 1911.

mander of the first rural zone (Chihuahua) with a force of rebel veterans. The commanders and garrisons were General José de la Luz Blanco with 350 men at Juárez, General José de la Luz Soto with 350 men at Hidalgo del Parral, and three corps in Chihuahua commanded by Lieutenant Colonel José Orozco and Colonels Agustín Estrada and Marceso Caraveo. Local prefects controlled contingents in several sierra villages such as Chínipas, Batopilas, and Guerrero City. These rural gendarmes were under the general supervision of the secretary of internal affairs, financed by the federal government, and paid by the state governors.

Before the government regularized its finances, the troops in the state capital were billeted in homes and hotels, but by early July two barracks had been provided for the men and rooms at a central hotel for the officers. A few senior officers and surgeons remained in private homes. The governor wanted to cut the garrisons to a minimum and planned reductions in troop numbers as conditions returned to normal. He ordered further discharges in the Casas Grandes district in August, reducing the garrison to eighty men.[15] Even for the men incorporated into the *rurales*, there remained the haunting possibility that they too might be discharged.

As part of the return to peaceful conditions, González wanted to heal the divisions in society caused by the revolution. Despite his accommodating attitude, however, he thoroughly altered the administration, removing anyone who might hinder his performance as governor. When Ahumada resigned, other officials, particularly state judges and bureau chiefs, followed him. González named replacements, selecting Hernández as secretary general to ensure a loyal subordinate as his principal administrative aide.[16] He evaluated incumbent officials for their honesty and efficiency before removing them and allowed a few to continue at their posts. He asked two in particular to stay on: state treasurer José Lamelas, a relative by marriage of the Terrazas family, and the director of state administration (Oficial Mayor de la Secretaría del Gobierno), José María Ponce de León. Both agreed to remain, although Lamelas resigned in late July and was replaced by a rebel sympathizer, Tomás Gameros. Even with his circumspect policy of dismissal, González made over one hundred appointments during his first month of ad interim government. He spaced the replacement of officials over a two-month period to allow for a smooth change of government.[17] To make it feasible for men of

15. Almada, *Vida González*, p. 54; *Fall Committee*, 2: 2933; *EPMT*, July 8, August 5, 1911.

16. Almada, *Gobernadores*, p. 456; *EPMT*, June 3, 1911; *PO*, vol. 31, no. 47 (June 11, 1911), p. 5.

17. *El correo*, June 12, 1911; *EPMT*, July 10 and 20, 1911.

modest income to serve in the government as well as to curtail the graft attendant on low-paying positions, the governor raised the salaries of workers in all
public offices. He also asked the legislature to increase his monthly wage to
1,000 pesos and the secretary general's to 750.[18]

González chose his replacements carefully, selecting talented men but, in
most cases persons who lacked experience in government service. The governor explained that the state would be "administered by men selected because
of their ability and moral standing." "The people's trust," he promised, "will
not be turned over to the aristocracy for their private looting." For the sensi-
tive elite, the extreme of this policy was the appointment of Gabriel Gardea,
a shoemaker before the revolution, as the prefect for Chihuahua City.[19] Besides seeking capable men, González also tried to find positions for veterans
as municipal presidents, police superintendents, or judges. Colonel Cástulo
Herrera was named inspector of a rebel security force in Chihuahua City in
June, and the following month he became the capital's chief of police. Juan
N. Medina, a rebel lieutenant colonel, was designated as the municipal president of Juárez, and many other rebels received bureaucratic appointments.
Widows and daughters of rebels killed during the insurrection were not for-
gotten. Several were given positions as stenographers in public offices as
González replaced even clerks and office help who had openly supported the
porfirian regime during the fighting.

Although the governor wanted to make positions elective in the districts
and municipalities, he decided to make appointments to these posts. Many of
the elections he had supervised during the revolution were challenged by
porfirian attorneys who loitered around the state legislature, and González
found he had difficulty enough obtaining sanction of those elected officials
to try to change over completely to local elections. Despite the inexperience
of the new bureaucrats he appointed, they mastered their duties quickly.
Antagonists tended to denigrate their work, but a disinterested observer reported that they soon adjusted to the routine of their jobs.[20]

The governor also tried to intercede with the central government in behalf
of the state's citizens. The national administration intended to provide indemnification to those who suffered loss of property and to the survivors of men
killed in the revolution. The interim president's decrees of May 31 and June
30 established a commission in the Ministry of Finance to oversee such pay-

18. Almada, *Gobernadores*, p. 456; *EPMT*, July 29, 1911.
19. *EPMT*, June 14, 1911.
20. Ibid., July 1, 4, 18, 19, and 21, 1911; Dearing to Secretary of State, September
5, 1911, RDS, 812.00/2346.

ments and set September 30, 1911, as the deadline for applications. González expressed his sympathy for the victims of the war as well as for those veterans who had not yet received their complete discharge pay. He warned them not to make the expensive trip to Mexico City, but to wait while he tried to arrange for a subcommission to come to Chihuahua. He argued that since most of the revolutionary fighting had occurred in his state, the federal commission should open a branch office in Chihuahua City or send representatives to the city.

Federico Moye, a former porfirian official, prodded González's efforts, trying to take advantage of the situation by speculating in claims against the federal government. He reportedly purchased about four hundred thousand pesos worth of them, which he planned to present in Mexico City.[21] Because the national government delayed its consideration of the governor's request for a subcommissioner's office in Chihuahua while Moye continued to buy claims at discount prices, González tried to facilitate the application process. He opened a special civil registry in the state palace for the collection of the documents required for the applications and to provide assistance with the necessary paperwork.[22] Nevertheless, he could not completely offset Moye's offer of immediate payment. Many found the payment procedure difficult; it embittered some.

Two cases called for the governor's special consideration. The first involved the survivors of the massacre at Cerro Prieto which had been committed by the federal army commanded by Juan Navarro. González sent Baltazar Anaya, his personal secretary, to the village at the end of July to distribute a small indemnity to each of the surviving widows and orphans. Anaya assured them that the governor was working to obtain federal pensions for them.[23]

As in other parts of northern Mexico, there were difficulties with the Chinese population in Chihuahua. In Torreón, Coahuila, rebels had rampaged through the city on May 13-15 and massacred a number of Chinese,[24] and outbreaks of violence against the Orientals followed in Sonora, Sinaloa, Durango, and Nuevo León. In Chihuahua, the Chinese were threatened and

21. *PO*, vol. 31, no. 61 (July 30, 1911), p. 1; no. 66 (August 17, 1911), p. 4; Almada, *Vida González*, pp. 55, 178-79; *EPMT*, July 21, 1911.

22. *PO*, vol. 31, no. 75 (September 17, 1911), p. 1.

23. *EPMT*, August 9, 1911.

24. Turner, *Mexican Nationalism*, pp. 203-5; Charles C. Cumberland, "The Sonora Chinese and the Mexican Revolution," *Hispanic American Historical Review* 40 (1960): 191-211; John Reed, *Insurgent Mexico* (New York: International Publishers, 1969), p. 295; Moisés González Navarro, "Xenofobia y xenofilia en la Revolución Mexicana," *Historia mexicana* 18 (1969): 594-614, especially 594-605.

many forced to leave their jobs. The hostility to them extended beyond a simple expression of xenophobia against the citizens of a weak nation. Mexicans charged that the Chinese monopolized the operation of grocery stores and laundries throughout the North. Violence broke out against the Chinese in Juárez and left the colony in a desperate condition. Because of job discrimination and commercial boycotts, the city's Chinese were destitute. González appointed J. W. Kim Yuen as a special representative to distribute three hundred pesos among them. Yuen in turn asked Carlos Perry, a respected member of the community, to give the funds to those in greatest need and told him to keep 10 percent for his own expenses. Perry kept all the money, however, and soon a commission of Chinese complained to the German vice-consul in Juárez, who notified González. The governor had Perry arrested and the funds turned over to the Chinese chamber of commerce for distribution to indigent families.[25]

II

While making replacements in public offices and providing relief for the most destitute members of society, the governor also attempted to improve conditions among the rest of society. Although the banner of the movement was political democracy, González stressed social and economic programs. He relied primarily on grants of extraordinary power to accomplish his goals and resorted to the legislature only for those measures that required either its acquiescence or amendments to the state constitution.

The governor developed a new taxation policy to encourage redevelopment of commerce and industry disrupted by the revolution and to equalize taxation by giving relief to the middle and lower classes while increasing the tax burden of the upper class. Reporting that the revolution had been particularly severe for the small merchants and farmers, González told the state deputies that he planned to facilitate the recovery of that sector of the economy by remitting unpaid state and municipal taxes for the first six months of 1911. The proposed exoneration would extend neither to mining and smelting companies, controlled chiefly by United States corporations, nor to "merchants, industrialists, ranchers, or landholders, whose tax evaluation exceeded 25,000 pesos."[26] His proposal was not without precedent. During the

25. The episode is recounted in González to the President of the Supremo Tribunal de Justicia, December 28, 1912, Archivo del Supremo Tribunal de Justicia, Chihuahua, bulto 1912, no. 2126 (hereafter cited as ASTJ).

26. *El correo*, June 15, 1911.

revolution Ahumada had made an effort to rally support for the porfirian cause by offering a revised tax schedule, reducing the cost of public vehicle licenses, and removing meters on water mains in the capital, but his program was never approved by the state legislature. González did not wait for an affirmative nod from the deputies. Using his authority to issue decrees in fiscal matters, on July 1, 1911, he remitted all taxes for the period of the revolution (from November 20, 1910, to May 31, 1911).[27] He excluded agricultural land belonging to one person and assessed at more than five thousand pesos and urban property assessed at more than six thousand pesos. Neither mining and smelting companies nor liquor stores and cantinas received tax relief.[28] Favorable to middle-class businessmen and small farmers, the decree shifted the financial burden to the wealthier classes and the foreign companies. It struck particularly businesses in the capital city, since many of the mining and lumbering enterprises there had paid taxes to the rebels during the revolution. One contemporary estimated that the Terrazas family owed some $750,000 in taxes unpaid during the revolution.[29]

In another step to make the state's financial laws favor the merchant and the farmer, González directed assessors to revalue all property for a more equitable assignment of taxes in 1912. He also provided for reassessment every four years and codified minimum rates for large holdings. Previously, hacendados had described their land as poor pasture or unused forest and paid from five centavos to one peso per hectare. The new code specified that agricultural holdings larger than 8,776 hectares, depending on use, would be charged between one and four pesos per hectare. The small householder, on the other hand, was to pay an annual 1.5 percent tax on urban property used as the owner's residence and assessed at twenty-five hundred pesos or less.[30]

The governor explained in an official report that his guiding philosophy had been to favor the poorer classes at the expense of the wealthier. He contended that such taxation at best might force the subdivision of large estates and at least would compel the owners to share proportionately the costs of government. González wanted to shift even more taxes from the poorer classes, and in September he used the authorization provided in a 1904 state

27. *EPMT*, February 19, 1911; *PO*, vol. 31, no. 59 (July 23, 1911), pp. 2, 3. A grant of special power had been made to Ahumada, May 22, 1911. González continued to use the right to rule by decree in military, financial, and general police affairs. See *PO*, vol. 31, no. 42 (May 23, 1911), pp. 2-3; no. 75 (September 17, 1911), p. 6.

28. *PO*, vol. 31, no. 53 (July 2, 1911), pp. 1-2.

29. Letcher to Secretary of State, March 24, 1913, RDS, 812.00/6952.

30. Almada, *Revolución en Chihuahua*, 1: 81; *PO*, vol. 31, no. 59 (July 23, 1911), pp. 2-3.

law to revoke the municipal monthly tax of one to ten pesos paid by small farmers and rural workers. He expected his program not only to equalize tax payments but also to increase state revenues, perhaps by as much as 100 percent.[31]

The oligarchy's economic preeminence also came under the governor's scrutiny. He particularly opposed their opportunities to expand their landholdings. The accumulation of large tracts by surveying companies and tax-exempt corporations had been a hallmark of the porfirian era and continued during the most hectic months of the revolution. González directed all *jefes políticos* to suspend the alienation of state land, because he wished "to follow the spirit of the Plan of San Luis Potosí to divide the lands for the workers and the proletariat of the city."[32] He designated a committee to study means of selling municipal lands to members of the working classes and admonished it to set low prices and long-term credit and to provide safeguards against speculators.[33]

III

Tax revision and prohibition of land alienation, although favorable to the middle and lower classes, were essentially negative actions. The governor's goal of ameliorating the conditions of the workers required a positive program. He devised new policies that acquired a sense of urgency from the rash of strikes during the summer of 1911. The labor unrest began in late June in the mineral district of Naica, where workers lived in a company town. González dispatched Tomás Ornelas to mediate the issues and confirmed a settlement which allowed the men to live off the company's property, obtaining land for them from a bordering hacienda. He indicated his opposition to one of the most honored mechanisms of exploitation when he directed railroad contractor J. B. Chandler to stop issuing scrip and to pay his employees in national currency. The action reflected González's sympathy with all the workmen who received chit payments negotiable only at company stores. He made his attitude explicit when he informed the public in mid-June that his government would seek the abolition of company stores.[34]

31. *PO*, vol. 31, no. 75 (September 17, 1911), p. 4; no. 78 (September 28, 1911), p. 1; *EPMT*, August 6, 1911.
32. Directives to suspend the alienation process, dated July 6, 1911, are printed in *PO*, vol. 31, no. 57 (July 16, 1911), p. 1. For examples of land acquisition, see ibid., no. 2 (January 5, 1911), pp. 22-24.
33. *EPMT*, July 17, 1911.
34. Almada, *Vida González*, pp. 46, 60, and copies of directives, pp. 173-74; *EPMT*, July 24, 1911.

Union agitation encouraged laborers to take advantage of the government's favorable disposition. Gutiérrez de Lara in particular was active in inciting the men to demand their rights from tax-exempt companies, and in the strikes that followed, the workers made the abolition of the *tiendas de raya*, the management-owned stores, one of their principal demands.

In the capital city, the streetcar workmen struck on June 30 demanding shorter hours and pay raises. Conductors wanted increases of from seventeen to twenty-five cents and motormen from twenty-two to thirty cents per day. The management, directed by state deputy Martín Falomír, immediately rejected the requests for higher salaries and the workers shut down the trolleys. Falomír countered with an effort to bring in strikebreakers from Torreón, but they refused to work for the wages offered. The workers then called on the governor for support. González promised to do everything "humanly possible" to advance their demands. Without scab labor, and under pressure from González, Falomír and the workmen reached an agreement within two days that returned the trolleys to their regular schedules and gave the workers half of their wage demand, with the promise of the full pay boost at the end of two months. During the strike the workers had paraded daily through the streets with placards denouncing the management, but no violence occurred.[35]

Impressed with the streetcar workers' quick victory, laborers at the American Smelting and Refining Company in the capital walked off the job on July 2. On the same day, workers at the largest foundry in the state, the Terrazas-owned Companía Industrial Mexicana, walked out. The company managers made no effort to import strikebreakers because of the governor's support for the workers. Two days later, on July 4, employees of the La Concordia textile factory left their jobs in a demand for a ten-hour day, higher pay for piecework, accident insurance, and increased wages for child and female labor.[36]

With strikes breaking out throughout the city, on the night of July 5, there was a mass meeting of labor organizations and workers. About two thousand people marched through the streets to rally at the Teatro de Héroes, where government officials spoke to the crowd. González assured the workers of his support for their actions, and his statement was endorsed by Hernández and Herrera. The discussion then turned to city-wide labor organization and the possibility of unionizing the entire state. Speakers expressed particular

35. *El correo*, July 1 and 2, 1911; *EPMT*, July 2 and 3, 1911.
36. *El correo*, July 5, 1911; *EPMT*, July 5, 1911.

sympathy for women workers, immediately prompting talk of a strike in the garment factories. Rumors also circulated of a threatened strike at the Santa Eulalia mines and a possible walkout by workmen on the Chihuahua section of the national railroad. The labor ferment remained remarkably free of violence and intimidation.

Turning speculation into prophecy, women in the La Paz textile factory struck at the end of the week. The strikers marched to the governor's residence, where they waited patiently for him to appear on the balcony. After a rousing speech, but one in which González stressed the need for peaceful settlement of grievances, the women cheered loudly and dispersed. They wanted an increase of twenty to seventy cents in their daily wage. The company offered some individual raises, but the women determined to remain off the job until increases were made across the board. The management recognized their limited alternatives and conceded the demands.

The mass rally also incited the miners at Santa Eulalia to action. The next day they formulated a petition to the governor asking that certain foremen be removed and requesting a small raise. González generally agreed that an increase in wages would be necessary because of the higher cost of living in the state following the revolution, but the mine owners threatened to close down the mines if the workers struck. The miners called on González to make good his promises at the rally, and for ten days or so the situation remained suspended.

New strikes closed garment factories and workers picketed the smelters and the foundry in the capital city, while miners and owners fenced for advantage without resort to strike or lockout in Santa Eulalia. Laborers throughout the state, with the exception of those in Juárez, began demanding better wages and shorter hours.[37] Although González supported their demands, he declared that strikes should be a last resort. He cautioned miners in Madera, who struck in protest against company stores and Chinese-owned grocery stores, that they should seek a solution which would prevent the mutual injury of a prolonged strike.[38] Within a few days he received word from Madera that the company and the workers had resolved their controversy; the management began paying wages in cash and reduced prices in the company store to match those in the capital city. The situation generally improved around the state as the governor used his influence on both workers and

37. *EPMT*, July 8, 10, and 15, 1911; Dearing to Secretary of State, August 11, 1911, RDS, 812.00/2346.

38. González to Workers' Representatives, July 10, 1911, in Almada, *Revolución en Chihuahua*, 1: 234.

owners. Men returned to their jobs in Pearson and Cusihuiriáchic with modest raises of around fifty cents a day, and even more for foremen, but for less than the increases they had initially demanded. Strikes in the capital city were not so easily resolved, however. Smelter and garment workers remained off the job, creating growing tension in the city, and the situation worsened when women were hired to replace strikers at one factory.[39]

González had to take a strong stand to support the workers and to prevent a possible strike in Santa Eulalia, so he used his extraordinary authority on July 21 to decree an arbitration procedure. He required enterprises holding concessions or exemptions from the state government to submit the demands of their employees to a panel of arbiters. The committee comprised one member chosen by the governor, another by the workers, and a third by the company. The governor reserved the power to make decisions in cases where the companies refused to abide by the arbiters' decision. The penalty for refusing to submit to arbitration was forfeiture of the company's concession or tax exemption. The governor believed that the state had both the power and the responsibility to intervene in behalf of labor, but he told the legislature that his action was only a stopgap measure until more comprehensive laws could be enacted providing some recourse short of strikes for redress of workers' grievances.[40]

The decree had an immediate effect. On July 21 telephone operators won a pay increase after a three-hour walkout, and the textile strike ended with a salary increase for the workers. Only the smelter strike continued in the capital district. Outside the city the long-delayed Santa Eulalia strike, the state's largest, began on July 29 when about four thousand workmen walked off the job. The companies offered to remove some of the foremen whom the workers disliked but refused to discuss an increase in wages. The governor dispatched troops to the region to maintain order, since the managers announced they would keep the mines closed until the men agreed to return at their former salaries. Within three days the miners returned to their jobs after obtaining demands that they be paid every eighth day instead of every two weeks. The only violence in the strike occurred at the Chihuahua Mining Company when strikers entered company buildings to force nonstriking workers off the job. In addition to the new arrangement, the men won assurances that the prices at the company stores would be brought into line with those in the capital city and that they would be permitted to trade with inde-

39. *EPMT*, July 17, 21, and 27, 1911.
40. *PO*, vol. 31, no. 59 (July 23, 1911), p. 3; no. 75 (September 17, 1911), p. 7; the decree was issued July 21.

pendent merchants.[41]

Strikes also broke out elsewhere in the mining and lumbering zone of Chihuahua during the summer. Labor spokesmen traveled from the capital to the mountain areas encouraging the men to demand higher wages and reduction of company store prices.[42] The strikers avoided violence and leaned heavily on the governor's favorable attitude and policies. Even Gutiérrez de Lara believed the workers should remain within the bounds laid down by the governor. When strikes did occur, the governor tried to intervene for the mutual benefit of both sides. In October, for example, workers in the Boquilla district demanded higher wages and an end to the company stores. González supported labor on the company-store issue but accepted the management's argument that the workers were the highest paid in the state and that the company could not grant a raise. The workers were satisfied with the governor's position and quickly returned to work.[43]

IV

González's concern for the workers extended beyond management of labor-owner relations. He tried to foster a better life for working men by controlling what he considered the evils that tempted the common man, gambling and intoxicating beverages. He reported to the legislature that he had made a solemn resolution not to tolerate either of these vices,[44] but his policies were severely tested in Juárez.

The military prefect of Juárez after the revolution was General José de la Luz Blanco. Following the discharge of troops there and the departure of the governor for the capital, Blanco permitted the opening of a few saloons and soon allowed gambling and keno parlors to resume operation. Within a few weeks Juárez once again was a wide-open city with gambling rooms attached to all the bars, and with the major casinos, such as the Big Kid's Palace, attracting large crowds. In one instance a former kindergarten building was converted into a gaming house.[45] González directed *jefes políticos* to prohibit gambling in their districts and specifically ordered Blanco to close all games

41. *EPMT*, July 22, August 1 and 3, 1911.

42. Robert Linton, manager, Sierra Mining Co., to Letcher, January 13, 1911, enclosure #6, in Letcher to Wilson, January 23, 1912, PR, Consulate General, Monterrey, Correspondence (C8), 1912, class 8, file 800.

43. *EPMT*, July 26, 1911; *El correo*, October 16, 1911.

44. *PO*, vol. 31, no. 75 (September 17, 1911), p. 3.

45. *EPMT*, June 10, August 17, 1911. For the Big Kid, see Owen P. White, *Them Was the Days: From El Paso to Prohibition* (New York: Minton, Balch & Co., 1925), p. 230.

of chance in Juárez with the exception of keno, which had a two-year concession.[46] When the general made no effort to restrict gambling, González placed
the city under another official, Juan N. Medina, whom he appointed as municipal president.

Medina supported the governor's opposition to vice, but noted that because the city had no industries it had little public revenue. He proposed to
place a heavy tax on gambling and alcohol and use the money for civic purposes. González brushed aside his arguments and ordered an immediate closing of gambling houses. When Medina ignored his directions, the governor
sent General Orozco with a contingent of troops to the border on August 15.
Orozco ostensibly led an honor guard to return the purloined cannon, the
Blue Whistler, to the El Paso city government, but in the predawn hours of
August 17 the troops raided six gambling houses, seized about one hundred
thousand pesos, destroyed gaming equipment, and arrested Medina. The governor's action was applauded on both sides of the border.[47]

Following the Juárez episode, the governor spelled out his position on
gambling by publishing a list of the games that were still legal. It included
chess; cockfights; horse, foot, and vehicular races; raffles; lotteries; poker; and
whist. Other games, including those which required special machinery, might
be approved for use during fairs if they did not remain in operation in one
town longer than fifteen days. Except during fiestas, no gaming was permitted on the streets or in plazas. Although opposed to lotteries, González decided to allow them, but controlled the rates charged for tickets.[48] He specifically prohibited prize fights, which were almost always promoted by North
Americans who used the boxing ring in Juárez when they could not obtain a
license for a fight in Texas.[49]

The governor likewise imposed regulations on the liquor traffic. His hostility to the sale of alcoholic beverages first appeared in his remission of taxes.
The cancellation of back taxes had been intended as an inducement to small
merchants, but it excluded liquor stores and cantinas. González's opposition
to alcohol was strengthened in late June and early July as brawls occurred
nightly in the capital city's saloons. After closing the bars for a few days, the
governor permitted them to resume business on June 28. By eight o'clock
that evening he again ordered them closed because twenty-seven men had
been wounded in drunken arguments. Some injuries resulted from gun or

46. Almada, *Vida González*, p. 57; *EPMT*, July 22, 1911.
47. *El correo*, August 17, 1911; *EPMT*, August 17 and 18, 1911.
48. *PO*, vol. 31, no. 87 (October 28, 1911), pp. 6-9; no. 68 (August 24, 1911), p. 3.
49. *EPMT*, July 26, 1911.

knife fights, but most of the bruises and cuts came from blows with beer bottles. Within a few days González again allowed the provisional operation of cantinas, but on July 14 a former rebel officer, Marcelano Caracosa, now a city policeman, was murdered trying to disarm and send home two drunks.[50] The killing created a public sensation, and the governor moved to place stringent regulations on the liquor traffic. The sale of open bottles and drinks in pastry and grocery stores was prohibited and the sale of any alcohol was limited to specific hours and days. The first regulations had little effect, and later González directed the municipal president of Chihuahua City to restrict the hours of cantinas and bars to 6:00 a.m. until 10:00 p.m. The closing time was advanced to 2:00 p.m. on Sundays and fiesta days in the hope of reducing fights and other outbreaks that commonly followed an all-day drinking bout.[51] The antialcohol legislation also was directed at workers' absenteeism, the so-called San Lunes holiday, attributed to hangovers on Mondays and on days following holidays.

González wanted not only to improve the conditions of labor, but also to increase economic opportunities for the general public. Certainly he must have recognized that idle men could be organized into a powerful force by his political opponents. His programs for encouraging full employment ranged from offering state contracts for public works to demands that the vagrancy laws be vigorously enforced. He reminded prefects that the penal code allowed drifters ten days to find a job before being subject to a seventy-peso fine or six to thirty days in jail.[52]

The governor urged citizens to compete with former monopolies and he intervened to aid businessmen. He started this program in Juárez when he ordered cancellation of the butchering concession in Chuhuichupa on May 21, 1911. After arriving in Chihuahua City, he stepped up his program against corporations. Whenever possible, he cancelled exclusive concessions and tax exemptions; for example, he terminated the concession granted to Creel and Falomír for the construction and operation of the Tivolí en Nombre de Díos, a recreation and gambling center.[53] He told mining corporations that their privileged position was injurious to the people.

González planned not only to limit corporate expansion but also to give

50. Ibid., July 2 and 18, 1911.
51. *PO*, vol. 31, no. 77 (September 24, 1911), p. 3; vol. 32, no. 52 (December 1, 1912), p. 10.
52. Ibid., vol. 31, no. 52 (August 7, 1911), p. 2.
53. Ibid., no. 56 (August 27, 1911), p. 2.

middle-class Mexicans and foreigners an opportunity to compete with syndicates in the exploitation of the state's mineral wealth. At the same time, he singled out foreign businessmen for a special warning: "For years Mexico has been exploited by foreigners until the great body of the people have nothing. We were on the verge of becoming a nation of paupers, but now all special privileges have ceased. . . . there will be no more selling out the country by permit." Yet he did not reject foreign investment in the economy of Chihuahua.[54]

Reforming the streetcar company became González's special project. Even after the workers had obtained their demands, he continued to badger the managers, partly to harass the concessionaire, Martín Falomír. During the July lull in the strikes, González revealed plans to investigate the compliance with contract obligations by the owners of several concessions. Investigation began of several companies, including the concession to provide water to the state capital, but the probe was particularly directed at the streetcar company, which also provided the city's electricity under its franchise. Its permit called for two-class cars, but the company provided only first-class service. González hinted that if two-class service were not instituted, the concession would probably be revoked,[55] and on July 16 he gave the company official notice to that effect. In an interview, the governor said, "This company has not paid a dollar of taxes since its organization nor has it complied with the provisions of the law under which it exists." He threatened to collect delinquent taxes unless the company revamped its policies, warning that the "tax will be 5 per cent on the gross amount collected by the company since it began operations in October 1908."[56]

Before taking action, González appointed a committee to investigate the company and offer recommendations. On the basis of their report he decided to award a new concession for electrical power and streetcars to replace the former contract. Subject to the approval of the state legislature, he let the contract to José A. Yáñez. The concession offered a twenty-year contract with tax immunity. In return, the contractor had to invest at least three hundred thousand pesos over a three-year period, obtain government permission before transferring his concession, provide a reduction in the electric rate to firms by at least 25 percent, provide indemnification to workers injured on

54. Marvin D. Bernstein, *The Mexican Mining Industry, 1890-1950: A Study of the Interaction of Politics, Economics, and Technology* (Albany: State University of New York Press, 1964), p. 98, citing *Mexican Mining Journal*, July, 1911, p. 16.

55. *EPMT*, July 15, 1911.

56. Ibid., July 17, 1911.

the job, and agree to submit labor disputes to arbitration. The contract included the ominous clause that in the event that the contractor failed to meet his obligations, the company and its franchise would pass into government ownership. The trolley concession included authorization to build lines on the streets not already serviced by the old company.[57]

To prevent the loss of its concession, the Falomír-Creel streetcar company altered its customer policy on July 29. They did not add second-class cars, but simply reduced all fares on the first-class service to second-class rates, and made transfers available to any part of the city. After these changes, the state deputies, including Falomír, refused to approve the new electrical concession proposed by the governor. González was satisfied with the results of his threats against the streetcar company, but he did use his financial authority to levy a tax on all electrical companies in the state, including the capital city line.[58]

A better-known and less complicated example of González's policy of encouraging business was his suggestion that Pancho Villa open a butchering house in Chihuahua City. Villa imported refrigeration equipment and brought in technicians from the United States to start a modern enterprise. Although he provided the capital's first modern meat service, detractors alleged that the police closed their eyes to the manner in which the former cattle thief obtained his beef for slaughter.[59] The governor also issued a contract for an ice plant for the city, stipulating that the concession would immediately be revoked if the contractor failed to meet the specifications regarding the amount of investment and the deadline for construction of buildings. Moreover, the contract included a monthly tax of thirty pesos for the salary of a state ice inspector to be named by the governor.[60]

In order to expand public works projects and social services, and to establish a sound fiscal system, González tried to consolidate and fund the state's debts. It was revealed that a majority of the outstanding bonds were held by Luis Terrazas and the Banco Minero, who were drawing interest of from 8 to 10 percent annually. González named Silvestre Terrazas as chairman of a committee to investigate ways of converting the bonds into securities bearing a lower interest. The committee devised a plan to issue convertible bonds for the state's obligations of three and a half million dollars. When Terrazas was

57. *PO*, vol. 31, no. 58 (July 23, 1911), pp. 3-4; *EPMT*, July 28, 1911.
58. *EPMT*, August 1 and 3, 1911; *PO*, vol. 31, no. 66 (August 17, 1911), p. 7.
59. Clendenen, *U.S. and Villa*, pp. 183-86; Pinchon, *Viva Villa*, 183-86; Amaya, *Los auténticos revolucionarios*, pp. 328-29.
60. *PO*, vol. 31, no. 59 (July 23, 1911), pp. 3-4; no. 86 (October 23, 1911), pp. 4-5.

preparing for a business trip to El Paso, the governor asked him to interview bankers in that city about buying the bonds. Terrazas wired the governor from the border that the proposal had met a warm reception.[61] In contrast to the rebels' frustrated efforts during the revolution, apparently Terrazas placed the state's bonds with bankers in El Paso. With a source of funds, González had the state treasurer notify persons with claims and bonds against the government that repayment could be made. Luis Terrazas was one of the first to be paid so he would have no hold on the government.[62]

González's reform programs also extended to civil justice and education. The San Luis Plan had announced the goal of bringing justice to political prisoners jailed by the porfirian government; and when prisoners in the state penitentiary petitioned the governor to examine their sentences,[63] their request received a favorable hearing. At first González looked into each case and then recommended, subject to legislative approval, pardons for those whom he considered wrongly imprisoned by the previous administration. The lengthy process induced him to request discretionary powers of pardon to make decisions more rapidly. The deputies went further than González suggested; they revised the penal code to prohibit the use of solitary confinement unless approved by a judge, and authorized pardons for state prisoners who had served half of their sentences, provided they were not repeat offenders. Many prisoners were freed under this act, but González used his authority sparingly to alter the sentences of other prisoners.[64]

The Anti-reelectionists took a special interest in public education and had announced that educational reform would be a major aspect of their revolutionary program. González endorsed this position. It was especially important that the state governors support educational reform because education remained primarily a state responsibility until President Alvaro Obregón assumed national responsibility for it in 1921.[65] The states were also largely responsible for financing education. González reopened schools closed during

61. *EPMT*, July 20 and 25, 1911; González to Terrazas, July 16, 1911, STC, box 31, folder Abraham González; Terrazas to González, n.d., 1911, STC, box 83, folder 1911-1912.

62. Almada, *Vida González*, p. 64.

63. *El correo*, June 15, 1911.

64. Almada, *Vida González*, pp. 63-64; the grant of special authority to pardon prisoners is recorded in *PO*, vol. 31, no. 63 (August 6, 1911), p. 2. Pardons and reductions of sentences are reported in the same serial, particularly in the issues for July, August, and September, 1911.

65. James W. Wilkie, *The Mexican Revolution: Federal Expenditure and Social Change* (Berkeley: University of California Press, 1967), p. 162. For a discussion of the educational proposals and programs of the revolutionaries, see James Presley, "Mexican Views on Rural Education," *The Americas* 20 (1963): 64-71.

the revolution and began a construction program to increase the number of classrooms. For more effective administration of the school system, he dismissed incumbent officials and replaced the general director with directors for primary and secondary education. State funds were expended to repair the Instituto Científico y Literario in Chihuahua City and to purchase furniture, books, and other materials for schools throughout the state. The governor sent six delegates to represent Chihuahua at a national congress on national educational problems. His program was a step in the right direction, but during his brief tenure as governor, González could accomplish little against the widespread illiteracy. Moreover, the legislature blocked some of his education programs when it failed to include funding for them in the annual state budget.[66]

As a reformer González deplored the centralization of power in the hands of the local *jefes políticos*. Opposition to the office had been a major tenet of the Anti-reelectionist party since its inception, and the governor evinced great concern for its elimination. Appointed by the governors, the *jefes* were particularly corruptible and were responsible for most of the irregularities and abuses in local government. González proposed that the office be abolished by constitutional amendment.[67] The legislature complied and, in accordance with the constitution, left the amendment for second approval by the new state deputies who took office in September, 1911. At the opening session of the new legislature, González appealed for quick action on this matter because he considered it "one of the indispensable means to guarantee democratic liberties and practices."[68] Elimination of the *jefes* and reorganization of local government was passed into law on October 28, 1911, and took effect on January 1, 1912.[69]

The elimination of the prefects was only one aspect of a program to return local government to the citizenry. It was also necessary to reduce the political and economic influence exercised by corporations through their company towns. To curb their domination and to contribute to the independence of the Mexican worker, González made several company towns municipal dis-

66. *El correo*, June 16, 1911; *PO*, vol. 31, no. 75 (September 17, 1911), pp. 5, 8; Almada, *Vida González*, p. 58.

67. *PO*, vol. 31, no. 56 (July 27, 1911), p. 5, and the discussion of the proposal in *El correo*, July 26, 1911.

68. *PO*, vol. 31, no. 76 (September 21, 1911), p. 2.

69. Legislative action on the proposal was recorded in *PO*, vol. 31, no. 90 (November 9, 1911), p. 2. Changes in local government to handle the duties previously performed by the *jefes* are included in the law of November 10, 1911. A copy of the statute is contained in STC, box 33, folder Francisco G. Hernández. For the implementation of the law, see Almada, *Gobernadores*, p. 461.

tricts of the state, establishing free municipalities. This action gave the residents civil government by putting them under elected administrators rather than corporation managers.[70] The company towns of Madera, Naica, and Dolores were elevated to municipalities, and the mining camps of Río de Plata, San Isidro, and La República were given village status.

The creation of new municipalities did not always occur smoothly. Residents of the former company towns, once removed from the paternalistic company regulation, became the prey of the gamblers and saloon owners who appeared almost simultaneously with the announcement of the towns' new status. Some legitimate stores opened to compete with the company-owned general warehouses, but an even greater number of cantinas sprang up. Gambling and drunkenness was common for about a month in Dolores, until the men adjusted to their freedom and the governor cracked down on the vice vendors. Other problems between company management and local authorities resulted because the creation of new towns did not include surveys, and boundary disputes invariably ensued.[71]

Throughout his administration, González attempted to develop empathy with the population by making himself accessible to the people and by harassing members of the old regime. His emphasis on a close relationship between governor and citizen was a reaction to the exclusive nature of the old oligarchical rule. He demonstrated this attitude in his warm reception of representatives from the Tarahumara Indians of the sierra who called on him requesting relief from their poverty; and he further revealed his congenial nature at Pancho Villa's wedding, when he reportedly took the part of the bride's father during the ceremony.[72] Whether or not the story is true, it demonstrates the type of image that González wanted to create.

In a popular decision, the governor reopened the investigation of the Banco Minero robbery of March 1, 1908. Whether he hoped to indict or simply embarrass members of the Terrazas-Creel family who were popularly suspected of contriving the robbery, certainly González used the affair to bully family members who were state deputies. The robbery had brought a public reaction against the Terrazas' predominance in 1908, and the pro forma police inquiry had convinced no one that the real criminals had been cap-

70. *PO*, vol. 31, no. 75 (September 17, 1911), p. 7. See also printed documents in Almada, *Vida González*, pp. 178-83.

71. Almada, *Revolución en Chihuahua*, 1: 242; *PO*, vol. 31, no. 60 (July 27, 1911), p. 2; W. H. Paul, Dolores Mining Co., to Letcher, January 20, 1912, enclosure #7 in Letcher to Wilson, January 23, 1912, PR, Consulate General, Monterrey, Correspondence (C8), 1912, class 8, file 800.

72. Ellsworth to Secretary of State, November 7, 1911, RDS, 812.00/2485; Pinchon, *Viva Villa*, p. 185.

tured, although three bank employees were jailed.[73] The zealous new investigation forced Enrique Creel to ask Madero to intercede. Creel charged that the grand jury was harassing his family and that the judge, Jesús Dozal, bore a personal grudge against him. Madero, hoping to end this old irritation, sent in a federal judge, whose allegedly impartial but obstructionist tactics caused the case to die a lingering death. Madero also asked González to temper his investigation. The governor made the president's letter public to avoid criticism for not pursuing the case,[74] and then released the men originally imprisoned for the crime.

The governor's assaults on the old regime culminated in orders that all pictures of living persons be removed from government buildings. He further ordered that all names of streets, schools, and parks that recognized the Terrazas-Creel regime be changed to honor heroes of the nation's past.[75] The campaign became so widespread that José María Sánchez, in exile in Los Angeles, feared he might be jailed by the rebel administration if he returned to Chihuahua. Sánchez wrote the governor in regard to the rumor that González intended to prosecute him for electoral fraud when he was governor during the 1910 elections. Sánchez pointed out that as governor he had had no part in validating the elections and asked González to give him guarantees against legal proceedings so he could return to his home. González petulantly responded that his government provided protection for everyone's civil rights, although he personally believed that Sánchez had connived at fraud and was morally culpable.[76]

The collapse of the porfirian government and the harassment of members of the old regime had forced many Mexicans into exile, and González wanted to prevent counterrevolutionary incursions back into his state by exiles. He decided to combine business with pleasure in October when he was invited to attend a jubilee in El Paso. Despite rumors that exiles would make an attempt on his life, González went to the border city, where he met an enthusiastic reception.[77] While there he hosted a banquet with Vice-Governor Eugenio Gayou of Sonora for the governors of Texas and Arizona and Albert B. Fall, representing New Mexico's executive. The dinner offered an opportunity to

73. For a detailed account of the robbery, see Sandels, "Silvestre Terrazas, the Press," pp. 136-55.

74. Almada, *Revolución en Chihuahua*, 1: 90-92, includes a copy of Madero's letter.

75. See, for example, the circulars from Hernández to local officials in Hidalgo del Parral of June 26 and July 14, 1911, reprinted in Almada, *Vida Gonzalez*, p. 184.

76. See the exchange of letters: Sánchez to González, September 18, 1911; González to Sánchez, October 6, 1911; González to Madero, October 9, 1911, in *DHRM*, 2: 141-44, 149-52.

77. Camacho to Secretary of Foreign Relations, October 12, 1911, AREM, L-E 851; *EPMT*, October 21, 1911.

discuss extradition procedures and a common patrol of the international frontier.[78] The visit to the United States proved a great success; federal officials, with the assistance of the Texas Rangers, arrested General Bernardo Reyes, the former porfirian governor of Nuevo León, in San Antonio the same month. A short time later, González received inquiries from the United States about whether or not the Mexican officials planned to seek the extradition of Emilio Vázquez Gómez, a declared opponent of the Madero government.[79] These incidents indicate the practical results of the governor's visit to El Paso and his effort to create an attitude of cooperation between officials on both sides of the international border.

Shortly after González returned from the El Paso celebration, he received the president-elect. Madero had not come to the state simply to justify his selection of Pino Suárez to the Anti-reelectionists there. He also wanted to invite Chihuahua's principal veterans of the revolutionary movement to accompany him to the inauguration. González accepted the invitation, joining Orozco and De la Luz Soto in the presidential coach to Mexico City.[80] The governor expected to be absent from his duties no longer than two weeks, and as he departed Chihuahua, he could feel some pride in his accomplishments during the summer.

While the national government had marked time under the provisional presidency of Francisco León de la Barra, González had initiated a comprehensive program in Chihuahua. He combined a reformer's paternalistic zeal with sympathy for the lower class and antipathy for the upper class. His policies smacked of a Calvinism that his name and nationality denied. His apparent goal was a society in which workers were sober, industrious men who worked in secure circumstances for an equitable wage, in which farmers were freed from the harassment and threatened expansion of large estates and from excessive taxation, in which tradesmen could do business without unfair competition from tax-exempt companies, and in which foreigners could participate in the economy without smothering Mexican enterprises. To achieve his

78. Albert B. Fall to C. B. Colquitt, March 13, 1914, reel 35, Albert Bacon Fall Collection, Papers from the Senate Office Files of Senator Albert Fall relating to Mexican Affairs, Huntington Library, San Marino, California, microcopy (hereafter cited as ABFC). The governors who attended were O. B. Colquitt of Texas and Richard Sloan of Arizona; Ellsworth to Secretary of State, October 9, 1911, RDS, 812.00/2420, and October 17, 1911, RDS, 812.00/2430.

79. Vic Niemeyer, "Frustrated Invasion: The Revolutionary Attempt of General Bernardo Reyes from San Antonio in 1911," *Southwestern Historical Quarterly* 67 (1963-64): 220-21. United States agents arrested Reyes in November, but the general jumped house arrest and fled to Mexico to begin his revolution. His effort failed, and he was arrested in Mexico in December and sent to a federal prison in Mexico City.

80. Agustín Victor Casasola, ed., *Historia gráfica de la revolución, 1900-1940*, 6 vols. (Mexico: Archivo Casasola, n.d.), 1: 375.

Governor Abraham González, October, 1911

Juárez during the battle for that city, 1911

El Pasoans watching the Battle of Juárez

Battle of Juárez

Pancho Villa and Pascual Orozco, Jr., dining in El Paso, May, 1911. Villa is seated at the left, Orozco at the center with his hat on his knee.

The Hotel Sheldon, El Paso, a center of rebel intrigue and United States counterintelligence activity.

Provisional government of Mexico, April 30, 1911: 1. Francisco Madero; 2. Francisco Vásquez Gómez; 3. Francisco Madero, Sr.; 4. Governor Abraham González; 5. Venustiano Carranza (governor of Coahuila); 6. J. La Luz González (governor of Zacatecas); 7. José María Maytorena (governor of Sonora); 8. Alberto Fuentes (governor of Aguascalientes); 9. General Pascual Orozco; 10. Alphonso Madero; 11. Juan Sánchez Azcona; 12. General de la Luz Blanco; 13. Federico González Garza; 14. Colonel Giuseppe Garibaldi; 15. Gustavo Madero; 16. Colonel Pancho Villa

Members of Villa's army and civil government stand vigil at the funeral of Abraham González, February, 1914.

goals, the governor attempted to use state authority to restrict the prerogatives of the porfirian oligarchy, at the same time offering positive encouragement to the middle and lower segment of the population. To develop moral fiber and to provide the incentive for Mexicans to use their opportunities, González strongly supported public education while turning the power of his office against alcoholism, gambling, and vagrancy.

The governor had the chance and the obligation to initiate social and economic reforms because of the constitutional environment in which he operated and Madero's ideas on government. The newly elected president remained loyal to the nineteenth-century conception of administration. This meant that most social and economic programs either fell to the state governments or were ignored. Education, corporate assistance, even public health remained primarily the province of the state governments. Thus, González could implement many local policies, but they had to be accomplished within the outline formulated by the Anti-reelectionists. Both Madero's pronouncements and the governor's personal views dictated that the reforms in Chihuahua be realized through constitutional forms, and González spent the summer establishing his reforms in the state's laws. In some instances this required him to work with the state deputies. For example, he was forced to lobby in the legislature for an amendment to the state constitution to abolish the office of *jefe político.* Similarly, revisions in criminal laws and tax assessments required legislative enactment.

In the process of pushing through his reforms, González proved to be an astute opportunist who employed to revolutionary account the powers formerly held by the porfirian governors. On assuming office as interim governor, he arrogated the power granted to his predecessor to rule by decree in financial, military, and governmental affairs. That authority allowed him to require arbitration of labor disputes, to move against company stores, to suppress most gambling, and to regulate the liquor traffic. No doubt it alarmed stalwarts of the old regime to see the centralized authority which had made porfirian governors near-autocrats become the vehicle of the revolutionaries.

The threat to the entrenched remnants of the porfirian regime was much greater in Chihuahua than elsewhere because legislation unfavorable to their interests had been incorporated into state law, often as provisions of the state constitution. Concomitantly, the governor's policies heightened the expectations of the people who wanted fulfillment of revolutionary promises. By the end of October, increased popular aspirations on one hand and potential reactionary opposition on the other created an administrative problem that required delicate handling to prevent an outbreak of fighting by the conservatives, the radical revolutionaries, or both. The new governor had made a dramatic start in using his powers for reform and his official appointees had learned the routine of bureaucracy, but the new administration had not yet had time to follow the programs through. While the porfirian oligarchs remained defensive and the revolutionaries impatient, González planned to continue his efforts after attending Madero's inauguration.

7

Cabinet Interlude and Aftermath

As early as the formation of the provisional cabinet following the Battle of Juárez, Francisco Madero had recognized that only a few rebels possessed the experience and the national stature for ministerial posts. He had to reconcile his need for able administrators with his obligation to replace porfirian appointees with revolutionaries. The new presidential cabinet in the fall of 1911 revealed a compromise as he selected men formerly associated with the Díaz regime for their experience and rebels who demonstrated leadership capabilities. Because he made personal loyalty the sole prerequisite, whatever the man's previous political allegiance, Madero was compelled to appoint relatives and former associates. He intended to bring into the government three staunch revolutionaries: Manuel Bonilla, José María Pino Suárez, and Abraham González.

On October 12, 1911, *El correo de Chihuahua* repeated Mexico City rumors that González would be selected as minister of public instruction and fine arts in the cabinet of President-Elect Madero. Although the report remained unconfirmed, Madero provided sketchy evidence for second-guessers when he visited Chihuahua at the end of the month, ostensibly to invite prominent rebels to his inauguration and to soothe supporters ruffled by the vice-presidential victory of Pino Suárez. After several meetings with Madero, González accepted the invitation to the inauguration and took the train for the capital city with him.

During the journey, Madero offered the governor the portfolio of public instruction and fine arts.[1] Rumors had been correct that Madero had intended since early October to make the offer over the objections of other prospective cabinet members. Manuel Calero, chosen minister of foreign relations, was appalled by the decision. He expressed the haughty attitude that would become common among the citizens of Mexico City when he referred to González as a rustic from the remote North. Calero claimed that to place such a callow man in the office insulted the memory of the former minister, Justo Sierra.[2] Nevertheless, Madero persisted in his plans and offered González the post.

By selecting him, Madero paid tribute to his organizational work during the revolution, his successful administration as governor, and his forthright loyalty to the president. Madero also hoped that by choosing Chihuahua's executive for the national cabinet, he might placate the state's citizens who were antagonized by the rejection of Vázquez Gómez as a candidate for vice-president. These plans were aborted when González, explaining that he did not want to neglect the obligations of his state office, rejected the offer.[3]

González's refusal complicated Madero's appointment of ministers. He offered the post to Miguel Díaz Lombardo, who accepted it, but Pino Suárez further upset the new president's plans by refusing the position of minister of internal affairs (gobernación) because of the obvious parallel with Ramón Corral, who had served Díaz both as vice-president and internal affairs minister.[4] Short on revolutionaries, Madero again pleaded with González, who was still in Mexico City, but he demurred once more and telegraphed Chihuahua's newspapers announcing the date of his return to the state capital.[5] Before González could leave Mexico City, however, Madero sent prominent party members to persuade him to change his decision. These presidential emissaries argued that González was first Mexican, then Chihuahuan; therefore, he was

1. *El correo*, November 10, 1911.

2. Manuel Calero y Sierra, *Un decenio de política mexicana* (New York: Middleditch Co., 1920), pp. 76-77.

3. *El correo*, November 10, 1911.

4. Francisco Cosío Robelo to Madero, October 20, 1911, and Adolfo Huerta Vargas to Madero, November 1, 1911, *DHRM*, 2: 184-90, 227-31. Both correspondents discussed the importance of the cabinet selections and offered suggestions to the president.

5. Letcher to Secretary of State, March 20, 1912, RDS, 812.00/3424.

obligated to serve when his nation called.[6] Swayed by this nationalistic appeal and Madero's persistence, González accepted and took the oath of office as minister of internal affairs on November 6, 1911.[7]

Madero's difficulties did not end with the selection of his cabinet. After the president's inauguration, the ministers were taunted by incessant jokes. Enemies and friends alike attacked the administration because it included known supporters of Díaz, because of its tendency to nepotism, and because it included rebels of little experience.[8] Newspapers and political magazines filled their columns with snide, often malicious remarks. Theatrical performances disparaged the members of the government, particularly Madero, Bonilla, and González. Reporters portrayed González as a country bumpkin without education, culture, or experience with city life. The rude, boorish caricature was capsulized in the sobriquet *ñor Abram*, the contraction of *señor*, emphasizing the peculiarities of the Spanish spoken in the North to connote his provincial origins.[9]

González did little to remove popular misconceptions of his behavior. A succession of minor gaucheries proved evidence enough for his detractors and prompted stories that spread throughout the nation. One afternoon he set off in frock coat, top hat, and stick to attend an affair of state. But when he arrived at the national palace, he discovered that he had appeared improperly, since Mexico followed European customs that called for evening clothes even in the daytime. On another occasion, although in correct attire for an official function, he walked to the Zócalo rather than arriving by coach-and-four.[10]

Critics drew on actual incidents as well as their own active imaginations to

6. *El correo*, November 10, 1911. The newspaper account is based on a statement to the public from González which was also published in the official state records, *PO*, vol. 31, no. 92 (November 16, 1911), p. 2. See also Calero, *Decenio de política mexicana*, pp. 76-77.

7. Calero to González, November 6, 1911, and Circular to State Governors and National Officials, November 6, 1911, AREM, L-E 135 (s-1), I/13.9, Abraham González, Su Expediente Personal.

8. Members of the cabinet were Calero, Foreign Relations; González, Gobernación; Manuel Vázquez Tagle, Justice; Miguel Díaz Lombardo, Public Instruction and Fine Arts; Ernesto Madero, Finance (Hacienda y Crédito Publico); Rafael Hernández, Development (Fomento); General José González Salas, War and Marine; and Manuel Bonilla, Communications and Public Works. See Casasola, ed., *Historia gráfica*, 1: 393. The revolutionaries in the cabinet were González and Bonilla. Calero, Vázquez Tagle, and Díaz Lombardo were tied to the porfirian regime. Rafael Hernández and Ernesto Madero were related to the president. See Portes Gil, *Autobiografía*, p. 101.

9. Ibid., p. 105; clipping from the *Mexican Herald*, February 8, 1912, RDS, 812.00/2953; Manuel Bonilla, Jr., *El regimén maderista* (Mexico: Talleres de "El universal," 1922), pp. 3-4.

10. *EPMT*, January 5, 1912.

ridicule the revolutionary government. Madero firmly believed in freedom of the press, but, faced with *zapatista* revolt in Morelos and the need to establish the authority of his government, he finally tried to deal with the newspaper attacks by proposing that Congress temporarily suspend the guarantee of freedom of the press. Congress, still comprised of men elected during Díaz's tenure, rejected the proposal. González, pointing out their links to the old regime, denounced the congressmen and suggested that it might be desirable to dissolve the assembly in order to remove one obstacle to the success of the new administration.[11] His hint went unheeded, and the cabinet remained the subject of jests and malicious stories.

González was assailed not only in Mexico City, but also in his home state. If Madero intended to reward Chihuahua with González's appointment, he misread the state. Although *El correo* reported the president's decision as an honor for Chihuahua, veterans of the revolution resented having their leaders dispersed throughout the nation. Already Madero had posted Orozco as commander of the *rurales* in Sinaloa. Moreover, the state's citizens disliked the similarity between the Díaz government's practice of appointing absentee governors and the removal of González to Mexico City.[12] González did not resign his office to become minister, but merely obtained a license from the legislature to leave the state.[13] During his absence the deputies appointed an interim governor whose powers were closely controlled. Under these conditions, little could be accomplished by the substitute executive.

The selection of an alternate stimulated divisiveness among Chihuahua's revolutionaries. The deputies passed over Orozco, still one of the state's most prominent revolutionaries although on duty outside Chihuahua, and Braulio Hernández, secretary general, to name Aureliano González. Both Orozco and Hernández had held responsible positions during the fighting, while Aureliano had been imprisoned for the duration.[14] The legislature's choice particularly irked Hernández. As the state's second-highest official, he felt the interim governorship should have been his by the logic of succession. He was also

11. Almada, *Vida González*, pp. 77-79, 201-2.

12. *El correo*, November 5, 1911; Letcher to Secretary of State, March 20, 1912, RDS, 812.00/3224; Meyer, *Mexican Rebel*, pp. 41, n. 13; 44.

13. The legislature granted González a fifteen-day license on October 31, 1911, to attend the inauguration (*PO*, vol. 31, no. 88 [November 2, 1911], p. 2). On the last day of his permit, the deputies extended his leave for three months so he could serve in the cabinet. The license expired February 15, 1912 (*PO*, vol. 31, no. 92 [November 16, 1911], p. 3).

14. Aureliano González assumed office on October 31, 1911. See *El correo*, November 1, 1911; PO, vol. 31, no. 88 (November 2, 1911), p. 2, and no. 92 (November 16, 1911), p. 3. For a biographical sketch of González, see Almada, *Gobernadores*, pp. 462-64.

miffed that González had not arranged his elevation to the executive position. Scarcely a week after González departed, Hernández resigned from the government, charging that Abraham "loves Madero more than he does justice." Hernández soon pronounced against the rebel government and became the leading Chihuahua veteran to support the prospective Vázquez Gómez rebellion.[15]

II

Confronted by popular opposition in his home state and open hostility in the capital, González must have wondered if his position was worth it. As minister of gobernación, he held an office with great power and heavy responsibilities that included the administration and supervision of general police powers, public health, *rurales*, internal security, and elections. National conditions seemed to conspire against the successful fulfillment of his duties; the preliminary selection of new administrators and the development of a coordinated policy were sacrificed to the immediate problem of insurrections against the Madero government. González did carry through the appointment of several departmental superintendents, but apparently no general reorganization or wholesale reappointment of staff occurred.[16] Little could be accomplished in his brief tenure of three months, even under the most ideal circumstances.

As internal affairs minister, González handled a number of problems in a random fashion. His actions revealed a superficial, stopgap approach rather than a coherent effort to seek out the origins of problems. Illustrative of his administration was his circular to state governors concerning federal prison farms. A sentence of removal to the plantations in Quintana Roo under the Díaz government had meant a life of slavery in the henequen fields with an early death the customary reprieve. González did nothing to close the labor camps, but he directed all the governors to submit full explanations of the crimes and sentences of the prisoners sent there.[17]

15. Ellsworth to Secretary of State, December 22, 1911, RDS, 812.00/2660. It was commonly known that Hernández felt he should take González's place during the governor's absence from Chihuahua. Letcher to Secretary of State, March 15, 1912, RDS, 812.00/3313. After his defection from Madero's government, he joined the Vázquez Gómez conspiracy and on April 22, 1912, was arrested in the United States by Justice Department officials for violation of neutrality legislation. See W. H. Llewellyn to Attorney General, February 10, 1912, RDS, 812.00/2873; Ellsworth to Secretary of State, February 8, 1912, RDS, 812.00/2785; *Fall Committee*, 2: 2518-20.
16. Secretaría de Gobernación, *Diario oficial*, vol. 117 (November 18, 1911), p. 219.
17. Ibid.

Since his ministry included the division of public health, González took steps to control outbreaks of cholera and other epidemic diseases that resulted from the disruptions of the revolution. The rudimentary federal health services had been launched in 1902 and included supervision of medical practices and inspection of public markets, but generally the efforts of the bureau were negligible. Medical and sanitary programs remained the concern of state governments. González, for example, did more for public health as governor of Chihuahua than as a national administrator. In the fall of 1911 he had organized a medical corps in Chihuahua to vaccinate residents in threatened regions against smallpox. Only after the return to more normal civilian government in the 1920s did the national bureau develop into a well-run agency.[18]

As part of his responsibility for political affairs, González maintained surveillance of elections in the states and localities to ensure that they were open. Charges of election fraud led to investigations and, in the case of the alleged election violations in Tlalnepantla, the setting aside of the results. The government also tried to realize one of the principal goals of the revolution by formulating a law for direct and popular election of local officials, congressmen, and justices of the Supreme Court. The proposal went to Congress and González urged state governors to present it to their legislatures to expedite its approval throughout the nation. As he had done when governor, González also ordered the removal of all pictures of living persons from public buildings, and he recommended to state governors that names of streets, schools, and offices honoring living persons be changed to commemorate heroes of the nation's past. He thus aimed at halting one form of coercion and glorification used by incumbent officials. The minister also had the job of recommending the suspension of constitutional guarantees when the situation in a state could not be managed by the federal government. In January, after consultation with the president and the approval of Congress, he suspended individual civil rights in several states, particularly Morelos.[19]

Generally, González could do little more than take responsive actions, but he did manage more consistent policies in regard to labor and the rural constabulary. Following a series of strikes in Mexico City, he directed members of his staff to collect data on working conditions and information on the

18. Ibid., vol. 117, contains weekly health and disease reports. See also Xavier de la Riva Rodríguez, "Salubridad y assistencia Médico-Social," in *Mexico: Cincuenta años de revolución* (Mexico: Fondo de Cultura Económica, 1963), pp. 226-27. For the minister's efforts in Chihuahua, see *EPMT*, August 7, 1911.

19. Madero to González, January 22, 1912, Archivo General de la Nacion, Libro Copiador 1, folio 273 (hereafter cited as AGN); Almada, *Vida González*, pp. 75-76, 201.

issues dividing labor and management. His assistants investigated numerous factories and used their reports to formulate a labor code. It called for the installation of safety devices in all factories, abolition of company stores, regulation of child and female labor, minimum wages, maximum work days, labor organization, and collective bargaining. The preliminary results of the survey and Madero's favorable disposition resulted in the formation of a department of labor in December, 1911. The office became a bureau within the Ministry of Fomento, but González continued to draw up labor legislation.

In January, 1912, González made a direct contribution to the labor movement on the basis of his experience in Chihuahua. When a new wave of strikes began in Mexico City's textile factories, González called together representatives of the workers and the management to settle their differences. Despite opposition from the company's spokesmen, he successfully concluded the bargaining in favor of the workers, achieving a 10 percent raise in salaries and a ten-hour working day.[20] The settlement emphasized the need for labor legislation. Madero supported González's labor policy; he intended to set a ten-hour working day and to ask Congress to pass reformist labor legislation.[21] Before a code could be considered, however, alarming reports of a potential insurrection in Chihuahua reached Mexico City. Madero turned his attention to questions of national security, and González had to return to Chihuahua to confront a rebellious situation.

Dissatisfaction among rebel veterans in Chihuahua resulted in part from González's policies regarding the *rurales.*[22] As minister of gobernación, he had general responsibility for this constabulary. The Madero government maintained it both as a mounted police force and as a militia. Following the revolution some of the rebel veterans had been incorporated into *rurale* units instead of being discharged. Revenue for the national government was meager, and as an economy move González, forced to reduce expenses, mustered out some *rurales.* This measure was also consistent with his efforts to demilitarize society by reducing the number of men in arms whenever possible.

20. González Garza, *Mi contribución político-literaria*, pp. 88-90; Cumberland, *Mexican Revolution*, p. 223. González Garza was subsecretary of the Internal Affairs Ministry and directed the labor survey under the supervision of González. Because he acted as González's representative in some arbitration meetings, González Garza claimed personal credit for the settlement.
21. Valadés, *Madero*, 2: 231; José C. Valadés, *Historia general de la Revolución Mexicana,* 5 vols. (Mexico: Manuel Quesada Brandí, 1963-65), 2: 47-48.
22. For general discussions of the *rurales,* see John W. Kitchens, "Some Considerations on the *Rurales* of Porfirian Mexico," *Journal of Inter-American Studies* 9 (1967): 441-55, and Paul Vanderwood, "Genesis of the Rurales: Mexico's Early Struggle for Public Security," *Hispanic American Historical Review* 50 (1970): 323-44.

Shortly after he took office, González withdrew the federal troops in Chihuahua for deployment elsewhere and placed the state's protection in the hands of the *rurales* under the command of Orozco, who had returned from Sinaloa. As a further step in his economy program he ordered in January, 1912, that the expenses of state forces must be assumed by state governments. Well acquainted with the situation in Chihuahua, González believed the *rurale* units there were larger than necessary, and he ordered a reduction from 350 to 250 men in each garrison.[23] The troop discharge proved particularly troublesome for the Madero government because rebellion soon threatened the state.

González initiated several other programs in his ministry. He required the superintendent of the *rurales* to introduce competitive bidding in the purchase of uniforms and other equipment. He directed the operations of the indemnification board to settle claims for the revolution, and he was placed in charge of the irrigation and land development program established under a new land law passed in December, 1911.[24] But he could do little in any of these fields, as he was forced to turn his attention to Chihuahua. His leave of absence from his gubernatorial duties had nearly expired and conditions in the state appeared increasingly ominous.

González had access to information on his home region and knew that as his reform program remained only law, unimplemented, it aggravated popular discontent. The interim governor had administered with little effort to carry out any reforms; he allowed state government to drift. Aureliano González signed into law González's constitutional provision eliminating the *jefes políticos*, and he called for an expanded program of primary school instruction, but he exercised initiative only in his plans for the state prison. He commuted a number of sentences and limited the employment of prison labor to prevent competition with free workers.[25] Otherwise, inaction characterized the interim administration.

Administration throughout the state reflected the inexperience of the men who had come to power after the revolution. Their programs were conceived without political insight, and government enforcement of the law was lax. Here Chihuahua missed González's leadership. Weak enforcement prompted

23. Letcher to Secretary of State, February 13, 1912, RDS, 812.00/2844; Almada, *Revolución en Chihuahua*, 1: 275-78.

24. Almada, *Vida González*, pp. 75-76.

25. *PO*, vol. 31, no. 97 (December 3, 1911), p. 3; Aureliano González granted numerous reprieves to prisoners, and his pardons are contained in ibid. for the months of November, 1911, through January, 1912. The stipulation against prison workers competing with free labor is in ibid., vol. 32, no. 4 (January 14, 1912), p. 3.

disrespect for the law and its executors. Crime, especially petty thievery and misdemeanors, spread throughout the state. Most observers condemned the lack of firm enforcement, which, businessmen complained, encouraged law breaking. After the federal troops left, charges were also made that *rurales* maintained poor discipline and did little to keep order.[26]

Municipal elections in January, 1912, to select officials to replace the local prefects did little to improve administration. Voters generally chose rebel veterans who lacked experience, but inexperience alone did not account for the decline in the government's authority. Squabbling followed a number of elections. In some cases they were set aside and new votes taken. Offices remained vacant as opponents hurled charges of electoral violations or ineligibility of some candidates. The city council in Chihuahua City disqualified the election winner, José Gardea, because he had not fulfilled the residency requirement. The election for the office of mayor in Juárez led to a legal dispute that reached to the state legislature before it was resolved.[27] Irresolute civil government contributed to agitation by opponents of the regime.

After González joined the cabinet in Mexico City, sidewalk sages confidently predicted that Orozco would lead an insurrection against the national government. Rumors in popular saloons and government offices linked his name with several counterrevolutionary movements. Reports circulated that he was negotiating with representatives of the Reyes conspiracy. Stories about the impending success of a *reyista* uprising spread throughout Chihuahua. The charges were little more than wishful thinking on the part of Madero's antagonists. While they created a general mistrust of Orozco's intentions, Madero and his minister of internal affairs continued to rely on him to command the *rurales*. Both publicly attested to his loyalty to the government. When word circulated that incriminating letters from Orozco to Reyes had been uncovered, Orozco immediately asked that a denial of the existence of such letters be published in the press throughout the North.[28] Unperturbed, Madero wrote to Orozco alerting him that Reyes might try to initiate his uprising in Chihuahua. He suggested the *rurales* give the old porfirian general "a reception so that he will not want to return to the state again." A few

26. Wilson to Secretary of State, February 7, 1912, RDS, 812.00/2776; James O. Colbath to James I. Long, U.S. consular agent, Hidalgo del Parral, January 4, 1912, enclosure # 4, and Roy H. Allen to Long, enclosure # 3 in Letcher to Wilson, January 23, 1912, in PR, Consulate General, Monterry, Correspondence (C-8), 1912, class 8, file 800.

27. *EPMT*, January 4, 16, 1912.

28. Ellsworth to Secretary of State, December 9, 1911, RDS, 812.00/2613; December 14, 1911, RDS, 812.00/2634; Letcher to W. L. Wilson, January 23, 1912, PR, Consulate General, Monterrey, Correspondence (C8), 1912, class 8, file 800; Meyer, *Mexican Rebel*, pp. 42-46.

days later in a letter to Chihuahua's provisional governor, Madero avowed that Orozco's "loyalty to my government is unquestionable."[29]

Chihuahua faced more serious threats when a series of outbreaks occurred in late December. The trouble began in the region of Dolores, where a local rivalry flared into a battle between the municipal president, Elfugo Bencomo, and the rebel veteran Antonio Rojas. The arrival of *rurales* forced Rojas to retreat into the mountains, but he began raiding in the area in the name of the Vázquez Gómez revolt. Within two weeks government troops captured Rojas and took him along with two other conspirators, Luis Fernández and Blás Orpinsel, to the state prison in Chihuahua City.

This incident alone would have aroused little apprehension. Even had Rojas been linked with the sinister but rhetorical revolution of Reyes, he might have been easily dismissed. Concern stemmed from his possible alignment with Emilio Vázquez Gómez. After serving briefly in the cabinet of the provisional president, De la Barra, at the end of October, 1911, Vázquez Gómez declared a revolt against the Anti-reelectionists, alleging they had discarded the San Luis Plan. He fled to San Antonio, Texas, and appealed to former rebels to redeem their victory at Juárez. The Madero government made no move to extradite him, but episodes such as that involving Rojas brought an anxious reaction because of insistent rumors of a conspiracy to overthrow Chihuahua's government.[30] Other outbreaks followed in late December and early January, all in the name of the *vazquista* cause.

The threats quickly dissipated when Orozco directed the suppression of the incipient insurrections. With a return to peaceful conditions, Orozco went to Mexico City to consult with President Madero. The substance of their discussion remained confidential. Both men probably had plans they believed the other must implement if the administration were to succeed. Orozco came as the champion of the rebel veterans, and he must have reiterated his suggestions to aid them. Earlier he had written to Madero requesting pay raises for the *rurales* and expressing dismay at the government's maintenance of the federal officer corps intact at the same time the rebels received discharges. Madero's appointments to federal administrative positions also reflected no effort to make a place for the rebels. Orozco warned that many of the former rebels were forced into banditry because they could find no work. He proposed that Madero begin public works or induce the foreign companies to

29. Madero to Orozco, December 4, 1911, AGN, Libro Copiador I, folio 37; Madero to Aureliano González, December 13, 1911, ibid., folio 50.

30. Almada, *Vida González*, pp. 86-87; *EPMT*, December 29, 1911, and February 23, 1912.

take on extra workers so the people could support themselves. The capstone of Madero's apparent disregard for the men who had brought him victory was González's announcement of further discharges scheduled for the end of January, 1912. Certainly the general sought some redress for his men.

Madero had two important requests of Orozco. He wanted the general to persuade Chihuahua's legislature to extend González's license so he could remain in the national cabinet. As peace had returned to that state, Madero also proposed that Orozco become the *rurale* commander in Morelos to deal with the Zapata revolution. The discussions satisfied neither man. Orozco probably offered his resignation orally, because as soon as he returned to Chihuahua he sent a message "through proper channels" to the president that he wanted to retire. Madero feared that Orozco's resignation would spark an uprising in the state, so he persuaded the general to stay at his post until March 1.[31]

Although Madero induced the general to continue his support for the government for another six weeks, Orozco's men had no such commitment. González's order discharging two hundred men came on January 31, 1912, in Juárez and brought on another crisis. The former *rurales* and their comrades who were still in arms revolted and seized the city after very little fighting. One of the officers, Santiago Masas, was chosen municipal president. He told reporters that his men supported the cause of Emiliano Zapata. Confusion soon developed as other insurgents indicated the rebellion had connections with the Vázquez Gómez conspiracy.[32]

The outbreak in Juárez sparked a similar mutiny in Chihuahua City. After the discharges in the state capital on February 2, rumors of an uprising spread through the city. Fearing that the conspiracy extended to the men guarding the federal prison, the officials ordered all guards disarmed. Ninety *rurales,* led by a discharged colonel, revolted and went to the state prison, where they freed Rojas and others arrested the previous month. The prison commander released his charges on the condition that Rojas meet with Orozco and Acting Governor Aureliano González. The conference did not lead to a settlement, but Rojas did secure his release and with other discharged *rurales* fled to the Sierra Madre. Orozco then restored order in Chihuahua City, and the following day he went to the border to secure a settlement in Juárez. He demonstrated his prestige among the men as he successfully reconciled his former

31. Meyer, *Mexican Rebel*, contains a cogent discussion of the meeting, pp. 47-50, and a translation of the letter of resignation, pp. 136-37. See also Madero to Orozco, December 4, 1911, AGN, Libro Copiador I, folio 37; Orozco to Madero, December 5, 1911, *DHRM*, 2: 386; Almada, *Revolución en Chihuahua*, 1: 275.
32. *EPMT*, February 1, 1912, and extra editions of the same date.

comrades to their discharges.[33]

González believed that the upheaval in Chihuahua demanded his return. Madero insisted that he retain his position in the national government, but news that Aureliano González had resigned made González's return imperative. The legislature accepted Aureliano's resignation on February 6, 1912. Some deputies wanted Orozco to assume the vacant post and Madero also encouraged him to serve as interim governor so González could stay in the cabinet.[34] Orozco was disinclined to accept, but took a few days to consider his answer. Meanwhile, the legislature assumed he did not want the office and telegraphed González to return. As the deputies suspected, Orozco refused to serve as governor.[35]

On learning that Orozco had rejected the position, González complied with the demands of the state assembly and departed for Chihuahua City. On the train trip he wrote Madero that the legislature would certainly oppose an extension of his license. Their hostility to his absence, he wrote, reflected an "opinion of the people that elected me constitutional governor." He could not ignore their sentiment, and must resign his cabinet office. The president accepted it with regret.[36] As González traveled to his home state, Madero sent an expression of his concern for the rebel veterans in an effort to hold the loyalty of General Orozco. He repeated that the new land law would provide cheap land on easy credit, and even named the districts in which land would be sold to former rebels.[37]

At Camargo City in southern Chihuahua, González was met by Silvestre Terrazas and other close advisers. Here his return to Chihuahua City was halted because the tracks to the north had been cut by raiders commanded by Hernández. González and his colleagues doubled back to Torreón, then took a circular rail route through Coahuila and Texas and reentered Chihuahua at Juárez.[38] Arriving in the border city, the governor again had to delay his jour-

33. Letcher to Secretary of State, February 13, 1912, RDS, 812.00/2844; *EPMT*, February 4, 1912.

34. Letcher to Secretary of State, February 4, 1912, RDS, 812.00/2737; February 6, 1912, RDS, 812.00/2744; Madero to Orozco, February 7, 1912, AGN, Libro Copiador I, folio 37; *El correo*, February 5-8, 1912.

35. Amaya, *Los auténticos revolucionarios*, p. 364, says the telegram was sent February 5, 1912; Letcher to Secretary of State, February 7, 1912, RDS, 812.00/2753.

36. González to Madero, February 9, 1912, and Calero to González, February 17, 1912, AREM, González Expediente, L-E 135 (s-1); Madero to González, February 20, 1912, *DHRM*, 3: 112-13.

37. Madero to Orozco, February 8, 1921, reprinted in Almada, *Vida González*, pp. 118-19.

38. Almada, *Revolución en Chihuahua*, 1: 287.

ney to the state capital because rebels had torn up the rails to the south. When his first-class coach was coupled to a locomotive for the run to the capital, he went through with twenty guards commanded by Félix Terrazas. Because of the recent mutinies, many wondered if the *rurales* were escorts or captors, but on his arrival in Chihuahua City on February 12, González immediately resumed his duties as governor.[39]

III

Back in office, González consulted with Orozco and Aureliano González, then announced investigations into the incidents in Dolores and the *rurales'* mutinies in Juárez and Chihuahua City. He also planned to assuage popular unrest by easing economic hardships. He proclaimed that all public lands in the state were to be surveyed and sold at the lowest possible cost with easy credit to the lower classes, and added that he had three hundred thousand pesos to distribute among widows, orphans, and injured. He closed his statement by affirming his trust in Orozco.[40]

Despite grumbling by old porfirians that his plan represented the most flagrant kind of bribery, González immediately put his recovery program into operation by appearing at a session of the state legislature. He requested approval of a six-million-peso loan, with the principal and 5 percent interest guaranteed by the national government. He explained that the money would be expended in the following manner: two and a half million pesos for irrigation projects, two million pesos for the expropriation and purchase of lands, one million pesos for the establishment of an agricultural credit bank for small farmers, and fifty thousand pesos for the construction of school buildings and purchase of school furniture. The proposal was immediately approved and published as state law.[41]

This action illustrates the role of the state governor in the implementation of national programs and shows how González resorted to federal laws to handle the delicate state situation. In December, 1911, the national Congress, at Madero's instigation, had passed a law that allowed state governments to make loans backed by the national government for irrigation projects, for the purchase of land, and to establish easy credit facilities for land purchases by

39. Puente, *Orozco*, p. 92; *EPMT*, February 11 and 13, 1912; *El correo*, February 13-14, 1912.

40. *PO*, vol. 32, no. 15 (February 22, 1912), pp. 1-2.

41. Almada, *Revolución en Chihuahua*, 1: 290; Ellsworth to Secretary of State, February 11, 1911, RDS, 812.00/2808.

Mexicans of limited means. Nothing was done, however, to utilize its provisions before González's return. The official state newspaper did not even publish the law for over a month,[42] and then Aureliano González did not act on it. The reforms instituted after Abraham González's return were actions to buy allegiance for the Madero government, positive efforts to use federal legislation to redeem the revolutionary pledges for improvement of Mexican society and an attempt to quiet opponents of the regime.

Along with proposals to reform the economy, the governor offered a program to end the threat of insurrection in the state. He called for the formation of auxiliary units because of the burning of railroad bridges to the south of the capital, the periodic interruption of service north to Juárez, and marauding by rebel bands in the more remote districts. Once they were formed, he directed the locally based volunteers to notify the nearest public official so some coordination might be developed to prevent depredations by "bandits who use a 'political plan' as pretext for their activities."[43] Several militia units commanded by former rebel officers were created; Pancho Villa organized a group in the municipal districts of Satevo and Zaragoza. Tómas Ornelas, Toribio Ortega, and José de la Cruz Sánchez followed Villa's example in the regions of Camargo, Cuchillo Parado, and Ojinaga.[44] To arm the auxiliaries and to stockpile arms in the event of a siege of the state capital, González arranged for the delivery of military supplies. He purchased one hundred thousand cartridges in the United States and dispatched Orozco and a detachment of *rurales* to bring the shipment to Chihuahua City.[45]

Despite the reform and defense programs, rumors undermined much of the remaining sentiment in favor of the Madero and González governments. Gossip had it that González would soon be recalled to Mexico City. The stories apparently resulted from the loose talk of Daniel Madero in the Chihuahua City Casino, the aristocratic meeting place in the state capital. The president repudiated his relative's statement and wrote González that he had no intention of asking him to return to the cabinet,[46] but the speculation persisted.

In mid-February, opponents of the González government captured Casas Grandes and proclaimed Pascual Orozco their leader. Other units had virtual

42. "Decreto del 18 de diciembre de 1911 para favorecer el riego fraccionamiento de terrenos y para preparar la organización de crédito agrícola en la república," *DHRM*, 2: 430-35; *PO*, vol. 32, no. 8 (January 28, 1912), pp. 1, 16.

43. *PO*, vol. 32, no. 17 (February 12, 1912), p. 1.

44. Almada, *Revolución en Chihuahua*, 1: 287-88.

45. González to Mexican Consul, El Paso, February 14, 1912, in *DHRM*, 2: 97.

46. See exchange of letters, Madero to Daniel Madero, February 22, 1912, and Madero to González, February 24, 1912, *DHRM*, 3: 125, 142-43.

control of the Galeana district, while a guerrilla force of six hundred men operated in the sierra and another band of two hundred men plundered in the northeastern section of the state. The fear that Orozco would join the rebels was compounded by the rumor that Villa and his auxiliaries planned to enlist if it appeared the rebellion would succeed.[47] Orozco had agreed to continue as commander of the *rurales* until March 1. Rumors spread that he would lead a revolt as soon as he completed that commitment. The deposed oligarchs in Chihuahua had made a concerted attempt to enlist Orozco against the revolutionary government since his January meeting with Madero, and their efforts were intensified at the end of February as Orozco prepared to step down as commander of the *rurales*.[48]

The state seemed on the verge of revolution. Reports circulated that Orozco had been exchanging communications with a force under José Inéz Salazar in Juárez and with another commanded by Hernández, camped along the railroad at a midpoint between the state capital and the border. It was anticipated that these troops would take the train to Chihuahua City and occupy the capital. One engineer, loyal to Madero, believed the stories and switched cars off the main line in Juárez to obstruct any effort to seize them to transport rebels south. Tension mounted as opponents of the government traded idle talk within hearing of González's friends. Trying to intimidate the governor's supporters, those rumormongers threatened the lives of all the incumbents and talked of a conspiracy to kidnap González and compel his resignation. González prudently spent several nights with friends rather than staying alone in his own residence.

On the evening of March 2, a crowd gathered in front of the state palace to protest against the Madero government and to demand that González resign. Demonstrators carried large placards that proclaimed: "The People of Chihuahua do not recognize the Treasonous government of Madero"; "The People of Chihuahua confide in Pascual Orozco, their only Hope"; and "The People of Chihuahua demand the immediate resignation of Abraham González as governor of the state." González went onto the balcony to respond to chants for his resignation. He refused to recognize the rally as the expression of the state's voters. He said that he had been elected by an absolute majority of forty-eight thousand votes and that the crowd represented only a small portion of that electorate. A legislative deputy, Alberto Talavera, also spoke in

47. Letcher to Secretary of State, February 2, 1912, RDS, 812.00/2725; February 20, 1912, RDS, 812.00/2931; Almada, *Gobernadores*, p. 458.
48. Letcher to Secretary of State, March 2, 1912, RDS, 812.00/3146; Meyer, *Mexican Rebel*, pp. 56-57, 65-66; Cumberland, *Mexican Revolution*, p. 215.

support of the governor. The rally disbanded, but rioting continued through-out the night.

The demonstration against the governor had been staged by Antonio Cor-tazar, a relative of Creel, and Rafael Trejo, who had unseated the Anti-reelectionist incumbent in elections for the municipal presidency of Chihua-hua City. Earlier in the evening, under instructions from Trejo and Cortazar, streetcar workers had rousted out men in the suburbs, offering free drinks and passes on the trolleys to those who would take part in the rally. That kind of appeal brought out a crowd of young men who joined the procession for beer and a chance to listen to the music of "an unusually good orchestra" that accompanied the marchers.[49]

González remained calm, partly because he expected military aid the next day. He had already called Villa to bring his force of volunteers from Bustillos to Chihuahua City. After the rally broke up, the governor left his office and began walking home. When he was within two blocks of his house, he met three workmen, one of whom he knew. They persuaded him to stay in one of their houses because of stories circulating among the working people that his arrest would be attempted in the early hours of March 3.[50] The following morning, Orozco announced a rebellion against the Madero government, using the approach of Villa's auxiliaries as a pretext for his troops to occupy the city and to declare martial law. The general ordered the arrest of two *rurale* officers loyal to González.[51]

Once the governor learned that Orozco had rebelled and his men had driv-en off Villa's force as it approached Chihuahua City on March 3, he decided to remain hidden in the home of a working-class family until he found an opportunity to slip out of the city and join a loyal military unit.[52] No one in the city, except those hiding him, knew where González was. Many suspected he had received political asylum from the United States consul, Marion Letcher, although Letcher published a denial in the city's newspapers. His protestations were to no avail, and a squad of Orozco's soldiers kept the con-sulate and the consul's residence under constant surveillance, hoping for a

49. Almada, *Revolución en Chihuahua*, 1: 297-98; José Llorente, Mexican consul, El Paso, to Secretary of Foreign Relations, March 4, 1912, AREM, L-E 735; Letcher to Secretary of State, March 4, 1912, RDS, 812.00/3192.
50. González to the Editor, March 6, 1912, in *EPMT*, March 14, 1912.
51. Meyer, *Mexican Rebel*, p. 52.
52. Juan Sarabía to Secretary of Foreign Relations, March 5, 1912, *DHRM*, 3: 152-53; *El correo*, August 15, 1912; Calzadíaz Barrera, *Hechos reales*, 1: 88.

glimpse of the missing governor.[53]

The constitution required that the state legislature appoint a successor if the governor did not reappear within four days. After waiting for the interval to pass, the permanent commission tried to call the legislature into session. Deputies loyal to Madero refused to attend on a variety of pretexts, so the commission called alternates to fill those seats. The pro-Orozco body then declared the governor's position vacant and appointed Felipe Gutiérrez to succeed González. Gutiérrez had ties of wealth, education, and social position to the upper class, but eleven of fifteen deputies who voted for him were confirmed supporters of Orozco. The legislature also voted to turn over the state treasury of two hundred thousand pesos to Orozco and to issue bonds for two hundred thousand more to support the revolution.[54] The next month the legislature, manipulated by Orozco, removed those deputies who had opposed the rebellion and permanently seated their alternates. Then they voted for the state of Chihuahua to secede from the Mexican federation.[55]

The Orozco rebellion tested Madero's government. The general won several military victories in the first weeks of the movement until a federal army finally succeeded in halting his advance and turned the rebels back to Chihuahua. The movement was rooted in the conditions created by Governor González and President Madero.[56] Orozco and his followers justified their insurrection in the Plan Orozquista, issued on March 25, which included a combination of vituperative, but often true, charges against the Madero government and a well-conceived program of social reform. It reiterated and expanded proposals made in other pronouncements as diverse as the Liberal Plan of 1906, the Anti-reelectionist platform of 1910, the San Luis Plan, and Emiliano Zapata's agrarian program, the Ayala Plan. The most glaring difference between Orozco's document and the previous pronouncements was in its exaggerated anti-American sentiments.

Although the Plan Orozquista appealed to Mexicans throughout the nation, it cannot be separated from the unique situation that González had

53. Letcher to Secretary of State, April 25, 1912, RDS, 812.00/3773. Amaya accepted the rumor and said González remained in the consulate for three months. See *Los auténticos revolucionarios*, p. 372.

54. *PO*, vol. 32, no. 19 (March 7, 1912), p. 1; Letcher to Secretary of State, March 7, 1912, RDS, 812.00/3188; *Hearings, 1913*, testimony of Felipe R. Gutiérrez, pp. 274-75. For a biographical sketch of Gutiérrez, see Almada, *Gobernadores*, pp. 465-76.

55. *PO*, vol. 32, no. 31 (April 18, 1912), pp. 2-3; Letcher to Secretary of State, March 31, 1912, RDS, 812.00/3525.

56. Meyer, *Mexican Rebel*, pp. 53-93, discusses the Orozco movement in great detail.

helped to create. The authors of the document inserted among their scurrilous assaults on Madero charges that he had defaulted on the promises of the San Luis Plan. While the *zapatistas* and other anti-Madero rebels charged that the Plan of 1910, by calling only for political reforms, had not proposed essential social and economic changes, the *orozquistas* first cataloged the failure of the Madero government even to redeem its political pledges. They denounced the selection of Pino Suárez as vice-president and the selection of many of the state governors, pointing out that the Constitution of 1857 made no provision for the office of vice-president but that Madero had continued that porfirian innovation and contrived the nomination of Pino Suárez. In the case of the governors, Orozco's followers charged that the threat of military intervention (probably a reference to the appointment of Carranza in Coahuila) and the official backing given to candidates (doubtlessly a reference to González among others) had precluded the open elections promised in the San Luis Plan. Both the vice-presidential selection and the gubernatorial election had caused divisions among the revolutionaries in Chihuahua.[57] In a similar fashion demands in Orozco's plan for the eventual incorporation of *orozquista* troops into state national guard units with a minimum of discharges reflected the dissatisfaction of many former rebels who had been mustered out immediately after the Battle of Juárez.

Apart from the charges against Madero's government, the rebels included plans for social reform. These were for the most part an extension of the program developed in Chihuahua by Governor González, calling for mandatory arbitration of labor disputes, an end to company stores, guaranteed payment of workers in national currency, and regulation of child and female labor. Other sections of the plan called for the sale of national lands with easy credit to the lower classes, the revitalization of local and district government through the elimination of prefects, and the equalization of taxation by abolishing head taxes and setting new tax levies. Although the authors of the Plan Orozquista went further than González in their provisions for land distribution and tax revaluations, their proposals were not different in kind from those he had established in state law either through decree or constitutional amendment. Because the *orozquistas* also demanded rigorous enforcement of these reform measures, their program suggested that in Chihuahua, González's administration had raised expectations by legislating reforms it had not put

57. Many particularly stressed the violations of the San Luis Plan's electoral provisions. See, for example, statements by two Chihuahua deputies in *Hearings, 1913*, testimony of Alfonso Iberri, pp. 342-43, and testimony of José Cordova, p. 501.

into practice and that these reforms served as a model of which the rebels could offer to other Mexicans.[58]

The anti-American passages of the document repeated rumors current in both Mexico and the United States that Madero had allowed himself to be compromised by North American corporations in order to borrow large sums of money to carry out the revolution of 1910. The anti-Yankee statements also reflected the near-hysteria in Chihuahua occasioned by the story that the United States planned to intervene in northern Mexico. That anxiety had become increasingly strong during the last months of 1911, yet Madero and González did little more than ignore what they considered a ridiculous rumor. An appeal to *yanquí*-phobia, always popular in Mexico, increased the plan's attractiveness to the public.

The ease with which Orozco rallied the people of Chihuahua in support of his insurrection testified to the astuteness of the authors of the plan in identifying issues that had general appeal. Moreover, the rebels offered two pesos a day to new recruits. But neither the provisions nor the pay explained the rebellion's attraction completely. From the leaders through the ranks, the rebels exuded an air of expectation. The insurrection joined together disgruntled veterans of the Madero revolution with the disinherited beneficiaries of the porfirian regime.

The defection of Orozco and others resulted from the Madero government's failure to reward their services following the revolution of 1910. The tremendous popularity of Orozco as a military hero warranted some recognition, if only to attract his followers to the new government, but Madero offered him what seemed to be only minor posts, while major preferments went to men of questionable sympathies. Like Orozco, José Inés Salazar, a former rebel officer, had been disappointed by his rewards. Discharged in the summer of 1911, Salazar sought an appointment as a *rurale* commander. For several months his appeal was lost in bureaucratic channels, until finally he received a position in Juárez, only to face the possibility of demobilization in early 1912. Salazar became one of the most important *orozquistas.* With the rank of general he signed the Orozco Plan, and in the early critical days of the insurrection he won the first major battle at Santa Rosalía.[59] Disbanding the

58. For a cogent discussion of the plan and its provisions, see Meyer, *Mexican Rebel*, pp. 62-65, and the translation of the Plan included as Appendix B, pp. 138-47.

59. Jesús Flores Magón to González, January 30, 1912, *DHRM*, 3: 57; Meyer, *Mexican Rebel*, pp. 59-60, 69. For a recent attempt to assess the charges that the Standard Oil Company loaned money to rebels, including Madero, with the hope of favorable treatment in Mexico, see Kenneth J. Grieb, "Standard Oil and the Financing of the Mexican Revolution," *California Historical Society Quarterly* 49 (March 1971): 59-71.

Anti-reelectionist army without adequate provisions for returning the men to civilian life helped create the dissatisfied element that seconded the call for rebellion.

Other rebels also expected more than they got following victory. Cástulo Herrera, one of the first Anti-reelectionists in Chihuahua, a member of the El Paso junta, and an officer in the rebel army, received an appointment as police chief of Chihuahua City. The change from the excitement of international gun smuggling to the routine of rousting drunks and pickpockets moved Herrera to resign his post in August, 1911. During the Orozco rebellion, he resumed his conspiratorial activities in El Paso.[60] Even better known was the case of Hernández. After he failed to receive an appointment as interim governor during González's tenure in Mexico City, the former secretary of state decided his principles required him to renounce his allegiance to Madero. Other rebels, who had received only twenty-five pesos, sometimes a minor government post, and confronted either a journey to Mexico City or business with a speculator to make their claims for indemnification, felt aggrieved enough to join Orozco.

The visible dissatisfaction of Orozco and other rebels tempted the state's conservatives to try to split the Madero movement in early 1912 by cajoling the general. Two developments particularly goaded them to action. First, the fiasco of the Reyes revolution ended for a time the possibility that a porfirian aristocrat would lead the assault against Madero. Second, the return of González threatened the initiation of a land reform program and stricter enforcement of various reform laws in matters of taxation and corporate privileges. A deep-seated sentiment that they had been denied their birthright drove them as well.

Ambitious in their expectations, the Terrazas sons, relatives, and clients had dutifully served the patriarch Luis. But the old man lived a long time, and only Enrique Creel had made a career outside Luis's tutelage. Following the revolution, Luis had been content to retire from the state, and shunned complicity in the Orozco rebellion for relaxation at the end of a rich career. Creel and other members of the family had aspirations in Chihuahua, however,[61]

60. *EPMT*, August 9, 1911; March 15 and 29, 1912.

61. Juan Neftalí Amador to Manuel Calero, July 20, 1912, STC, box 4, Juan Neftalí Amador folder. Luis's denial of any participation in the Orozco revolt is contained in a letter to Enrique C. Creel, April 3, 1912, and a letter to the *EPMT*, February 22, 1916, both reprinted in Fuentes Mares, . . . *Y México se refugió en el desierto*, pp. 250-51, 263-70. He made the same denial to a U.S. Senate committee in September, 1912. See *Hearings, 1913*, p. 314.

and their spokesman, Gonzálo C. Enrile, formed an alliance of convenience with Orozco.

Those who remained loyal to Madero believed that the reactionary elite had simply flattered and bribed Orozco into rebellion. As for the general's disappointment over his share of the spoils of victory, González declared that those who fought only for pay and preferment were mercenaries, not soldiers.[62] Popular opponents of the *orozquistas* adopted the same view, and soon expressed it in the couplets of a common *corrido*:

> They say that Pascual Orozco has turned his coat
> Because don Terrazas seduced him.
> They gave him many millions and they bought him
> And sent him to overthrow the government.[63]

Observers from the United States, including newspaper reporters and the American consul, also believed that members of the old regime had duped Orozco.[64]

The combination of rebel apples and porfirian oranges developed from a mutual desire for power, status, and possible wealth. Both groups initially faced confusion over which cause to embrace. Many expected to link up with the Vázquez Gómez movement, and Emilio had moved his headquarters-in-exile to El Paso in anticipation. For two months a tenuous agreement existed between Orozco and Vázquez Gómez, but in May, Governor Gutiérrez informed Vázquez Gómez that the rebel state of Chihuahua no longer recognized him as its leader. Hernández denounced Orozco as "the multitraitor hero of the seven somersaults and unnumbered back-slidings" because of his break with the *vazquistas*,[65] but rank-and-file rebels felt greater discontent with the prominent role Orozco allowed the porfirian aristocracy.[66]

While the rebel army moved south, clearing the state of government troops and smashing a federal army at Rellano, disagreements arose between Orozco and Enrile. During April wild reports circulated that Enrile had replaced

---

62. González to the editor, *El correo*, August 6, 1912, reprinted in Almada, *Vida González*, pp. 222-27.
63. Reed, *Insurgent Mexico*, p. 42. For a detailed discussion of all possible causes of the revolt, see Almada, *Vida González*, pp. 103-23, 133.
64. *EPMT*, March 5, 1912; Letcher to Secretary of State, March 20, 1912, RDS, 812.00/3424.
65. *Hearings, 1913*, testimony of Hernández, p. 556.
66. *PO*, vol. 32, no. 38 (May 12, 1912), p. 1; Letcher to Secretary of State, March 12, 1912, RDS, 812.00/3268.

Orozco as commander of the army and planned to hand him over to United States Justice Department officials for executing an American citizen. Soon stories reported that Orozco had been intimidated by Enrile and José Cordova, the general's secretary, and that Enrile had withdrawn financial support for the insurrection. When the federal army commanded by Victoriano Huerta defeated the *orozquistas* at Conejos on May 12, the divisions in the rebel camp became wider. Disagreements climaxed the day of the defeat when an attempt to assassinate Enrile almost succeeded. Despite bullet and knife wounds, the hardy oligarch survived the attack. Orozco made no move to investigate the incident; after Enrile recovered, he escaped from Chihuahua to exile in California.[67]

After Enrile had been removed, Orozco faced no internal challenges to his authority, but the zenith of his rebellion had passed. Twelve days after the battle at Conejos, Huerta's forces soundly defeated Orozco's troops at the second battle of Rellano. Throughout June the federal army applied pressure on the rebels, forcing them to the north. Finally the strength of the *orozquistas* was shattered at Bachimba on July 3. A few days later the federals whipped the survivors and reoccupied the capital. Orozco's forces were reduced to guerrillas, although they still held Juárez and a few towns in the north of the state.[68]

During the months of the Orozco rebellion (March to June), Abraham González had remained hidden. For a few days he stayed in Chihuahua City, then slipped away to meet Villa. When Pancho left the state to coordinate his movements with those of federal troops, the governor had to remain in Chihuahua or forfeit his claim to the office. González joined a group of loyal troops commanded by José de la Cruz Sánchez in the region of Ojinaga, and when the federal army reentered the state, he met their advance patrols on June 16 near Camargo City.[69] During González's absence, Madero's government had appointed an interim governor, José María Luján, to comply with the state constitution. Luján traveled with the federal army until he could relinquish gubernatorial authority to González, who returned to Chihuahua City with Huerta's men.[70]

67. The disputes between Enrile and Orozco can be followed in the *EPMT*, March-May, 1912. See especially April 10 and 15, May 12, and June 4, 1912.
68. A military account of the rebellion is contained in Meyer, *Mexican Rebel*, pp. 67-93.
69. *El correo*, August 15, 1912; *EPMT*, March 11 and April 14, 1912.
70. *EPMT*, April 14, 1912.

IV

González's service in the national cabinet had little to distinguish it. Although a colleague testified to his regular attention to duty, three months allowed little opportunity for accomplishment.[71] His hasty departure, moreover, exacerbated the instability of the cabinet. Madero had to shuffle his ministers to different posts. He brought Vice-President Pino Suárez into the cabinet, causing critics of the regime quickly to point out the similarities between Pino and Corral. The new assignment of ministerial positions lasted barely a month before further changes became necessary. The hostile United States ambassador, Henry Lane Wilson, commented that "the cabinet was divided into warring factions . . . absorbed in petty intrigues and lilliputian politics which had little to do with the salvation of the country."[72]

The heritage of González's tenure as minister of internal affairs was one of unrealized expectations in Chihuahua. Because there had been little effort to enforce the revolutionary legislation González had fostered in the summer of 1911, many persons believed the revolutionaries had failed to redeem their pledges, creating a situation in which the Orozco insurrection flourished. González probably could not have prevented the mutiny by Orozco's followers even if he had remained at his post as governor, but his departure to Mexico City encouraged the conspiracy against the state government and provided another charge—that he was an absentee governor—which could be used to demonstrate that Madero and his colleagues had ignored the San Luis Plan. Once González was restored to power in July, 1912, he had to contend with the problems of pacification and reconstruction of a devastated economy and society. The progress made in the summer of 1911 vanished in the summer of 1912.

71. Calero, *Decenio de política mexicana*, pp. 76-77; Almada, *Revolución en Chihuahua*, 1: 297.

72. Bonilla, *Regimén maderista*, p. 6; Henry Lane Wilson, *Diplomatic Episodes in Mexico, Belgium, and Chile* (Garden City: Doubleday, Page & Co., 1927), p. 240.

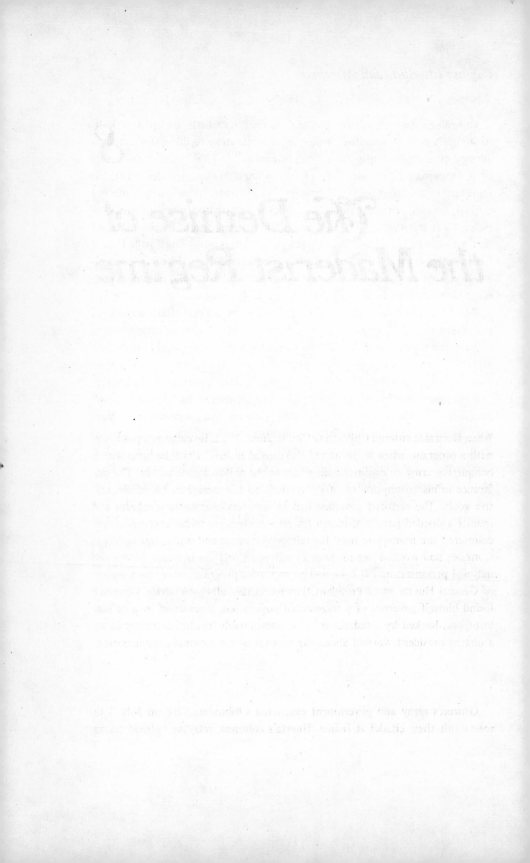

8

The Demise of the Maderist Regime

When González entered Chihuahua City in June, 1911, he came as a politician with a program; when he reentered the capital in July, 1912, he came with a conquering army to command allegiance to the national government. The difference in his assumption of office symbolized the change in his administrative goals. The restored governor had to suppress *orozquista* renegades and reunite a divided people. Concern for reform flickered as his government encountered the immediate need for reimposing peace and order. During 1911, González had worked out his policies independently, in isolation from most national pressures; in 1912, he had to improvise programs under the scrutiny of General Huerta while President Madero occasionally gave advice. González found himself governor of a fragmented population, threatened by a defiant insurgent, backed by a federal army of questionable loyalty, and directed by a distant president worried about the survival of his national administration.

I

Orozco's army and government evacuated Chihuahua City on July 5 to reestablish their citadel at Juárez. Huerta's columns, relaying railroad tracks

139

as they advanced, occupied the capital two days later. González made a triumphal entry into the city at the head of the army and took up office again. He quickly restored transportation and communications with the help of the railroad workers, postal clerks, and telegraphers who trailed the army.[1] He hoped to reestablish normal state administration, but first he had to restore order. The capital was in chaos. As stragglers scurried away to rejoin Orozco and loyalists flocked to reclaim their posts, an uneasy excitement gripped the unfortunate residents who abided each victor in the malignant game of musical chairs. Huerta's victory they celebrated, tight-lipped, with a hope of peace; González they cheered with reservation, waiting to learn his plans for reconstruction.

The governor began his new era with a purge of government. He appointed loyal men to the state bureaucracy and local governments, and he intended to dismiss every official who had supported Orozco by so much as remaining in office. Most major positions were vacant since Orozco's administration formed the rear guard of the insurgent army. González named Aureliano González as his secretary general and reinstated Tómas Gameros as state treasurer,[2] then he reconstituted the state judiciary and legislature. Eight deputies and substitutes had refused to yield to Orozco and he had replaced them. González now called the eight into session in the council chambers and offered them his annual report, justifying his proscriptive policy. "The work of reconstruction since the revolution [of 1910]," he explained, "has been interrupted by malicious citizens dissatisfied with their loss of power . . . and traitors to the revolution who joined them." He concluded with a conciliatory reference to amnesty and the old saw that history would judge his opponents.[3] But his actions presaged an obdurate attitude toward Orozco and his sympathizers.

Finding men to serve in the renewed administration presented difficulties. The number of available Anti-reelectionists had been sharply reduced by the rebellion. Most of González's intimates and lieutenants were gone: Hernán-

1. Letcher to Secretary of State, July 5, 1912, RDS, 812.00/4355, and August 29, 1912, RDS, 812.00/4822; Wilson to Secretary of State, July 9, 1912, RDS, 812.00/4385. The *orozquista* legislature had approved the removal of the state capital anywhere convenient for the governor in an anticipatory action on June 27, 1912. See *PO*, vol. 32, no. 52 (June 30, 1912), p. 1.

2. Almada, *Vida González*, p. 135. González later appointed Isidro Fabela as Chihuahua's *oficial mayor*. See documents in *DHRM*, 4: 108-9, 138.

3. González recognized Ismael Aguierre, Gil Rico, Sebastían Vargas, Sr., Pedro Gómez Ornelas, Agustín Flores, Daniel Rodríguez Marín, Miguel Baca Roquillo, and Guadalupe J. Balderriau. See *PO*, vol. 32, extra edition to 54 (July 29, 1912), p. 1; no. 55 (August 4, 1912), p. 3.

dez, his closest adviser during the 1910 presidential campaign and revolution, had defected, then departed for exile. His rival within the party, Orozco, remained in the field against him. His fellow conspirator in El Paso and long-time friend, Herrera, had been arrested in the United States as an insurgent gunrunner. His personal secretary, L. S. Elizondo, was soon killed in the fighting. His legislature had deserted en masse to Orozco. Alberto Talavera, Manuel Chico, and at least a dozen other deputies had gone into exile rather than face the governor. His military comrades from the 1910 struggle, except for Villa and a handful of others, had followed Soto's defection to the insurgents. Many of his adherents had despaired during his absence and sought exile.[4] After the Treaties of Juárez, González had established an administration by selecting capable men from the Anti-reelectionist ranks; now in the wake of Huerta's victories the governor had to use anyone who had remained loyal.

The wholesale replacement of administrators, some of whom were only slightly sympathetic to the rebellion, came as a surprise in the national capital. Rafael Martínez, a Chihuahua journalist, wrote in *La patria*, "González is a good choice to continue as governor . . . because he is not a demagogue and represents neither a red, white, nor black threat of terror to the state." Madero also expected conciliation, and cautioned González that even though he did not intend vengeance, he was being overly intransigent. The president suggested that González moderate his policies to restore tranquillity without causing injuries which would lead to future tumult in the state. "Open your arms to everyone," he advised; "forget the wrongs they have done." He conceded that the rebellion's leaders deserved to be brought to justice, but added that it would be better if everyone could be pardoned. Moreover, Madero urged González to begin working with General Huerta, who argued for a program of pardon.[5]

Despite Madero's suggestions, González remained intractable in his condemnation of Orozco's supporters. Months of hiding had nurtured his resentment and he sought revenge. He became apprehensive that the same crowd who had plotted with Orozco was conspiring to replace him as the state's

4. *Hearings, 1913* is a catalog of testimony not only by persistent porfirians against the Madero and González governments, but also by former Anti-reelectionists. For example, see the statements of Talavera, p. 288; Chico, p. 287; Génaro Dozal, p. 289; and José María Ponce de León, p. 282. The decision of others to join Orozco or quit the country can be found in *EPMT*: De la Luz Soto, March 20, 1912; Herrera, March 29, 1912; Demetrio Ponce, March 6, 1912. For Elizondo, see the report of Rafael E. Múzquiz, October 11, 1912, in *DHRM*, 4: 157-58.

5. *El correo* reprinted the article on July 23, 1912. See also Madero to González, July 20, 1912, AM, reel 12.

chief executive. His fears gained substance when he learned that a member of Madero's cabinet, Rafael Hernández, who was also Madero's uncle, had made a tour through the southwestern United States, conferring in El Paso with Orozco and in Los Angeles with Luis Terrazas and insurgent governor Gutiérrez. Hernández believed the rebels would surrender, but because they feared González's rancor, their spokesmen maintained that reconciliation would be possible only if the governor left office. Hernández reported his findings first to General Huerta, who agreed that González must resign his position, and then to the president. In El Paso, Orozco announced that arrangements had been made to end the fighting and that he would soon meet with Huerta to complete the terms.[6] Madero immediately reaffirmed his support for González and told him that he had not authorized Hernández's negotiations and that he disavowed any agreements with the rebels. Nevertheless, the president admitted that some members of his government recommended González's retirement.[7]

Madero tried to settle the differences between the governor and Huerta as Chihuahua quickly proved cramped quarters for the two. Huerta's attitude was as rigid as his military posture, and González, his dignity injured, took an inflexible stand. Each man looked on the other as a subordinate. The president urged González to become more conciliatory and reminded Huerta that the governor was a stalwart of the revolutionary party,[8] but his pleas for amiable cooperation between the civil and military leaders had little chance of success because of their mutual animosity. As soon as González joined the federal army in June, he learned that Huerta had sentenced his protégé, Pancho Villa, to death before a firing squad for stealing a horse. Madero's timely intercession had saved Villa's life, but he had been taken to the national prison in Mexico City.[9] González suspected that Huerta had trumped up the charges against Villa. Mistrust further strained relations between the two men, particularly after the reoccupation of Chihuahua City. González was anxious for the elimination of the insurgents so he could launch a reconstruction program, but Huerta was slow to pursue the enemy, ostensibly seeking a reconciliation with the rebels.

Huerta had taken charge of the federal troops in March, 1912, and dis-

6. Edwards to Secretary of State, August 6, 1912, RDS, 812.00/4584; August 12, 1912, RDS, 812.00/4614; Hernández to Madero, August 24, 1912, *DHRM*, 4: 101-5.

7. Madero to González, August 30, 1912, AM, reel 12.

8. Madero to Huerta, July 20, 1912, AM, reel 12; Bonilla, *El regimén maderista*, p. 18.

9. Villa's arrest, sentence to death, and last-minute reprieve by Madero are recounted in Cumberland, *Mexican Revolution*, p. 199.

played great ability in defeating the rebels in Chihuahua. But his once relentless advance slowed to a halt after his men arrived in the state capital. A seasoned campaigner, Huerta had demonstrated his army's ability to defeat the *orozquistas* in massed battles, but he refused to order his troops to attack the rebels in Juárez.[10] Following the general's orders, other field officers carried out a correct, though restrained, pursuit of the enemy. Indications were that the army felt no inducement to strengthen the Madero government by a quick defeat of Orozco. Federal forays against the rebels "proceeded with equal slowness and apparently equal indifference." Many observers suspected that the army officers wanted to drag out the struggle until the strain toppled Madero's government. The United States consul believed that the officers, concerned to pave the way for their own eventual accession to power, took care that the military occupation did not alienate state residents, whether they backed Madero or Orozco.[11]

The army's dilatory advance was hardly justifiable and gave credence to rumors that Huerta was conspiring against the governor. González believed that the general was trying to induce Madero to appoint a military governor. Shortly after the occupation of the state capital, Madero called Huerta to Mexico City. Gossip had it that Huerta had instigated the trip to extol the army's partial victory so as to cajole the president into giving him the governorship. Madero tried to end the rumor by telling González that he had reiterated to Huerta his faith in González's ability to govern the state.[12]

While González remained cautious in his relations with Huerta, the general also hesitated to come to any agreement with the governor. Huerta had taken the command against the rebels with the understanding that he would have a free hand, but he felt that Madero meddled too much in military affairs. He and his army were cheered in Mexico City and acclaimed throughout the nation for their triumphs, but in Chihuahua City they were viewed as conquerors. The state's society ostracized the federal officers and refused to receive them.[13]

10. William L. Sherman and Richard E. Greenleaf, *Victoriano Huerta: A Reappraisal* (Mexico: Centro de Estudios Mexicanos, 1960), pp. 52-53. For an account of Huerta's early career and military experience, see George J. Rausch, Jr., "The Early Career of Victoriano Huerta," *The Americas* 21 (1964): 136-49.

11. Letcher to Secretary of State, August 29, 1912, RDS, 812.00/4822; September 15, 1912, RDS, 812.00/5056; October 17, 1912, RDS, 812.00/9483.

12. Letcher to Secretary of State, September 15, 1912, RDS, 812.00/5056; Madero to González, August 5, 1912, AM, reel 12.

13. See an explanatory letter from Madero to Huerta, June 22, 1912, AM, reel 12; Sherman and Greenleaf, *Huerta*, pp. 52, 55; Letcher to Secretary of State, October 16, 1912, RDS, 812.00/5324.

The conflicting policies of González, Huerta, and Madero became obvious in August. First Huerta made clear his decision not to press the rebels when he announced a thirty-day amnesty, urging the rebels to surrender to federal officers.[14] Before the interval lapsed, Madero, sensing his shaky hold on the government, declared a suspension of constitutional guarantees in several states, particularly the strongholds of Zapata and Orozco. González publicized the decree and announced its implementation for a six-month period beginning with the expiration of Huerta's amnesty. He explained that the new law removed constitutional protections from highwaymen and anyone disrupting traffic on the roads or interfering with the operation of the railroads or telegraph.[15]

The suspension of guarantees was only one indication of Madero's determination to pacify the country. He called on the Congress to provide additional funds for the purchase of guns and to enlarge the army to seventy thousand men. After urging from the president, Huerta advanced with sudden vigor against Juárez. Orozco angrily responded that the amnesty had been an effort to deceive him and that he would renew the fight, but he withdrew his men from the border city. Federal army units arriving in Juárez on August 20, 1912, were greeted by newly appointed city officials loyal to the González government.[16] The fall of the last large town under rebel control convinced many that the rebellion had ended. The army settled into garrison routine, sending out patrols along the railroads but making little effort to rout rebels even when they appeared within sight of the right of way. It remained complacent and refused to force a confrontation. When the government sent two airplanes to Chihuahua, the officers never bothered to have them uncrated.[17]

The insurgents did not surrender, but split into small bands and continued to fight. Although their strength declined from September, 1912, to January, 1913, they maintained a capital at Ojinaga, threatening to launch a full-blown rebellion at any moment. Guerrillas carried out attacks on foreigners calculated to discredit the state and national governments. In Batopilas, rebels

14. Letcher to Secretary of State, July 10, 1912, RDS, 812.00/4393; *PO*, vol. 32, extra edition to 54 (August 15, 1912), p. 5.

15. The suspension of guarantees applied to the states of Chihuahua, Morelos, Guerrero, Tlaxcala, Durango, and Sonora, and some districts of other states. See Wilson to Secretary of State, July 24, 1912, RDS, 812.00/4481; Cumberland, *Mexican Revolution*, pp. 198-99. González's statements were reported in *PO*, vol. 32, extra edition to 54 (August 15, 1912), pp. 1-4.

16. Valadés, *Madero* 2: 235; Edwards to Secretary of State, August 14, 1912, RDS, 812.00/4628; August 16, 1912, RDS, 812.00/4643; August 20, 1912, RDS, 812.00/4672.

17. Letcher to Secretary of State, October 17, 1912, RDS, 812.00/9483.

robbed a Chinese-owned shoestore on September 9 and returned a week later to collect any money they had missed.[18] Most of the rebel raids, however, fell on North Americans, who made up the overwhelming majority of foreigners in the state. After several years of forcing a living out of the harsh Chihuahua soil, the Mormon colonists in the northwestern corner of the state found the torment inflicted by José Inés Salazar too much. Salazar collected all of their guns and ammunition in exchange for the safe conduct of the women and children to the United States border, and during the late summer, most of the religious immigrants left their once promised land.[19] Other North Americans complained of their treatment at the hands of the rebels who had turned foraging into strategy. Cattlemen and miners watched their property being plundered, while army troops a few miles away refused to leave the railroad except to repair telegraph lines. William N. Fink, a mine superintendent, was kidnaped and held until the rebels received a five-thousand-peso ransom.[20] The raids, Letcher believed, were "systematic lawlessness or . . . well ordered disorderliness, arranged . . . to affect such persons as would cause the most clamor throughout the exterior world." These incidents convinced Letcher that the insurgents and certain other men along the border wanted "to provoke the intervention of the United States to discredit Madero."[21] Whether seeking to goad the United States or simply trying to maintain their struggle, Orozco's renegades presented the most serious problem for the González government.

The turbulence led the governor to organize small auxiliary units at the state's expense. The irregular forces were made up of regional volunteers and were deployed in Sancillo, Rosales, Cusihuiriáchic, Temóchic, Santa Eulalia, and Bachíniva, all districts threatened by the insurrectionists. González also asked the federal government to station two corps of *rurales* in Chihuahua under his command. For his state militia, he had to provide arms and ammunition. He requested the secretary of gobernación to supply three hundred rifles for the volunteers.[22] The minister apparently complied, because González then directed an agent to purchase ammunition in the United States.

18. Meyer, *Mexican Rebel*, pp. 87-88; Report of September 2, 1913, ASTJ, no. 2065.

19. B. Carmon Hardy, "Cultural 'Encystment' as a Cause of the Mormon Exodus from Mexico in 1912," *Pacific Historical Review* 34 (1965): 439-54, especially 451-52.

20. *Hearings, 1913*, testimony of H. S. Stephenson, p. 372; C. L. Cain, p. 606; Thomas Holmes, p. 610; William N. Fink, pp. 692-97.

21. Letcher to Secretary of State, October 17, 1912, RDS, 812.00/9483.

22. *PO*, vol. 32, no. 62 (September 22, 1912), p. 3; *El correo*, September 17, 1912.

The Mexican consul in El Paso obtained permission from the United States government to export war materiel through the El Paso port of entry. In September he shipped twenty-five thousand cartridges to Chihuahua and the next month sent an additional one hundred rifles. The governor's agents acquired more weapons when he authorized them to buy guns collected by the federal army from surrendering rebels. By mid-September, González reported to the state legislature that he had spent nearly seven thousand pesos for expenses and armament of the volunteers.[23]

The recruitment of a loyal force that reduced his reliance on the federal army must have eased the governor's apprehensions. His suspicions further diminished when Madero recalled Huerta and reorganized the military in Chihuahua. During the general's visit to Mexico City in August, the two men had clashed over a number of issues. Madero had been upset, as was González, over the near-execution of Villa. Moreover, Huerta made no attempt to account for one and a half million pesos assigned for the campaign against Orozco. Huerta had complaints, too. He resented Madero, regarding him as a busybody with a bookkeeper's mentality. The president's promotion of other officers also piqued him. By October, Madero had had enough of the army's hesitant campaign. He promoted Huerta but removed him from command. Then in the best porfirian manner he offered the general a European commission, but Huerta refused and retired to sulk in a cantina for the next few months.[24]

Although he was as eager as González to suppress the guerrillas, Madero was dismayed by the cost of supporting the federal army in Chihuahua. In November he ordered the commanders in Juárez and Chihuahua City to reduce their garrisons to the minimum. Since the dispersed rebel bands made pitched battles impossible, he suggested that the cavalry be reorganized into flying columns which could pursue the enemy. He proposed to model the federal units after González's auxiliaries and suggested that perhaps they should incorporate some of the volunteers who were familiar with the sierra terrain. Uncertain of the loyalty of the federal troops, the president began

23. The purchase of ammunition broke down as follows: ten thousand cartridges for .44-caliber and twenty-five thousand cartridges for .30-.30-caliber rifles. The ammunition was obtained from the Winchester Arms Company of New Haven, Connecticut. Rifles were purchased from Parley, Spalchavre and Fay of New York. See Llorente to Secretary of Foreign Relations, September 27 and November 5, 1912, AREM, L-E 848; Lomelí to Llorente, November 19, 1912, AREM, L-E 848; Almada, *Vida González*, pp. 136-37; *El correo*, September 17, 1912.

24. Sherman and Greenleaf, *Huerta*, pp. 55-56, 58.

rotating new men into the state's garrisons.[25] Within two months, he recognized that the suppression of the guerrillas could not be accomplished quickly without an exorbitant investment financially and in personnel, so he decided to reinstitute the military zone of Chihuahua under the command of General Antonio Rábago.[26]

González continued to press his campaign against Orozco, extending his efforts in the fall to international law. Orozco had been wounded in September and had crossed into the United States. The governor immediately initiated extradition proceedings to bring Orozco, Sr., and his private secretary, José Córdova, to Chihuahua for trial. United States officials hesitated to arrest the men, however. Throughout the summer of 1912 they had jailed insurgents, including David de la Fuente, Agustín Estrada, and Gonzalo Enrile, but the Mexican government had never provided the evidence on which to justify extradition.[27] Acting on instructions from González, the Mexican consul in El Paso pressed for the arrest of the two Orozcos and Córdova. General Orozco remained out of sight, but marshals captured Pascual Orozco, Sr., and Córdova, who had come across the river from Ojinaga. The two were taken to El Paso and jailed, awaiting extradition to Chihuahua. The consul presented the governor's charges that Córdova had instigated several murders allegedly carried out in Juárez by the elder Orozco. When he found he had insufficient proof, he reportedly offered amnesty to another insurgent prisoner in El Paso if he would sign affidavits that implicated Orozco and Córdova. The ploy failed, and eventually the two men obtained their liberty.[28]

Although unsuccessful in dealing with the Orozcos, González survived the clash of personalities that hampered his restored administration. The president had removed Huerta, the governor's nemesis, from Chihuahua, and González had organized his own military force. Taken together, these developments allayed his fears. Since his reoccupation of the governor's office, González had given little attention to reform. But rather than initiating social programs now, the governor devoted his last months to an effort to resolve the question of amnesty.

25. Madero to Generals Fernando Trucy Albert and Joaquín Téllez, November 12, 1912, AM, reel 11; Madero to Emilio Madero, November 15, 1912, AM, reel 11.

26. Madero to Gen. Fernando Trucy Albert, December 25, 1912, AM, reel 12.

27. *Hearings, 1913*, W. D. Howe (an El Paso attorney) to Senate Subcommittee, October 5, 1912, pp. 623-24.

28. González to Secretary of Foreign Relations, September 17, 19, and 30, 1912, AREM, L-E 826; *Hearings, 1913*, testimony of Pascual Orozco, Sr., pp. 472-81; testimony of Charles A. Boynton, p. 627; testimony of Félipe López, pp. 665-69.

II

From July, 1912, until the end of his administration, González could accomplish little to improve social conditions; reconstruction occupied his administration. When he first returned to office, the governor appointed a loyal administration and moved to suppress the insurrection. At the same time, he found that his government faced bankruptcy. Orozco's forces had taken the state treasury with them; they had even removed the treasury records as they retreated. The financial need was so pressing that González borrowed fifteen thousand pesos from the paymaster of Huerta's army, which he repaid when the national government provided one hundred thousand pesos in aid to the state. González also demanded loans from the business community of the state capital. He argued that most of its members had assisted Orozco and must contribute funds for his use as well.[29] His harsh stand was supported by the city's loyalists who had suffered under Orozco. During the rebellion, the insurgent troops had abused known synpathizers of Madero and González. They had arrested several men suspected of spying for the federal government and others who refused to make "voluntary" loans. When Silvestre Terrazas, editor of *El correo*, refused to publish rebel propaganda, soldiers insulted him, stripped him, and then paddled him with the flat of a sword. The editor's secretary received the same handling.[30] Those who had suffered mistreatment eagerly backed the governor's rough handling of Orozco's sympathizers.

The army's dawdling advance against the rebels limited the activities of González's administration. But with the fall of Juárez, the governor pressed a somewhat more active program. He called an extraordinary session of the state legislature to abrogate all the laws passed from March 3 to July 4, 1912. The deputies declared all the legislative and administrative decisions of the Orozco regime void, although they recognized its criminal proceedings so as to preserve civil order.[31] The governor had weighed the possibility of collecting taxes for the period of the rebellion because of Chihuahua's financial difficulties, but Madero advised him that the people could not be blamed for paying taxes while Orozco occupied the state. Moreover, he added confidentially, the United States government would oppose efforts to collect taxes a second time from American citizens in Chihuahua. Madero cautioned the gov-

29. Almada, *Vida González*, p. 135; *Hearings, 1913,* testimony of Felipe R. Gutiérrez, p. 279.

30. Statement of Francisco Longería, April 26, 1914, STC, box 41, folder Francisco Longería; *EPMT*, April 17, 1912.

31. *PO*, vol. 32, extra edition to 57 (August 15, 1912), p. 8; no. 59 (September 5, 1912), p. 1; Madero to González August 19, 1912, AM, reel 12.

ernor to use all possible tact in handling the problem. González resolved the issue by asking the deputies to recognize taxes paid in good faith to the Orozco government, and they in return gave the governor discretionary powers in financial affairs, allowing him to judge which payments had been made in good faith and which had not.

The governor anxiously worked to restore business activity. The railroads were the first priority, but it was not until late November, 1912, that the Mexican National Railroad resumed regular freight and passenger service through the state.[32] Capital for business remained a problem. Ernesto Madero, minister of finance, wrote to Silvestre Terrazas suggesting that a group of businessmen open a mortgage bank in the state capital since Chihuahua's banks were all in the hands of *orozquista* supporters. Terrazas passed the letter on to the governor and inquired, if he decided to act on the suggestion, under what conditions the institution might operate. González approved the plan and assured Terrazas he would aid him in every way possible, indicating that the new bank could count on the business of the state government.[33] His administration fell before this mortgage institution could be established, however.

The government undertook modest social reform programs. The donation of land for the towns of Villa Ahumada and Madera was completed. Using his special authority, the governor also arranged to continue a program for the division of municipal land by lots, and he worked for improved water and sanitation systems for other villages. He made special efforts to increase the supply of drinking water in the capital and to provide a drainage system in Camargo, while ordering repairs on the water and drainage systems in Jiménez. Telegraph lines were extended to outlying towns to give them communications with the rest of the state and to provide the government with military intelligence in those areas.[34] Measures were undertaken to prevent threatened epidemics of communicable diseases, and a contract was signed for the construction and operation of a secular mortuary and cemetery to provide inexpensive burials in the capital city.[35]

32. Edwards to Secretary of State, November 26, 1912, RDS, 812.00/5594.

33. Ernesto Madero to Silvestre Terrazas, September 24, 1912; Terrazas to González, October 1, 1912; González to Terrazas, October 4, 1912, STC, box 6, folder Banco Hipotecario.

34. *PO*, vol. 32, no. 71 (November 24, 1912), p. 1; no. 62 (September 22, 1912), pp. 2-11; Almada, *Vida González*, p. 136.

35. *El correo*, September 17, 1912. The contract between González and Manuel Rodríguez Chávez, September 6, 1912, is contained in STC, box 31, folder Abraham González.

Education received special attention from the governor, and his concern for it induced him to moderate his retributive attitude: he allowed teachers appointed by Orozco to continue at their posts. Elsewhere he immediately appointed interim professors, and selected a new director of the state educational system. González called on the state legislature to approve funds for new school buildings and the renovation of old ones. Finally, he used his extraordinary authority to spend large sums of money for school furniture and materials and to raise teachers' monthly salaries by twenty pesos. He directed the administrators to evaluate the curriculum at the state preparatory school and to revise it in accordance with the course offerings at the national preparatory school in Mexico City.[36] The random character of these actions illustrated that while the governor worried over social matters, he had more pressing concerns.

After his recruitment of volunteers for the state militia and the recall of Huerta, González considered a more conciliatory attitude toward former rebels. In September, having completed his purge of officials, he began modification of his program to accommodate residents who had fled Chihuahua either out of fear of Orozco or to avoid reprisals by the restored government. The governor wanted to repatriate the state's exiles, but he refused to extend amnesty to the leaders and financial backers of the Orozco insurgency. Madero, on the other hand, renewed his argument that the government had to reconcile all former *orozquistas*. He insisted that many citizens had been implicated in the rebellion, but not all had been completely in accord with it. There were numerous requests for guarantees from former adherents of the porfirian regime, including one-time governor José María Sánchez. The president offered several suggestions for general amnesty, advising González to pardon all those who were willing to surrender their weapons.[37]

The difference of opinion between the president and the governor was brought out sharply in the case of Luis Terrazas. In July, 1912, Terrazas indicated to Rafael Hernández his desire to return home. Once he learned that Madero had proposed a conciliatory policy, Don Luis wrote the president, again declaring that he wanted to return to Chihuahua but asking for guarantees. He asserted that he had not been involved in Orozco's rebellion and that he had no wish to meddle in politics. Madero requested González's opinion

36. *PO*, vol. 32, no. 55 (August 4, 1912), p. 3; José María Pino Suárez to Isidro Fabela, October 22, 1912, *DHRM*, 4: 180.

37. *El correo*, September 17, 1912. For examples of the president's views, see Madero to González, November 16, 1912, and Madero to José López Portillo y Rojas, November 16, 1912, AM, reel 11.

and in his letter repeated that the reconstruction of the state would be complete only when its people had been accommodated by the government. Learning of the negotiations, United States Senator Albert B. Fall advised his friend Luis not to return to Chihuahua as long as González remained in office. Fall warned: ". . . you would be in danger of assassination, to say nothing of being subjected to petty annoyances and to being harassed continually." González delayed his answer, but finally in December he acceded and Terrazas returned home.[38]

González's willingness to allow Don Luis to enter the state resulted from the governor's approval of a program of pardons designed by the president. Madero had urged González to permit the return of all exiles on the condition that they appear before a district judge immediately on their arrival in Mexico. After confessing their culpability in crimes against the government, they would receive suspended sentences. Violation of their probation would lead to the execution of the sentence against them or deportation. Madero had moreover suggested that González extend a complete pardon in those cases where he judged it convenient.[39]

The governor accepted the president's proposal because he believed the civil war had nearly ended. Rumors circulated that the rebels would try to recapture Juárez, but they proved fallacious. González dismissed such stories as idle talk. The return of numerous exiles and North American businessmen demonstrated a general confidence in his administration,[40] although there was one disheartening incident. A peace envoy dispatched to negotiate a settlement with one guerrilla band was intercepted by another roving gang that robbed him and sent him back to the protected zone. Nevertheless, the governor announced that the rebellion against the constitutional government had ended. He said only a few bandits continued to plague the state, and offered amnesty to those men if they would surrender their weapons. He blamed the

38. The Terrazas case can be traced in the following correspondence: Madero to González, July 25, 1912, AM, reel 12; November 5, 1912, AM, reel 11; December 8, 1912, *DHRM*, 4: 235; Fall to Terrazas, October 2, 1912, ABFC, reel 35. Once Luis returned to Chihuahua, his trials did not end. After Villa's victory at the Battle of Tierra Blanca in November, 1913, Terrazas, with many other residents of Chihuahua City, left for Ojinaga, and from there Luis went into exile, first in El Paso, then in southern California. Villa harassed his family and plundered their properties. Terrazas was finally permitted to return to Chihuahua, where he died in June, 1923, within months of Villa. See Lister and Lister, *Storehouse of Storms*, pp. 230-32, 269.

39. Madero to González, December 7, 1912, AM, reel 11.

40. Madero to Gen. Joaquín Téllez, November 23, 1912, AM, reel 11; Madero to González, November 23, 1912, AM, reel 11; Edwards to Secretary of State, December 3, 1912, RDS, 812.00/5636.

sporadic opposition on the yellow press, which carried sensational accounts of retaliation against those rebels who surrendered to the government.[41]

González's conviction that the struggle had finally ended moved him to call for national legislation for a general amnesty. He wanted to pardon everyone who had participated in the Orozco revolt except criminals. In particular, he wanted the common citizens who had been led astray by demagogic leaders to return to their homes without fear of retribution. A thirty-day amnesty, González suggested, would bring peace to the nation. Madero fully supported his amnesty proposal, but pointed out that the legislation could not be considered until Congress reconvened in April, 1913. He did, however, recommend that the governor use his extraordinary authority to pardon those he saw fit. Madero believed the country had no more pressing need than to reestablish peace and to prevent incidents along the border with the United States.[42]

González's adoption of a policy of reconciliation ended the difference of opinion between the governor and the president, but pardon for the rebels was not the popular course in Chihuahua that Madero had predicted. Loyal adherents of the González government pointed out that many former rebels escaped penalties for supporting Orozco and for this reason held the governor in contempt. Moreover, the loyalists argued, his capricious program created suspicion and mistrust among the state's citizens and encouraged the rebels to remain in the field.

The recruitment of administrators from among men of known loyalty placed many inexperienced and incompetent men in office. Their bungling of administrative affairs created disregard for the government. The amnesty policy aggravated the situation, for a large number of loyalist officeholders resigned in protest, believing the governor had bent over backwards to conciliate his enemies. With numerous resignations the administration slipped into greater inefficiency as the governor searched for anyone to fill the posts.[43] Many citizens desired an end to the insurrection, but others who wanted compensation for their financial losses and their maltreatment from the rebels provided little support for the amnesty program and called on both the presi-

41. Letcher to Secretary of State, December 10, 1912, RDS, 812.00/5678; December 18, 1912, RDS 812.00/5719; *El correo*, December 16, 1912.

42. González to the Minister of Gobernación, January 3, 1912, STC, box 31, folder Abraham González; Madero to González, January 7 and 8, 1913, AM, reel 11.

43. The changes in personnel can be followed in ASTJ, reports 44, 91, 98, 318, 419, 431, 553, 673, and 716, for January and February, 1913; Letcher to Secretary of State, August 29, 1912, RDS, 812.00/4822, and October 16, 1912, RDS, 812.00/5324.

dent and the governor to arrange some indemnification for their losses.[44] Pardon also raised the question of what to do with those insurgents who had been captured and imprisoned. Many argued they ought to be freed.[45]

Nor did amnesty bring in all the rebels. Madero became particularly anxious to settle with the bands led by Rojas and Salazar, and González continued to seek an armistice agreeable to the remaining insurgents. In January, 1913, commissioners took peace terms into the mountains, but when the parleys with the rebels failed to result in an agreement,[46] Madero adopted a rigid policy of completing pacification by the use of *rurales* rather than federal troops. He informed the governor that the army, because of its awkward organization, had not prosecuted the war well, so he had decided to send in Alberto Guajardo, who had pacified Coahuila and Durango. Guajardo was bringing five hundred *rurales* and another two hundred irregular troops to Chihuahua. The president also sent Pablo González with three hundred men and suggested that the governor should relinquish command of his auxiliaries to González for the pacification of Chihuahua.

Madero's decision was a response to renewed rebel strength. The controversy over the correct amnesty policy, followed by less than exacting execution of pacification, contributed to popular mistrust of the government and strengthened the insurgents' position. The situation was exacerbated in January when González learned that one of the peace commissioners, Roque González Garza, also sent to Mexico City regular reports on conditions in Chihuahua.[47] The presence of an official agent implied that Madero had lost confidence in the incumbent state administration.

III

The resurgence of Orozco's forces demonstrated González's inability to rally the people of Chihuahua behind his government. In January the rebels

44. Madero to Silvestre Terrazas, November 29, 1912, AM, reel 11; Madero to González, August 7, 1912, AM, reel 12; Terrazas to González, December 9, 1912, STC, box 83, folder 1911-1912; Madero to Luis G. Rojas, August 23, 1912, *DHRM*, 4: 100; Elías de los Ríos to Santiago González Casavantes, January 18, 1913, AM, reel 11; A. G. Harris to Fall, August 3, 1912, ABFC, reel 35.

45. There are many letters of this kind in reel 11 of the AM; see as an example Madero to González, January 28, 1913.

46. Madero to González, January 7, 1913, AM, reel 11; Letcher to Secretary of State, January 29, 1913, RDS, 812.00/5969.

47. Madero to González, January 28, 1912, AM, reel 11; February 7, 1913, AM, reel 12; Roque González Garza to Madero February 1, 1913, AM, reel 18.

regained sufficient strength to threaten Juárez and Chihuahua City. The governor placed the blame squarely on the army officers. Suspicious of the military's motives, he sent Isidro Fabela on a confidential mission to Mexico City to report his misgivings to Madero, but developments in the national capital prevented an interview with the president.[48]

While the Orozco threat flourished again in Chihuahua, other insurgents who had been defeated and imprisoned in Mexico City plotted a coup d'état in the capital city. Bernardo Reyes and Félix Díaz, both of whom had sparked unsuccessful revolts, conspired with General Manuel Mondragón against the government. Confederates freed them from their cells early in the morning of February 9, and they advanced with troops against the national palace. In the initial battle opposing commanders were killed, and the surprise assault collapsed. Félix Díaz assumed command of the insurgent forces in place of the dead Reyes, and Madero had to call on Victoriano Huerta to direct his defense in the place of the dead army commander. Both sides settled into a protracted artillery duel that damaged much of the capital's business district and killed countless civilians but did little harm to military positions. The bombardment continued intermittently for more than a week and earned the name of Ten Tragic Days. The real tragedy was the resolution of the shelling.

The fighting ended with an arrangement between Huerta and Félix Díaz, assisted by the American ambassador, Henry Lane Wilson, to eliminate Madero from the government. In one of the most ignominious acts of the revolutionary era, Huerta arrested Madero and Pino Suárez on February 18, to conclude the ten days of turmoil. The capstone to the sordid affair came four days later with the assassination of the two deposed executives. Whether or not Huerta contrived the murders, his connivance was condemned by a large segment of the Mexican people. The Ten Tragic Days altered the situation in Chihuahua and shaped the course of González's last days.[49]

The uprising by the former porfirian army officers should not have been as startling in Chihuahua as it was. Pancho Villa had been imprisoned in Mexico City and knew of the conspiracy between Reyes and Díaz. After he escaped in December, 1912, he made his way to El Paso. He informed González of his

48. Isidro Fabela, "El Gobernador don Abraham González," *Boletín de la Sociedad Chihuahuense de Estudios Históricos* 11 (1964): 10-11.

49. For an account of the Decena Trágica and the assassinations, see Ross, *Madero*, pp. 278-330; Michael C. Meyer, *Huerta: A Political Portrait* (Lincoln: University of Nebraska, 1972), pp. 45-63, 69-82.

whereabouts and also of the prospective revolt in the capital.[50] González passed the word to Madero, but neither man gave it much heed. They had become immune to rumors and gossip, since the grist of everyday affairs included reports of impending rebellions. Villa's information was only another of the confusing and contradictory reports that the administration received. That the governor had dismissed the story was painfully obvious when the first notice of the upheaval arrived in Chihuahua.

Convinced that the overthrow of the government was imminent, González was overwhelmed. He prepared to flee from Chihuahua City and join his auxiliaries. He confided both his fears and his plans to the American consul, and asked Letcher to accept the state's treasury of 180,000 pesos to prevent it from falling into the hands of the army. Letcher refused the state's money and apparently calmed the governor. González reviewed his situation. There were five thousand volunteers in the state on whom he could depend; the federal army had three thousand men garrisoned in the city and reportedly they would be joined by twelve hundred *orozquistas* if the revolt succeeded in Mexico City.[51] Somewhat reassured, González called the legislature into special session to request special powers to rule by decree, then he began a period of "watchful waiting." The army officers and the rebels also stood at their posts waiting to learn the outcome of the struggle in the national capital. Because of the approximate balance of power, circumspect inaction marked state affairs until the coup d'état placed Huerta at the head of the new Mexican government.[52]

Immediately on arrogating national authority on February 19, Huerta demanded that state governors recognize his authority. González joined the governors of Coahuila and Sonora in refusing to accede to the interim president. Venustiano Carranza, in Coahuila, sent an officer of his state volunteers, Captain Alfredo Breceda, to see the governors of Chihuahua and Sonora, requesting that they join in organizing opposition to Huerta. González appointed Ismael Navarro as his delegate to a meeting for that purpose in Monclova.[53]

50. Villa escaped December 27, 1912 (see Schyler to Secretary of State, December 27, 1912, RDS, 812.00/5774). His lawyer, José Bonales Sandoval, then wrote to Madero explaining Villa's actions; see *DHRM*, 4: 262-63.
51. Letcher to Secretary of State, February 10, 1912, RDS, 812.00/6084; February 11, 1913, RDS, 812.00/6090.
52. Edwards to Secretary of State, February 20, 1913, RDS, 812.00/6283; *PO*, vol. 33, no. 7 (February 9, 1913), p. 1; no. 8 (February 23, 1913), p. 1.
53. Portes Gil, *Autobiografía*, pp. 130-31. The junta did not convene until after the death of González.

Because the governor had ignored Huerta's demand for recognition and had begun preparations for resistance, rumors circulated through the city that the army officers would take some proscriptive action. Fear for the governor's safety stemmed from stories from Mexico City of the probable assassination of the president and vice-president as well as other supporters of the regime. Among the rumors was one carried by Lorenzo Borreguero to a friend of González, P. H. Holguín. Borreguero confided that in a shop he had overheard several well-known enemies of the governor say that the army would arrest González at five in the afternoon and arrange his assassination within a few days. Holguín immediately reported the incident to the governor, but González refused to be concerned and dismissed the advice that he should abandon the city. Although Holguín's brother, Esteban, also argued with the governor, trying to convince him of his peril, González adamantly refused to leave his office.[54]

The same afternoon, February 22, 1913, Major José Alessio Robles, the officer of the day, ordered a squad of men to surround the government buildings at five o'clock. Then Manuel Gordillo Escudero entered the offices and arrested González. The soldiers escorted the governor to the headquarters of the second military zone, where General Rábago charged González, members of his administration, and Lieutenant Colonel Guadalupe Gardena and Major Trinidad Rodríguez of the volunteers with conspiring against the federal army. The evidence against González was his authorization for José Alcalá to purchase guns and ammunition to arm the state auxiliaries.[55] No action could be taken against the governor for the moment because he possessed immunity as the state executive.

The officers forced González to ask the state legislature for a license releasing him from his duties. The deputies convened and permitted him to depart from his office for one month. Three days later, again under duress, González resigned so he could be placed before a special military investigating tribunal. He told the state legislature that he had decided independently to resign, but the alternative had apparently been death at the hands of his captors. The legislature accepted his resignation and named Rábago as interim governor until new elections could be held.[56]

54. P. H. Holguín to Santiago González Casavantes, October 31, 1921, STC, box 33, folder Miscellany 5.

55. "Copía simple del simulacro del proceso instruído al extinto C. Gobernador del Estado, don Abraham González en el año de (1913) mil novecientos trece," STC, box 31, folder Abraham González.

56. *PO*, vol. 33, extra edition to 8 (February 26, 1913), p. 1; no. 9 (March 2, 1913), p. 1; Letcher to Secretary of State, March 1, 1913, RDS, 812.00/6456. His resignation was accepted February 28, 1913.

González's arrest and resignation sparked anxiety that he would be assassinated at the first opportunity. Concern for his life reached the United States, where telegrams were sent to President William H. Taft, the Department of State, and Senator Albert Fall requesting diplomatic intervention on the governor's behalf. Under this urging, the State Department inquired about the legality of the proceedings against González. Ambassador Wilson responded with a completely fallacious account of how the governor had escaped to the United States, then added that González had inspired numerous crimes against Americans. Wilson concluded, "His reputation is so limited and his character so doubtful that I doubt the wisdom of any vigorous intervention in his behalf." Consul Letcher obtained an interview with interim governor Rábago, who reported that González had been acquitted of conspiracy charges, although he was still detained for examination on lesser charges. He remarked that González's life was in no danger.[57]

Unconvinced by Rábago's disclaimer, Letcher tried to arrange diplomatic protection for González. He called on his counterparts from Great Britain and Germany and urged them to make representations to the army that an assassination would make an unfavorable impression on their governments. The other two consuls refused, however; their reticence, the American said, reflected their favorable disposition toward the counterrevolutionaries in Chihuahua. They expressed their hostility toward the former governor when they said that they believed it was the policy of the new government "to kill men like González."[58]

While Letcher attempted to protect the former governor with the pressure of his office, González's legal counsel, Aureliano González unsuccessfully sought to defend him before a special court-martial. On March 4 the military judges convicted González of violating a federal law forbidding the purchase of army weapons and ammunition. The court found that González had authorized Alcalá to secure arms for the state's volunteers. The army had captured equipment during the revolution of 1910 and from the Orozco rebels, and González had obtained Huerta's permission to buy some of the captured weapons. Thus a few of the guns acquired by the volunteers bore the imprint

57. Rumors of possible assassination were reported in Letcher to Secretary of State, February 23, 1913, RDS, 812.00/6343. For inquiries about González, see Price McKinney of Cleveland, Ohio, to President William Howard Taft, February 26, 1913, RDS, 812.00/6397, and J. F. Follansbee to Fall, February 26, 1913, ABFC, reel 31. See also Department of State to Letcher, February 27, 1913, RDS, 812.00/6397, and Letcher's report of an interview with Rábago in Letcher to Secretary of State, March 1, 1913, RDS, 812.00/6456.

58. Letcher to Secretary of State, October 17, 1913, RDS, 812.00/9483.

of the federal army. The court found him guilty of a misdemeanor that carried a sentence of three to five months in prison,[59] although the charges were merely a pretext to hold González in custody.

During González's trial, President Huerta had been discussing an alliance with Orozco's forces. Representatives of the two men negotiated in Villa Ahumada, where they concluded an agreement contingent on Huerta's acceptance of stipulations for incorporation of the rebels into the *rurales*, aid to widows of the struggle against Madero, and land reform. Huerta readily agreed, and Orozco announced his support for the new government on February 27. Huerta, Orozco's secretary, José Cordova, and the minister of internal affairs then planned the pacification of the northern states by Orozco.[60] González, who had believed there were several snapping dogs at his heels, learned he was pursued by Cerberus, as the alignment united his staunchest opponents, Huerta, Orozco, and the army.

The details of González's last days are obscured by a thicket of official reports, military secrecy, and accusations by contemporaries who charged Huerta with all the murders in Mexico. On March 6 a military detail arrived in Chihuahua to escort the former governor to Mexico City. Three officers, Major Benjamín Camarena, Captain Hernando Limón, and Lieutenant Federico Revilla, presented an order from General Huerta for the transfer of González. To comply with the order without exciting popular curiosity, Rábago arranged for the commission to take the prisoner the same night. The escort and González boarded a special Pullman car and the train departed at 11:30 p.m. without lights or whistles that might attract attention.[61] They traveled roughly forty miles south to a place near Bachimba Pass, where Camarena signaled a stop with a hand lantern, then ordered González to step down from the coach. After the soldiers climbed out, the officer told the engineer to move the train down the tracks three kilometers and wait half an hour before returning. The pulling away of the train was the only preliminary before Camarena shot González to death. The escort then buried his bullet-riddled body in a shallow grave where he fell.[62]

59. "Copía . . . proceso . . . González . . . ."
60. Meyer, *Mexican Rebel*, pp. 97-98.
61. Letcher to Secretary of State, March 24, 1913, RDS, 812.00/6952. Letcher based his account on a report from an unnamed informer who had examined the records of the railroad dispatcher. See also Fidel Avila to Juan G. Cabral, August 28, 1914, STC, box 5, folder Fidel Avila.
62. Fabela, "Gobernador González," p. 14; "Notes from a Map showing the Spot where González was Assassinated in the First Hours of March 7, 1913," signed by J. R. Braca [Brasa]?, STC, box 6, folder Miscellany 6. Braca had been a member of the train crew.

IV

The following day friends despaired for González's life when they learned that guards had taken him from the city, allegedly for a journey to the national capital. When no word of his arrival in Mexico City reached his family, they became increasingly worried and asked Consul Letcher to use the good offices of the United States to ascertain González's fate. North Americans who had done business in Chihuahua heard rumors and called on Senator Fall to have the government learn what had become of the former governor, and Secretary of State William Jennings Bryan, who had just taken office, instructed the ambassador to seek information about him.[63]

González's relatives became increasingly pessimistic about his survival when the Mexican government first reported they had no information, then said that he had been allowed to leave for exile in the United States with an escort of his own choosing.[64] In the atmosphere of uncertainty and political murder created by Huerta's assumption of power, sensational rumors tried to account for González's disappearance. One report said González, still handcuffed, had been pushed between the cars of the moving train. A second added the macabre touch that after the escort shot the governor to death, they had placed his body on the tracks and ordered the engineer to reverse directions, intending the train to mutilate it so that the gunshot wounds would not be apparent.[65] Inquiries grew more insistent and the national government decided to release an official account of the affair. The minister of internal affairs informed the United States ambassador that the train carrying

63. Letcher to Secretary of State, March 7, 1913, RDS, 812.00/6545; March 13, 1913, RDS, 812.00/6698; Bryan to Wilson, March 16, 1913, RDS, 812.00/6698; Fall to C. B. Colquitt, March 13, 1914, ABFC, reel 35; Memorandum by C. V. S. (Charles V. Safford, Fall's secretary), March 29, 1913, ABFC, reel 40. At their annual meeting in Amarillo, Texas, March 4-6, 1913, the Panhandle and Southwestern Stockmen's Association passed a resolution of concern about González's arrest and trial. Fall forwarded the resolution with a request that the State Department inquire about Chihuahua's governor. The resolution is contained in ABFC, reel 33, and RDS, 812.00/6727.

64. Wilson to Secretary of State, March 17, 1913, RDS, 812.00/6746; April 2, 1913, RDS, 812.00/6990.

65. Fall learned of the murder from an informant in Chihuahua, possibly Alberto Terrazas (he provided information to the senator on other occasions; see Fall to John R. Fulkerson, August 21, 1913, ABFC, reel 31), and Fall reported the story to Secretary of State Bryan. See Fall to Bryan, April 7, 1913, RDS, 812.00/7047; see also Fall to Colquitt, March 13, 1914, ABFC, reel 35. For another contemporary account, see Avila to Cabral, August 28, 1914, STC, box 5, folder Fidel Avila. The account that González had been killed or mutilated by the train has been repeated in numerous histories of that period. For examples, see Sánchez Azcona, "Marzo 7 de 1913," p. 15; Rafael Martínez and Eduardo Guerra, *Madero, su vida y su obra* (Monterrey, N.L.: n.p., 1914), pp. 45-46; and most recently in Ronald Atkin, *Revolution: Mexico, 1910-1920* (New York: John Day Company, 1970), p. 133.

González had been intercepted near Parral by armed men loyal to Madero. In the battle that followed, the minister said, González had been killed.[66] A certain logic attended the story. Since González's arrest, troops loyal to him had been operating along the railroad north and south of Chihuahua City, and in early March volunteers had besieged the army in Parral and held them there for several days.[67] But the official account had a familiar ring; the government had given out the same story about the assassination of Madero and Pino Suárez. Conclusive proof of the governor's assassination came several months later, when Lieutenant Colonel Euleuterio Hermosillo found the body and reburied it where it could be easily located.[68]

González's relatives and associates agreed with Consul Letcher's judgment on his assassination, ". . . civilization has been mocked in this act of stark, cold-blooded and vengeful murder."[69] But there were many others who could rejoice at his elimination and were suspected of having had a hand in it. Chihuahua's porfirian faction had tied themselves to the *orozquista* movement and borne the brunt of González's harsh terms of amnesty. Although they lacked the initiative to contrive the murder, they certainly felt no remorse. Pascual Orozco carried a grudge against the former governor. Since the first days of the revolution of 1910, he had run cross-current to González. The insurgent general had sufficient grievances to wish to remove González, and he may have included a confidential stipulation to that effect in his negotiations with Huerta. Orozco's desire to replace González as governor does not convict him of the assassination, however; murder was not necessary to eliminate the governor. Army officers also had definite reasons for opposing González. He was a civilian who had never shown ability in battle or interest in the military. He constantly worked against them, and even organized his own independent auxiliaries. While the porfirians, the army, and the insurgents all had motives, loyalists blamed Huerta for instigating the crime. As in the assassinations of Madero, Pino Suárez, Gustavo Madero, and other Antireelectionists, the people in the streets blamed the interim president. His harsh efforts to consolidate authority and his demand for the backing of state governors gave substance to the charges, but they only created an atmosphere conducive to assassination.[70]

66. Wilson to Secretary of State, April 5, 1913, RDS, 812.00/7028.
67. Edwards to Secretary of State, February 22, 1913, RDS, 812.00/6306; Letcher to Secretary of State, February 23, 1913, RDS, 812.00/6309; February 24, 1913, RDS, 812.00/6346; March 7, 1913, RDS, 812.00/6546.
68. Almada, *Revolución en Chihuahua*, 2: 19.
69. Letcher to Secretary of State, March 24, 1913, RDS, 812.00/6952.
70. Huerta's efforts to consolidate authority and conciliate or replace state governors is recorded in Kenneth J. Grieb, *The United States and Huerta* (Lincoln: University of Nebraska Press, 1969), pp. 31, 54-56.

The murder of González was more deplorable because it was probably the act of one man who saw an opportunity to ingratiate himself with his superiors. Benjamín Camarena, an obscure member of the army's general staff, was ordered to bring González to the national capital. Another member of the detail, Hernando Limón, asserted that Huerta had alluded to the timely use of the *ley fuga*, the execution of fleeing prisoners, but the ambitions of the escort probably caused them to read that meaning into his words. Camarena had no direct orders to kill González; he acted with the hope of obtaining favorable notice from his commanders, even the president. Later Camarena also killed his own brother for opposing Huerta, then received an assignment in Europe and reportedly a bonus for his contribution to the government.[71]

The immediate effect of González's assassination was to undermine efforts to resist the Huerta government. The military governor purged the administration and installed men who supported the new regime. The government systematically harried its opponents out of the state, and in Parral a number of public officials were executed because they refused to support Huerta.[72] Resistance faltered as González's death stripped Chihuahua of its most respected leader. But the loss was not simply one of leadership. During the first months of the Constitutionalist rebellion against Huerta, the rebels in Coahuila and Sonora had state funds to finance their campaigns, while the Constitutionalists in Chihuahua had difficulty supporting the military units they were able to field because the army had taken the treasury.[73]

Although González's death slowed the organization of resistance, it proved to be a powerful rallying symbol. The atrocity united the pro-Madero population as González had never been able to do after his return from the national cabinet. The Constitutionalists fought to vindicate Madero, Pino Suárez, and González. In 1914, after they had driven Huerta from Mexico, they began proceedings against the alleged killers of González. General Rábago was taken to Chihuahua, where he died in prison before the court could prove his complicity in the crime. In early 1915, former colonel Jovito Orozco was arrested and tried for participation in the assassinations of both González and Madero.

71. Hernando Limón, "Cómo fusilaron a don Abraham," *LO* (LA), July 12, 1936; Guillermo N. Mellado, *Crímenes del huertismo* (n.p., n.d.), pp. 57-60. Mellado asserts that Huerta ordered Camarena to murder González, but there is no evidence to substantiate the charge. The author does demonstrate that Camarena eagerly sought to win the confidence of the new government.
72. Appointments and dismissals of officials are contained in ASTJ, reports 861, 966, and 1036 for March and April, 1913; Letcher to Secretary of State, October 17, 1913, RDS, 812.00/9483.
73. Silvestre Terrazas and J. N. Amador to Ignacio L. Pesqueira, May 22, 1913, STC, box 83, folder 1913 (January-June); González Ramírez, *Las ideas. La violencia*, p. 247.

He was cleared of the first charge because he had not been in Chihuahua during March, 1913, but was executed by a firing squad for assisting in the arrest of Madero at the national palace in February, 1913. Charges were brought against Lieutenant Colonel José Alessio Robles of ordering the arrest of González, thus precipitating his murder. The court decided that even though Robles had been the arresting officer, he was not responsible for the governor's assassination. [74]

The most striking illustration of González's symbolic power came in Villa's reckless campaign against the Huerta government and his spectacular rise to prominence among the Constitutionalist revolutionaries. Villa led his men in vengeance against the executioners of González. [75] The general made constant references to his fallen hero, and when he began to print his own currency he decorated the bills with the images of Madero and González. Once Villa had driven the federal forces from the state, he led an honor guard to reclaim González's remains. The body was returned to Chihuahua City. At the railroad station, a huge crowd met the train, then followed through the streets as Villa walked beside the hearse that took the body to the Teatro de los Héroes. That night, February 22, 1914, a ceremony commemorated the martyrs of the revolution: Madero, Pino Suárez, and González. Deeply moved, Villa stood the first watch over the coffin of the former governor, and other soldiers kept vigil until the following morning, when the body was interred in the state's pantheon. [76]

74. Almada, *Revolución en Chihuahua*, 2: 20; Almada, *Gobernadores*, p. 461.

75. Pinchon, *Viva Villa*, p. 271; Clendenen, *U.S. and Villa*, p. 29.

76. *El legalista* (Hidalgo del Parral, Chihuahua), February 25, 1913, clipping in AM, reel 17; programs of the memorial service, February 22, 1914, in STC, box 13, folder Chihuahua, Chih.; Almada, *Revolución en Chihuahua*, 2: 19-20. A moving although slightly exaggerated account of Villa's role at the ceremony is contained in Reed, *Insurgent Mexico*, pp. 134-37. The closest station to the site where González was killed was named in his honor, and Villa Ahumada was also renamed for the governor. In an ironic twist, the town's residents preferred the name of the porfirian official and it was later restored. See Lister and Lister, *Storehouse of Storms*, p. 268.

Appendix

Program of the Anti-reelectionist Party
Established at the National Convention of April, 1910

First:

To reestablish the rule of the Constitution of 1857, making effective the obligations and rights that it prescribes, such as the independence of the authorities of the Federation and the responsibilities of civil servants.

Second:

To secure the reform of the Constitution, establishing the principle of no reelection of the President and Vice-President of the Republic. To secure the same reform in the constitutions of the states by which Governors are selected, and to make effective the stipulation of residence in the district, territory, or state, for the election of deputies and senators.

Third:

To secure the reform of the electoral law, in order to achieve the effectiveness of the suffrage. To increase the authority and freedom of the municipal governments and to secure the elimination of the *Jefaturas* and *Prefecturas Políticas*.

Fourth:

To regulate article seven of the federal constitution, to make effective the freedom of the press.

Fifth:

To improve and develop public instruction and break the bonds that restrain academic freedom.

Sixth:

To improve the material, intellectual, and moral condition of the worker, creating factory schools, securing the passage of laws for pensions or indemnification for labor accidents, and combating alcoholism and gambling. To have equal solicitude for the indigenous people in general, especially the Maya and the Yaqui Indians, repatriating those despoiled and founding agricultural colonies on national lands, or those that can be aquired for that purpose. To accelerate the employment of Mexican railroad personnel at all levels, putting into law the special educational schools that will be necessary.

Seventh:

To favor the development of public wealth; to assess taxes equitably, to abolish the system of inequities and to combat monopolies and privileges; and above all, to take care that the public funds are invested in the commonweal of the Nation.

Eighth:

To foster large, and especially small, agriculture and irrigation, to which will be assigned a portion of the public funds. Regarding mining, industry, and commerce, they will be conceded all the franchises that will assure their development and prosperity.

Ninth:

To study and to put into practice the most efficient methods to improve the army so that it be better able to accomplish the high duty that it is charged with: that of guarding the institutions and defending the honor and integrity of the Republic. Military instruction will be made obligatory as one of the principal means.

Tenth:

To tighten the good relations with foreign countries, especially with those of Latin America, and prudently to direct the policy of the government to obtain a union of the Central American Nations.

Mexico, April 26, 1910

Francisco I. Madero
Francisco Vázquez Gómez

Source: Roque Estrada, *La revolución*, pp. 220-22.

Note on Sources

The examination of González's public career presented a number of problems. None of his personal papers are known to be extant. His manuscripts in the state archive in Chihuahua were released to his brother, Santiago González Casavantes, who apparently intended to write a biography, and have since disappeared.[1] Other records in the Chihuahua State Archives and the United States consulate in Chihuahua City were destroyed by fire, and significant official records, such as the police file on the Anti-reelectionists in Chihuahua, have disappeared from the documentary collections.[2] The absence of personal papers and pertinent files made a biography out of the question; instead, I relied on the manuscripts of contemporaries and on newspapers to trace the public career of Chihuahua's revolutionary governor.

The correspondence between González and Francisco I. Madero began in early 1909 and continued until Madero's assassination. The extant letters are nearly all from Madero to his lieutenant. The Madero Archive, available at the Instituto Nacional de Antropología e Historia, is more extensive than the twenty-two reels of microfilm would suggest. The collection consists of Madero's letter books, which are carbon copies of his correspondence from 1900

1. See the exchange of letters, Santiago González Casavantes to Silvestre Terrazas, June 31, 1934, STC, box 28, folder "G" Miscellany; Terrazas to González, June 26, 1934, STC, box 105, folder June, 1934.
2. Almada, *Vida González*, pp. 33-34.

until his death, with a major gap from early 1910 until June, 1911. After the victory at Juárez, more often than not the letters were written by Madero's secretary, and some of the copy books remain in stenographer's shorthand. The last few reels contain incoming mail, pictures, and a large newspaper clipping file. The Mexican government purchased the collection from the family of Alfredo Alvarez; it has been previously cited as the Alvarez Archive. A description of the holdings was written shortly after its purchase, and the article, Jesús Castañón Rodríguez's "Archivo del Sr. Madero" (*Boletín bibliográfico de la Secretaría de Hacienda y Crédito Publico* 145 [November 20, 1958] :3), serves as an excellent introduction to the papers. There are letters to and from González and other revolutionaries. The archive is particularly rich on the organization of the Anti-reelectionist party and Madero's presidency.

The National Anthropological Museum's holdings should be supplemented by the correspondence edited by José C. Valadés and published as "Archivo de Madero" in *La opinión* (Los Angeles) in 1937 and 1938. Valadés's selection of letters includes some exchanges with González. Other collections published by the same editor include reports and letters from the archives of Corral, Creel, and Villarreal. These series and other historical articles were published simultaneously in the Lozano family's *La opinión* and *La prensa* (San Antonio, Texas). For an index to these newspapers, see "Indice de *la opinión*" (*La opinión*, February 13, 1938).

Three smaller but valuable collections include González-Madero correspondence. The Madero Papers at the Biblioteca Nacional cover the period from February to May, 1911, after Madero reentered Mexico. I saw only two boxes of manuscripts, but other historians have used as many as four. The records document the creation of the provisional government in Chihuahua and the establishment of prorebel district administrations under González. In the Archivo General de la Nación, four copy books include Madero's letters written during the first months of his presidency and are particularly important for the situation in Chihuahua in late 1911. Scattered material not readily available elsewhere was edited and published by Isidro Fabela in *Documentos históricos de la Revolución Mexicana: Revolución y régimen maderista*, 5 vols. (Mexico: Fondo de Cultura Económica, 1964; Editorial Jus, 1965).

Second in importance only to the various Madero collections as a source for the public career of Abraham González is the massive Silvestre Terrazas Correspondence and Papers in the Bancroft Library, University of California, Berkeley. The holdings comprise 119 boxes of incoming and outgoing mail, newspaper clippings, historical documents, and pictures. The first 82 boxes contain letters to Terrazas, alphabetically arranged, and boxes 83-108 contain Terrazas's letters to others, chronologically sorted. Although much of the useful material for this study was located in the Ricardo Flores Magón section (four boxes) and the Abraham González folder, some of the most valuable letters were found in the miscellaneous folders. A guide, with a partial list of correspondence, is available at the Bancroft Library, but the investigator should be prepared to search the entire collection.

The Bancroft Library also holds other materials useful for this study, including a file of *El correo de Chihuahua* on microfilm and the *Diario oficial* of the Mexican government. In addition, many hard-to-locate secondary studies of the Mexican Revolution are available there.

In the Archivo General de la Secretaría de Relaciones Exteriores de México, the section concerned with the decade of the Revolution comprises several hundred *legajos*. The material includes dispatches from Mexican consuls along the border, detectives' reports, and other intelligence collected by the agents of the Ministry of Foreign Relations. The extent of its coverage may be seen from an examination of Berta Ulloa Ortíz's excellent guide, *Revolución Mexicana, 1910-1920* (Mexico: Secretaría de Relaciones Exteriores, 1963). The personnel *expedientes* of various government officials should also be consulted.

Because González's public life was restricted to Chihuahua, with only the brief three-month stint in Mexico City, the destruction and disappearance of records and manuscripts in the state presented a particular problem. The Archivo del Supremo Tribunal de Justicia had only scattered records for the years from 1910 to 1913. Among these are court cases and reports of the rotation of public officials. Some very interesting information turned up on the problems of the Chinese in the state and González's efforts to assist them. The local press and the border newspapers had ignored the problems of Chihuahua's Orientals. The most useful state source was the *Periódico oficial del estado de Chihuahua*. This official serial apparently lacked a regular publication schedule, but appeared roughly once a week with additional issues for important decrees or legislation. The *Periódico* continued uninterrupted publication despite civil disturbances and revolts but only reported official actions. Events as critical as Orozco's arrogation of authority were signaled only by the announcement of the appointment of new interim officials in the government. Fortunately, detailed reports of government decisions and the public reaction to them were reported in Silvestre Terrazas's *El correo de Chi-*

huahua, which, despite interruptions during the revolution and the Orozco rebellion, proved a valuable source.

Because of Chihuahua's proximity to the United States, there was unusual interest among North Americans in the developments in the state. A good deal of information about González and the revolution appeared in the reports of the consuls stationed in Chihuahua, and occasionally their dispatches included details unavailable elsewhere. The huge Records of the Department of State Relating to the Internal Affairs of Mexico, 1910-1929 includes all available material from the consular posts at Juárez and Chihuahua City and the consular agency at Hidalgo del Parral. Amid requests for leaves of absence, increase in housing subsidy, and more official stationery, the Post Dispatches, Record Group 89 in the National Archives, provided a few useful notes. More interesting were the Dispatches of the Consulate General for Northern Mexico at Monterrey. The American consul at Chihuahua City, Marion Letcher, proved an exceptional observer who reported revolutionary events with insight.

El Paso was a center of rebel exile activity directed first against Díaz and later Madero. The city's residents had a keen interest in events in Chihuahua. The *El Paso Morning Times* gave front-page coverage to the Madero revolution; and beginning in June, 1911, the editor stationed in Chihuahua City a reporter, J. F. Neville, who filed daily reports on the activities and the problems of the González government. The newspaper provided a detailed, if sometimes overly sympathetic, source for the governor's administration. Many American businessmen had commercial and property interests in Chihuahua. As the revolution became increasingly anti-American, they turned to the United States government for aid. A major source for these business interests is the correspondence on Mexican affairs from the Albert B. Fall Collection now at the Henry E. Huntington Library, San Marino, California. Papers on Mexico from the senator's office files were microfilmed by the University of New Mexico. A handy introduction to and warning against the pitfalls of the collection is Michael C. Meyer's "Albert Bacon Fall's Mexican Papers: A Preliminary Investigation (*New Mexico Historical Review* 11 [1965]: 165-74).

Much information on United States citizens in Chihuahua and contemporary assessments of González were compiled in two published reports of hearings by subcommittees of the Foreign Relations Committee of the United States Senate. The 1913 hearings published as *Revolutions in Mexico* tried to ascertain if North American enterprises had provided financial assistance to either the Madero or the Orozco revolutionaries. The testimony is a catalog of charges by businessmen and politicians against Chihuahua's governor. As the rebels became increasingly anti-American, some business and political leaders demanded military intervention. The hearings of 1919-20 published under the title *Investigation of Mexican Affairs* reveals Fall's attempts to manipulate witnesses and to compile damaging evidence against the Mexican leaders. Statements against the rebels, including González, were reprinted from the 1913 report.

Publications by three scholars contributed greatly to this study. Between 1950 and 1970 Francisco R. Almada wrote a series of volumes on Chihuahua's past that range from a directory of the state's governors to a compendium of the state's history. Most helpful for research on González's career were Almada's two-volume *La revolución en el estado de Chihuahua* (Mexico: Talleres Gráficos de la Nación, 1962) and his brief biography, *Vida, proceso, muerte de Abraham González* (Mexico: Talleres Gráficos de la Nación, 1967). In the latter book, Almada included a number of documents no longer available. Michael C. Meyer's *Mexican Rebel: Pascual Orozco and the Mexican Revolution* (Lincoln: University of Nebraska Press, 1967) was the first dispassionate biography of that revolutionary. In the course of tracing the general's career, Meyer did much to untwist the knot of Chihuahua state politics during the Madero era. In the same fashion, Robert Sandels's "Silvestre Terrazas, the Press, and the Origins of the Mexican Revolution in Chihuahua" (Ph.D. dissertation, University of Oregon, 1967) assesses the role of this prominent journalist in fomenting the rebellion of 1910. The two preceding investigations complement and contributed to an account of Chihuahua's insurgent governor.

~Selected Bibliography

I. PRIMARY SOURCES

A. Manuscripts

Archivo del Supremo Tribunal de Justicia, Chihuahua. Chihuahua City. Records and Transactions, 1910-13.

Archivo General de la Secretaría de Relaciones Exteriores de México. Mexico City. Revolución Mexicana durante los Años de 1910 a 1920. Informaciones Diversas de la República y de las Oficinas de México en el Exterior. File series H/513-1910-20/1. Various sections and volumes, 1910-13.

———. Enrique C. Creel, Su Expediente Personal. I/131/455, L.E. 422.

———. Abraham González, Su Expediente Personal. I/131/9 (s-1), L.E. 135.

———. Antonio V. Lomelí, Su Expediente Personal. H/131/178, L.E. 11-86-1189.

Archivo General de la Nación. Mexico City. Libros Copiadores de Madero.

Bancroft Library. University of California, Berkeley. Silvestre Terrazas Collection. Correspondence and Papers.

Biblioteca Nacional. Mexico City. Archivo Madero. Correspondencia del Presidente Francisco I. Madero. File number 9 (72).

Huntington Library. San Marino, California. Papers from the Senate Office Files of Senator Albert Bacon Fall Relating to Mexican Affairs. Microfilmed by the University of New Mexico. Reels 30-40.

Instituto Nacional de Antopología e Historia. Mexico City, Archivo de Don Francisco I. Madero. Microfilmed by El Centro de Documentación Histórica.

National Archives, Washington, D.C. Dispatches from United States Consuls in Chihuahua, 1830-1906. Record Group 84. National Archives Microfilm Publication (microcopy 289).

————. Post Records of Embassies and Consulates. Record Group 84. Correspondence of the Consulate General, Monterrey, Mexico, 1900-1914.

————. Records of the Department of State. Numerical Files, 1906-1910. Record Group 59.

————. Records of the Department of State Relating to the Internal Affairs of Mexico, 1910-1929. Record Group 59. National Archives Microfilm Publication (microcopy 274). 1910-1914.

B. Published Documents

Casasola, Agustín Víctor, ed. *Historia gráfica de la revolución, 1910-1940.* 6 vols. Mexico: Archivo Casasola, n.d.

Fabela, Isidro, ed. *Documentos históricos de la Revolución Mexicana: Revolución y régimen maderista.* 5 vols. Mexico: Fondo de Cultura Económica, 1964; Editorial Jus, 1965.

González Navarro, Moisés. *Estadísticas sociales del porfiriato, 1877-1910.* Mexico: Talleres Gráficos de la Nación, 1956.

González Ramírez, Manuel, ed. *Manifiestos políticos, 1892-1912.* Mexico: Fondo de Cultura Económica, 1957.

María y Campos, Armando de, ed. *Las memorias y las mejores cartas de Francisco I. Madero.* Mexico: Libro Mex, Editores, 1956.

Periódico oficial del estado de Chihuahua. 1911-13.

Periódico oficial del estado de Coahuila. 1911-13.

Secretaría de Gobierno. *Diario Oficial.* Vols. 117 and 118. Mexico: Imprenta del Gobierno Federal, 1911-12.

United States. Senate Committee on Foreign Relations. *Investigation of Mexican Affairs.* Report and Hearings before a Sub-Committee on Foreign Relations, Senator Albert Fall, Presiding, Pursuant to Senate Resolution 106. 66th Cong., 2d sess. 2 vols. Washington: GPO, 1919-20.

————. *Revolutions in Mexico.* 62d Cong., 2d sess. Washington: GPO, 1913.

Valadés, Jose C., ed. "Archivo de Corral." *La opinión*, published weekly from October 15, 1933, to May 6, 1934.

–––. "Archivo de Madero." *La opinión*, published weekly from October 15, 1933, to May 6, 1934.

[Valadés, José C.?] , ed. "Siguiendo la pista a políticos mexicanos." *La opinión*, published weekly from April 16 to June 11, 1939.

C. Memoirs, Diaries, and Contemporary Accounts

Aguirre, Amado. *Mís memorias de campañas––apuntes para la historia.* N.p., n.d.

Bush, Ira J. *Gringo Doctor.* Caldwell, Idaho: Caxton, 1939.

Calero y Sierra, Manuel. *Un decenio de política mexicana.* New York: Middleditch Co., 1920.

Estrada, Roque. *La revolución y Francisco I. Madero: Primera, segunda y tercera etapas, 1911-1912.* Guadalajara: Imprenta Americana, 1912.

Figueroa Domenech, J., and Antonio P. González (Kanta Klaro). *La revolución y sus héroes.* 5th ed. Mexico: Herrero Hnos., Sucs., 1912.

Furlong, Thomas. *Fifty Years a Detective.* St. Louis: C. E. Barnett, 1912.

Garibaldi, Giuseppe. *A Toast to Rebellion.* Indianapolis: Bobbs-Merrill, 1935.

González-Blanco, Pedro. *De Porfirio Díaz a Carranza.* Madrid: Imprenta Helénica, 1916.

González Garza, Federico. *La Revolución Mexicana. Mi contribución político-literaria.* Mexico: A. del Bosque, 1936.

Guzmán, Martín Luis. *Memorias de Pancho Villa.* Mexico: Compañía General de Ediciones, 1968.

Hamilton, Leonidas L. *Hamilton's Mexican Handbook: A Complete Description of the Republic of Mexico . . . and a Commercial Directory of the Principal Business Men of Mexico.* Boston: D. Lothrop & Co., 1885.

Madero, Francisco I. *La sucesión presidencial en 1910.* San Pedro, Coahuila, 1908.

Martínez, Rafael, Carlos M. Samper, and José P. Lomelín, *La revolución y sus hombres (apuntes para la historia contemporánea).* México: Talleres Tipográficos de "El tiempo," 1912.

Martínez, Rafael, and Eduardo Guerra. *Madero, su vida y su obra.* Monterrey, N.L.: n.p., 1914.

Palavicini, Félix. *Mi vida revolucionaria.* Mexico: Ediciones Botas, 1937.

Puente, Ramón. *Pascual Orozco y la revuelta de Chihuahua.* Mexico: E. Gómez de la Puente, 1912.

Reed, John. *Insurgent Mexico.* New York: International Publishers, 1969.

Schuster, Ernest O. *Pancho Villa's Shadow*. New York: Exposition Press, 1947.

Taracena, Alfonso. *Mi vida en el vértigo de la Revolución Mexicana: Anales sintéticos, 1900-1930*. Mexico: Ediciones Botas, 1936.

Turner, Timothy G. *Bullets, Bottles and Gardenias*. Dallas: Southwest Press, 1935.

Vázquez Gómez, Francisco. *Memorias políticas, 1905-1931*. Mexico: Imprenta Mundial, 1913.

White, Owen P. *Them Was the Days: From El Paso to Prohibition*. New York: Minton, Balch & Co., 1925.

Wilson, Henry Lane. *Diplomatic Episodes in Mexico, Belgium, and Chile*. Garden City: Doubleday, Page & Co., 1927.

II. SECONDARY ACCOUNTS

A. Monographs, General Studies, and Special Accounts

Atkin, Ronald. *Revolution: Mexico, 1910-1920*. New York: John Day Co., 1970.

Aguirre Benavides, Adrián. *Madero el inmaculado: Historia de la revolución de 1910*. Mexico: Editorial Diana, 1962.

Almada, Francisco R. *Gobernadores de Chihuahua*. Mexico: Imprenta de la H. Cámara de Diputados, 1950.

———. *Juárez y Terrazas (aclaraciones históricas)*. Mexico: Libros Mexicanos, 1958.

———. *Resumen de historia del estado de Chihuahua*. Mexico: Libros Mexicanos, 1955.

———. *La revolución en el estado de Chihuahua*. 2 vols. Mexico: Talleres Gráficos de la Nación, 1962.

———. *Vida, proceso, muerte de Abraham González*. Mexico: Talleres Gráficos de la Nación, 1967.

Amaya, Juan Gilberto. *Madero y los auténticos revolucionarios de 1910 hasta la Decena Trágica y el fín del Gral. Pascual Orozco*. Mexico: n.p., 1946.

Barrera Fuentes, Florencio. *Historia de la revolución: La etapa precursora*. Mexico: Talleres Gráficos de la Nación, 1955.

Beals, Carleton. *Porfirio Diaz, Dictator of Mexico*. Philadelphia, n.p., 1932.

Bernstein, Marvin D. *The Mexican Mining Industry, 1890-1950: A Study of the Interaction of Politics, Economics, and Technology*. Albany: State University of New York Press, 1964.

Blaisdell, Lowell L. *The Desert Revolution: Baja California, 1911*. Madison: University of Wisconsin Press, 1962.

Bonilla, Manuel, Jr. *El régimen maderista*. Mexico: Talleres de "El universal," 1922.

Braddy, Haldeen. *Cock of the Walk: Qui-qui-ri-quí: The Legend of Pancho Villa*. Albuquerque: University of New Mexico Press, 1955.

Calzadíaz Barrera, Alberto. *Hechos reales de la revolución*. 3 vols. Mexico: Editorial Patría, 1961.

Clendenen, Clarence C. *Blood on the Border: The United States Army and the Mexican Irregulars*. New York: Macmillan, 1969.

Cockcroft, James D. *Intellectual Precursors of the Mexican Revolution, 1900-1913*. Austin: University of Texas Press, 1968.

Cosío Villegas, Daniel, ed. *Historia moderna de México*. 9 vols. México: Editorial Hermes, 1955-70.

Creel, Enrique C. *El estado de Chihuahua: Su historia, geografía, y riquezas naturales*. Mexico: Tip. el Progreso, 1928.

Cumberland, Charles C. *Mexican Revolution: Genesis under Madero*. Austin: University of Texas Press, 1952.

Fuentes Mares, José. *. . . Y México se refugió en el desierto: Luis Terrazas, historia y destino*. Mexico: Editorial Jus, 1954.

González Ramírez, Manuel. *Las ideas. La violencia*. Vol. 1 of *La revolución social de México*. México: Fondo de Cultura Económica, 1960.

Grieb, Kenneth J. *The United States and Huerta*. Lincoln: University of Nebraska Press, 1969.

Jordán, Fernando. *Crónica de un país bárbaro*. 3d ed. Mexico: B. Costa-Amic, Editor, 1967.

Leyva, José María. *Aportaciones a la historia de la revolución*. Mexico: n.p., 1938.

Lister, Florence, and Robert H. Lister. *Chihuahua: Storehouse of Storms*. Albuquerque: University of New Mexico Press, 1966.

Márquez Montiel, Joaquín. *Hombres célebres de Chihuahua*. Mexico: Editorial Jus, 1953.

Mártinez Nuñéz, Eugenio. *La vida heróica de Práxedis G. Guerrero*. Mexico: n.p., 1960.

Mellado, Guillermo. *Crímenes del huertismo*. N.p., n.d.

Meyer, Michael C. *Mexican Rebel: Pascual Orozco and the Mexican Revolution*. Lincoln: University of Nebraska Press, 1967.

———. *Huerta: A Political Portrait*. Lincoln: University of Nebraska Press, 1972.

México: Cincuenta años de revolución. Mexico: Fondo de Cultura Económica, 1963.

Moreno, Daniel. *Los hombres de la revolución. 40 estudios biográficos.* México: Libro Mex., 1960.

Naranjo, Francisco. *Diccionario biográfico revolucionario.* Mexico: Imprenta Editorial "Cosmos," 1935.

Niemeyer, Eberhardt Victor, Jr. *El General Bernardo Reyes.* Biblioteca de Nueva León. Monterrey: Universidad de Nuevo León, 1966.

Ortíz Rubio, Pascual. *La revolución de 1910: Apuntes históricas.* 2d ed. Mexico: Herrero Hermanos, Sucs., 1929.

Pinchon, Edgcumb. *Viva Villa: A Recovery of the Real Pancho Villa.* New York: Grosset & Dunlap, 1933.

Pletcher, David M. *Rails, Mines, and Progress: Seven American Promoters in Mexico, 1867-1911.* Ithaca, N.Y.: Cornell University Press, 1958.

Portes Gil, Emilio. *Autobiografía de la Revolución Mexicana: Un tratado de interpretación histórica.* Mexico: Instituto Mexicano de Cultura, 1964.

Reynolds, Clark W. *The Mexican Economy: Twentieth-Century Structure and Growth.* New Haven: Yale University Press, 1970.

Ross, Stanley R. *Francisco I. Madero, Apostle of Mexican Democracy.* New York: Columbia University Press, 1955.

Sánchez Azcona, Juan. *La etapa maderista de la revolución.* Mexico: Talleres Gráficos de la Nación, 1960.

Sherman, William L., and Richard E. Greenleaf. *Victoriano Huerta: A Reappraisal.* Mexico: Centro de Estudios Mexicanos, 1960.

Taracena, Alfonso. *Madero, el héroe cívico.* Mexico: Ediciones Xóchitl, 1946.

Turner, Frederick C. *The Dynamic of Mexican Nationalism.* Chapel Hill: University of North Carolina Press, 1968.

Valadés, José C. *Imaginación y realidad de Francisco I. Madero.* 2 vols. México: Antigua Librería Robredo, 1960.

———. *Historia general de la Revolución Mexicana.* 5 vols. Mexico: Manuel Quesada Brandí, 1963.

Wilkie, James W. *The Mexican Revolution: Federal Expenditure and Social Change.* Berkeley: University of California Press, 1967.

Zuno, José G. *Historia de la revolución en el estado de Jalisco.* México: Talleres Gráficos de la Nación, 1964.

B. Articles

Berbusse, Edward J. "Neutrality-Diplomacy of the United States and Mexico, 1910-1911." *The Americas* 12 (1956): 265-83.

Brown, Lyle C. "The Mexican Liberals and Their Struggle against the Díaz Dictatorship, 1900-1906." *Antología MCC, 1956*, pp. 317-62.

Cadenhead, Ivie E., Jr. "The American Socialists and the Mexican Revolution of 1910." *Southwestern Social Science Quarterly* 43 (1962): 103-11.

Casavantes González, Alberto. "Arbol genealógico de la familia del sr. don Abraham González y Casavantes," *Boletín de la Sociedad Chihuahuense de Estudios Históricos* 11 (1964), between pp. 7 and 8.

Calderón, Estebán B. "Maderismo en Chihuahua." *El nacional* (Mexico City), November 20, 1931.

Contreras Torres, Miguel. "Abraham González, enamorado de la democracia." *El universal* (Mexico City), March 25, 1958.

Creelman, James. "Interview with Porfirio Díaz." *Pearson's Magazine* 19 (1908): 241-44.

Cumberland, Charles C. "Mexican Revolutionary Movements from Texas, 1906-1912." *Southwestern Historical Quarterly* 52 (1948-49): 301-24.

―――. "Precursors of the Mexican Revolution of 1910." *Hispanic American Historical Review* 22 (1942): 344-56.

―――. "The Sonora Chinese and the Mexican Revolution." *Hispanic American Historical Review* 40 (1960): 191-211.

Esquer, Manuel R. "Reminiscencias históricas." *El Heraldo* (Chihuahua City), March 7, 1953.

Fabela, Isidro. "El Gobernador don Abraham González." *Boletín de la Sociedad Chihuahuense de Estudios Históricos* 11 (1964): 7-15.

García, Matías C. "Rasgos biográficos del sr. d. Abraham González." *El correo de Chihuahua*, September 21, 1911.

González Navarro, Moisés. "Mexico: The Lop-sided Revolution." In *Obstacles to Change in Latin America*, edited by Claudio Velíz. London: Oxford University Press, 1965.

―――. "Xenofobia y xenofilia en la Revolución Mexicana." *Historia mexicana* 18 (1969): 594-614.

Grieb, Kenneth J. "Standard Oil and the Financing of the Mexican Revolution." *California Historical Society Quarterly* 49 (1971): 59-71.

Hardy, B. Carmon. "Cultural 'Encystment' as a Cause of the Mormon Exodus from Mexico in 1912." *Pacific Historical Review* 34 (1965): 439-54.

Kitchens, John W. "Some Considerations on the *Rurales* of Porfirian Mexico." *Journal of Inter-American Studies* 9 (1967): 441-55.

Limón, Hernando. "Cómo fusilaron a don Abraham." *La opinión*, July 12, 1936.

McColl, Robert W. "The Insurgent State: Territorial Bases of Revolution." *Annals of the Association of American Geographers* 59 (1969): 613-31.

Magaña Cerda, Octavio. "Historia documental de la revolución." *El universal*, June 11, 1950.

Niemeyer, Vic. "Frustrated Invasion: The Revolutionary Attempt of General Bernardo Reyes from San Antonio in 1911." *Southwestern Historical Quarterly* 67 (1963-64): 213-25.

Presley, James. "Mexican Views on Rural Education." *The Americas* 20 (1963): 64-71.

Puente, Ramón. "La verdadera historia de Pancho Villa." *Excélsior*, March 30, 1931.

Rausch, George J., Jr. "The Early Career of Victoriano Huerta." *The Americas* 21 (1964): 136-49.

Salazar, Eulogio, Jr. "El protomártir del Antirreleccionismo." *El Heraldo* (Chihuahua City), March 7, 1951.

Sánchez Azcona, Juan. "Marzo 7 de 1913." *El Universal* (Mexico City), March 7, 1936.

Sandels, Robert L. "Silvestre Terrazas and the Old Regime in Chihuahua." *The Americas* 28 (1971): 191-205.

Sims, Harold D. "Espejo de caciques: Los Terrazas de Chihuahua." *Historia mexicana* 18, no. 71 (1969): 379-99.

Thurber, Mary. "'Soldier of Fortune' Who Fought with Madero Returns to El Paso." *El Paso Morning Times*, March 29, 1955.

Vanderwood, Paul. "Genesis of the Rurales: Mexico's Early Struggle for Public Security." *Hispanic American Historical Review* 50 (1970): 323-44.

Vargas Piñera, Luis. "El gobierno maquinó la sublevación de Pascual Orozco contra Madero." *Excélsior*, September 4, 1938.

C. Theses and Dissertations

Albro, Ward Sloan III. "Ricardo Flores Magón and the Liberal Party: An Inquiry into the Origins of the Mexican Revolution of 1910." Ph.D. dissertation, University of Arizona, 1967.

Bryan, Anthony. "The Career of General Bernardo Reyes: Continuity and Change in Mexican Politics, 1905-1913." Master's thesis, University of Nebraska, 1967.

Holcombe, Harold E. "United States Arms Control and the Mexican Revolution, 1910-1924." Ph.D. dissertation, University of Alabama, 1968.

Sandels, Robert L. "Silvestre Terrazas, the Press, and the Origins of the Mexican Revolution in Chihuahua." Ph.D. dissertation, University of Oregon, 1967.

D. Newspapers
El correo de Chihuahua. 1909-13.
El Paso Morning Times. 1908-14.

Index